Dialectical Behavior Therapy With Adolescents

Dialectical Behavior Therapy With Adolescents is an essential, user-friendly guide for clinicians who wish to implement DBT for adolescents into their practices. The authors draw on current literature on DBT adaptation to provide detailed descriptions and sample group-therapy formats for a variety of circumstances. Each chapter includes material to help clinicians adapt DBT for specific clinical situations (including outpatient, inpatient, partial hospitalization, school, and juvenile-detention settings) and diagnoses (such as substance use, eating disorders, and behavioral disorders). The book's final section contains additional resources and handouts to allow clinicians to customize their treatment strategies.

K. Michelle Hunnicutt Hollenbaugh, PhD, LPC-S, is an associate professor in the Department of Counseling and Educational Psychology at Texas A&M University, Corpus Christi. She has several years of clinical experience in a variety of settings and has spent the majority of this time researching and providing Dialectical Behavior Therapy (DBT). She is currently conducting several research studies on adaptations of DBT and continues to facilitate the implementation of DBT-based clinical services for the local community.

Michael S. Lewis, PhD, LPCC-S, is a clinical professor at Capital University and has extensive experience working with adolescents and young adults. He has also spent time working in substance-abuse treatment facilities and high-school settings. Michael specializes in wellness- and mindfulness-based innovative interventions. His research interests include college counseling, counselor development, and behavioral addictions.

Dialectical Behavior Therapy With Adolescents
Settings, Treatments, and Diagnoses

K. Michelle Hunnicutt Hollenbaugh
Michael S. Lewis

NEW YORK AND LONDON

First published 2018
by Routledge
711 Third Avenue, New York, NY 10017

and by Routledge
2 Park Square, Milton Park, Abingdon, Oxon, OX14 4RN

Routledge is an imprint of the Taylor & Francis Group, an informa business

© 2018 K. Michelle Hunnicutt Hollenbaugh and Michael S. Lewis

The right of K. Michelle Hunnicutt Hollenbaugh and Michael S. Lewis to be identified as authors of this work has been asserted by them in accordance with sections 77 and 78 of the Copyright, Designs and Patents Act 1988.

All rights reserved. The purchase of this copyright material confers the right on the purchasing institution to photocopy pages which bear the photocopy icon and copyright line at the bottom of the page. No other part of this publication may be reproduced, stored in a retrieval system, or transmitted in any form or by any means, electronic, mechanical, photocopying, recording or otherwise, without prior permission in writing from the publisher.

Trademark notice: Product or corporate names may be trademarks or registered trademarks, and are used only for identification and explanation without intent to infringe.

Library of Congress Cataloging-in-Publication Data
Names: Hollenbaugh, K. Michelle Hunnicutt, author. | Lewis, Michael S. (Michael Scott), 1977– author.
Title: Dialectical behavior therapy with adolescents : settings, treatments, and diagnoses / K. Michelle Hunnicutt Hollenbaugh, Michael S. Lewis.
Description: New York, NY : Routledge, 2018. | Includes bibliographical references.
Identifiers: LCCN 2017036111 (print) | LCCN 2017036683 (ebook) | ISBN 9781315692425 (eBook) | ISBN 9781138906020 (hbk) | ISBN 9781138906037 (pbk) | ISBN 9781315692425 (ebk)
Subjects: | MESH: Cognitive Therapy | Adolescent | Mental Disorders—therapy | Mental Disorders—diagnosis
Classification: LCC RC489.C63 (ebook) | LCC RC489.C63 (print) | NLM WM 425.5.C6 | DDC 616.89/1425—dc23
LC record available at https://lccn.loc.gov/2017036111

ISBN: 978-1-138-90602-0 (hbk)
ISBN: 978-1-138-90603-7 (pbk)
ISBN: 978-1-315-69242-5 (ebk)

Typeset in Frutiger
by Apex CoVantage, LLC

Visit the eResources: www.routledge.com/9781138906037

Contents

List of figures		vii
List of tables		ix
Contributors		xi

1 Introduction and Overview   1
K. Michelle Hunnicutt Hollenbaugh

2 Treatment Delivery and Implementation   19
K. Michelle Hunnicutt Hollenbaugh

3 Treatment Team and Continuity of Care   29
K. Michelle Hunnicutt Hollenbaugh and Jacob M. Klein

4 Outpatient Settings   39
K. Michelle Hunnicutt Hollenbaugh

5 Family Counseling   53
K. Michelle Hunnicutt Hollenbaugh

6 Partial Hospital Programs and Settings   63
Garry S. Del Conte

7 DBT in Inpatient Settings   85
K. Michelle Hunnicutt Hollenbaugh and Jacob M. Klein

8 Working Within School Sites   97
Richard J. Ricard, Mary Alice Fernandez, Wannigar Ratanavivan, Shanice N. Armstrong, Mehmet A. Karaman, and Eunice Lerma

9 Eating Disorders   109
K. Michelle Hunnicutt Hollenbaugh

10 Conduct Disorder, Probation, and Juvenile Detention Settings   123
K. Michelle Hunnicutt Hollenbaugh and Jacob M. Klein

11 Substance Use Disorders   137
K. Michelle Hunnicutt Hollenbaugh

12 Other Diagnoses for Consideration   149
K. Michelle Hunnicutt Hollenbaugh

13 Comorbid Diagnoses and Life-Threatening Behaviors   161
K. Michelle Hunnicutt Hollenbaugh

14 Summary and Conclusions   171
K. Michelle Hunnicutt Hollenbaugh

Handouts 177
Index 235

Figures

1.1	Biosocial Theory	4
6.1	Model of a Dialectical Milieu	66
9.1	Biosocial Theory as Applied to Eating Disorders	111
10.1	Biosocial Theory as Applied to Conduct Disorder/Criminal Behavior	126
11.1	Clear Mind, Clean Mind, Addict Mind	138
13.1	Behavior Chain Analysis	164

Tables

1.1	Definition of Terms in the Structure and Implementation of DBT	3
1.2	DBT Dialectical Dilemmas	7
2.1	Pros and Cons of Implementing Standard DBT vs. DBT Informed	20
3.1	Treatment Team Members and Roles	30
4.1	Traditional DBT Treatment Targets and Hierarchy	40
4.2	Sample Skills Training Schedule	47
5.1	Options for Implementing Family Counseling in DBT	54
5.2	Treatment Targets in DBT Family Interventions	55
5.3	Sample Format of Multifamily Skills Group (Six Weeks)	59
6.1	DBT Treatment Assumptions in an Adolescent Partial Hospitalization Program	69
6.2	Curriculum Template for a DBT Partial Hospital Program	70
6.3	Curriculum for Six-Week Parent Middle Path Skills	73
6.4	Hierarchy of DBT PHP Behavioral Targets by Role and Mode	75
6.5	Treatment Targets for a DBT PHP	77
6.6	Daybreak Treatment Center Staff Agreements	79
7.1	Treatment Targets for Inpatient DBT	89
7.2	Sample Skills Training Format for Inpatient DBT	92
8.1	Teen Talk: Treatment Team Members and Roles	101
8.2	DBT Treatment Targets in the Teen Talk Program	102
8.3	Overview of the Teen Talk Skills Group Sessions	103
9.1	Treatment Targets in DBT for Eating Disorders	113
9.2	Sample Skills Training Schedule for DBT-ED	117
10.1	DBT Treatment Targets and Hierarchy With Conduct Disorders and in Juvenile Detention Settings	127
10.2	Sample Skills Training Schedule for DBT for Conduct/Behavioral Problems	132
11.1	Adapted Treatment Targets for Treating Clients With SUDs	142
11.2	Sample Skills Module Format	144
12.1	DBT Treatment Targets and Hierarchy for Anxiety Disorders	150
12.2	DBT Treatment Targets and Hierarchy for Depression	153
12.3	DBT Treatment Targets and Hierarchy for Bipolar Disorder	155

Contributors

Shanice N. Armstrong, PhD is an assistant professor at Henderson State University. She has several years of counseling experience working with at-risk and marginalized youth populations. Her interests involve multiculturalism and strength-based approaches in counseling, resilience, supervision, and counselor education.

Garry S. Del Conte, PsyD, ABPP is clinical director at Daybreak Treatment Center in Germantown, Tennessee. He is a licensed psychologist and a Linehan Board-Certified DBT Clinician. His clinical specialization is working with children, adolescents, and families.

Mary Alice Fernandez, PhD, LPC-S, NCC is a retired assistant professor from Texas A&M University, Corpus Christi.

K. Michelle Hunnicutt Hollenbaugh, PhD, LPC-S, is an associate professor in the Department of Counseling and Educational Psychology at Texas A&M University, Corpus Christi. She has several years of clinical experience in a variety of settings, and has spent the majority of this time researching and providing Dialectical Behavior Therapy (DBT). She is currently conducting several research studies on adaptations of DBT, and continues to facilitate the implementation of DBT-based clinical services for the local community.

Mehmet A. Karaman, PhD is an assistant professor at the Department of Counseling and Guidance at the University of Texas Rio Grande Valley. He has practiced in psychiatric hospitals, community mental health agencies, school districts, and non-profit organizations. His research interests include achievement motivation, instrument development, cross-cultural studies, and counseling children and adolescents.

Jacob M. Klein, M.Ed., is a Licensed Professional Clinical Counselor in the state of Ohio, currently working in private practice with a focus on gender therapy, and is a Ph.D. candidate at The Ohio State University.

Eunice Lerma, PhD is an assistant professor at the Department of Counseling and Guidance at the University of Texas Rio Grande Valley.

Michael S. Lewis, PhD, LPCC-S, is a clinical professor at Capital University, and has extensive experience working with adolescents and young adults. He has also spent time working in substance abuse treatment facilities and high school settings. Michael specializes in wellness- and mindfulness-based innovative interventions. His research interests include college counseling, counselor development, and behavioral addictions.

Wannigar Ratanavivan, PhD, LPC, NCC is an adjunct graduate faculty member at Texas A&M University, Corpus Christi.

Richard J. Ricard, PhD, LPC-S is assistant dean and professor of Counseling and Educational Psychology at Texas A&M University, Corpus Christi. He is also the founder and director of the Teen Talk program at the Student Success Center in Corpus Christi, Texas. His research focuses on program evaluation and implementation of evidence-based counseling interventions in schools.

Introduction and Overview
K. Michelle Hunnicutt Hollenbaugh

Dialectical Behavior Therapy (DBT) is considered a 'third wave' Cognitive Behavioral Therapy—which means it's a type of CBT that also includes other interventions and approaches (for example, dialectics and mindfulness). Marsha Linehan began developing this treatment several decades ago, and since then it has saved communities thousands of dollars by helping clients avoid inpatient hospitalizations and acute mental health care (Linehan, 2015). This is accomplished by working with clients so they are reinforced for using new skills to cope with and manage emotions, instead of resorting to life-threatening behaviors such as self-injurious or impulsive behaviors. Originally, Linehan developed DBT for individuals (primarily women) diagnosed with borderline personality disorder (BPD). However, since then, research on DBT has expanded substantially. Researchers have used DBT in many different settings for both adults and adolescents struggling with a variety of diagnoses (Fleischhaker et al., 2011). This research includes but is not limited to: eating disorders (Salbach-Andrae, Bohnekamp, Pfeiffer, Lehmkuhl, & Miller, 2008), bipolar disorder (Goldstein, Axelson, Birmaher, & Brent, 2007), inpatient treatment (Katz, Cox, Gunasekara, & Miller, 2004), residential settings (The Grove Street Adolescent Residence, 2004), and schools (Ricard, Lerma, & Heard, 2013).

Currently, there aren't many evidence-based treatments available that focus specifically on treating adolescents struggling with pervasive emotion dysregulation (the inability to effectively manage emotions in most life situations). There are also a lot of adolescents who do not respond well to traditional treatment methods—or they may simply benefit from supplemental interventions in addition to the treatment they are currently receiving. For these reasons, DBT is a great option for clinicians who are working with adolescents.

WHY DBT IS DIFFERENT

When Linehan originally started working with clients with borderline personality disorder, she noticed the type of intervention she was using was not always effective. When she used a behavioral, problem-solving approach, she found it was too focused on change, and clients became resistant. When she used a more person-centered approach, she found the focus was too much on validation, and clients were unable to problem solve in order to make necessary changes. As a result, she developed DBT as a new type of approach that provides flexibility to use both validation and change in the context of the client's current situation (Linehan & Wilks, 2015). DBT also addresses several problem behaviors at the same time. Treatment targets (goals) are addressed through several modes (types of treatment): including skills groups, individual sessions, and family sessions. This increases the intensity of treatment, but it also increases the adolescent's success in learning and using skills while decreasing problem behaviors.

HOW TO USE THIS BOOK

Our goal in writing this book is to share approachable material for you to use in your practice. Hopefully you will find this information useful on its own; however we also recommend reading the foundational texts by Linehan (1993's *Cognitive-Behavioral Treatment of Borderline Personality Disorder*) and Miller, Rathus, and Linehan (2007's *Dialectical Behavior Therapy With Suicidal Adolescents*). Though we will give basic explanations of the foundational principles of DBT here, those texts go much more in depth and will help you understand the material.

We organized this book for maximum utility. This introduction will give an overview of DBT, including all of the basic principles, functions, and modes of treatment. Chapter 2 will include specifics on implementing DBT in your setting, decisions to consider when adapting DBT, and the importance of commitment strategies. Additionally, it will explore multicultural considerations. Chapter 3 will discuss how to develop a consultation team and describe DBT as a collaborative approach to treatment. Then, Chapters 4 through 8 will discuss considerations for implementation in specific settings (different levels of care, schools, and forensic settings). Chapters 9 through 13 will discuss specific diagnoses, and adaptations for adolescents struggling with eating disorders, conduct disorders, substance use disorders, other diagnoses, and how to address comorbidity and non-suicidal self-injury (NSSI) specifically. Finally, Chapter 14 will include a summary and conclusions. The text will include usable handouts based in DBT for each corresponding chapter.

TERMINOLOGY

Counselors, social workers, psychologists, and other professionals alike will find this text helpful, but for the sake of brevity we will use the term *clinician* to refer to any professional working in these capacities. We will also use the term *client* when discussing the adolescents you will be treating, though we are aware that you may refer to them as patients, students, etc. There are a lot of different terms used in DBT that will be described in this chapter and the next chapter—refer to Table 1.1 for a basic definition of all of these terms.

Table 1.1 Definition of Terms in the Structure and Implementation of DBT

Term	Definition
Treatment Mode	A treatment mode describes how DBT will be provided. This includes skills groups, individual counseling, phone coaching, and consultation team. You can decide which modes to implement based on the needs of your settings and your clients.
Skills Module	In DBT skills training with adolescents, there are five psychoeducational skills modules: *mindfulness, interpersonal effectiveness, emotion regulation, distress tolerance*, and *walking the middle path*. These modules are usually taught via psychoeducational skills groups.
Treatment Strategies	There are several types of treatment strategies in DBT. The strategies discussed in this book include *dialectical, core* (validation and problem-solving), *stylistic, case management*, and *commitment*. We believe these will be the most applicable to readers; however there are more strategies discussed in depth in Linehan's (1993) original text.
Stages of Treatment	There are four stages in DBT treatment. Stage one has received the most attention, and is the most common, as this is when skills groups take place.
Treatment Targets	There are several hierarchical treatment targets that are identified for each individual client. These include *decreasing life-threatening behaviors, decreasing therapy-interfering behaviors, decreasing quality-of-life-interfering behaviors*, and *increasing behavioral skills*. These are addressed via the modes of treatment and facilitated by the strategies employed by the clinician.
Treatment Functions	Miller et al. (2007) stated that treatment targets cannot be addressed unless the program as a whole addresses the following treatment functions: *improving motivation to change, enhancing capabilities, ensuring skill generalization, structuring the environment to support clients and clinicians*, and *improving therapist motivations*.

THE BIOSOCIAL THEORY OF EMOTION DYSREGULATION

Dialectical Behavior Therapy is based on the biosocial theory of emotion dysregulation. Emotion dysregulation is "the inability, despite one's best efforts, to change or regulate emotional cues, experiences, actions, verbal responses, and/or nonverbal expressions under normative conditions" (Koerner, 2012, p. 4). Basically, the biosocial theory states that pervasive emotion dysregulation is the result of two interacting phenomena—biological predisposition to emotional vulnerability and an invalidating environment (see Figure 1.1). Biological predisposition means the adolescent's brain is biologically different, and therefore he or she is more vulnerable to volatile

Invalidating Environment

- Stress-Filled Home
- Indiscriminately Rejects Private Experience
- Punishes Emotional Displays While Intermittently Reinforcing Emotional Escalation
- Oversimplifies Ease of Problem-Solving and Meeting Goals

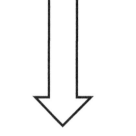

Biological Vulnerability

- High Emotional Sensitivity
- High Emotional Reactivity
- Slow Return to Emotional Baseline
- Biological Predisposition

Emotional and Behavioral Dysregulation

- Doesn't Know How to Express Emotions Appropriately
- Negative Coping Techniques Such as Substance Abuse, Eating Disorders, and Self-Harm

Figure 1.1 Biosocial Theory

emotions than others. These adolescents may experience emotions more frequently and intensely, and they may have more difficulty managing those emotions. The invalidating environment is often experienced as emotional neglect or harm from parents or other significant adults, siblings, and peers. They learn that their emotions are not important, wrong, or they are simply ignored. As a result, these adolescents do not learn effective methods of regulating emotions, and then they experience pervasive emotion dysregulation. The interaction of these two variables can lead to behaviors with potential harmful consequences—including self-injury and suicide attempts (Linehan, 1993). See Handout 1.1 for a handout that explains the biosocial theory to adolescents and parents. Without intervention, pervasive emotion dysregulation can develop into more severe disorders. By using DBT, clinicians (and parents) can stop reinforcing the harmful, life-threatening behaviors that the adolescent is currently using to manage his or her emotions, and instead teach him or her new and effective ways to cope.

DIALECTICS

The term *dialectic* may be new to some readers. It means the synthesis of opposites—that two, seemingly opposite, ideas or phenomena can both be correct and co-exist (Linehan, 1993, p. 30). DBT treatment is, in itself, dialectical as clinicians work with clients to validate them in their current situation, while also helping them make changes for the better. One of the most important underlying assumptions in DBT is that the client is doing the best that he or she can, *and* he or she can also do better (Linehan, 1993). This highlights the dialectical nature of DBT—two ideas that appear to be contradictory are both correct. Clinicians can take a dialectical approach to counseling by being flexible and viewing reality as something that is always changing, and that all aspects of reality are interrelated. In session, clinicians are encouraged to find balance (Linehan referred to this balance as being on a "teeter-totter" with the client on one side, and the clinician on the other, 1993, p. 30) and to ask "what are we leaving out?" When teaching dialectics to clients, it is important to emphasize the use of the terms "both" or "and" as opposed to "either" and "or." In fact, one of the key concepts of DBT, the *Wise Mind*, is the dialectic between the emotional and the reasonable minds (Linehan, 2015).

Initially, I (the first author of this book) found the concept of dialectics to be vague and ill defined at times—but after spending time with it I think that ambiguity is in itself a description of being dialectical. Nothing is set in stone; nothing is black or white. Everyone perceives reality through his or her own lens and that is what makes two sides of a situation equally correct. For individuals, it *is* correct for them to see the situation in *their* own manner, based on their own experiences.

MODES OF TREATMENT

By now, you have probably discovered how complex DBT treatment is. In traditional DBT, there are several modes of treatment—that is, different facets that make up the complete course of treatment. Fortunately, there is a lot of research that shows that not all modes of DBT treatment are necessary for positive treatment outcomes. Instead, clinicians should focus on what will work best given the setting they work in and the clients they are treating. However, if the program does not offer all of the standard DBT modes, it does not meet the requirements to be considered full DBT. Clinicians should disclose this readily to clients—Linehan and colleagues suggest terming the program as *DBT informed* instead. The standard DBT modes include psychoeducational skills groups, individual sessions, intersession phone coaching, and a clinician consultation team (Linehan, 2015).

Skills Groups

Psychoeducational skills groups are adapted to fit the needs of the setting and can be altered for the needs of the adolescents. Traditionally, they last for two hours weekly. The first hour consists of reviewing homework and diary cards and the second hour consists of learning new materials. Mindfulness practice is conducted at the beginning and the end of each session, to emphasize the importance of this skill, and increase the adolescents' ability to use this skill. Typically, groups are closed during each module and then opened again at the beginning of a new one. This provides the group a sense of cohesion and comfort necessary to build skills, and then adolescents who have experience with the material can support and give tips to new members (Rathus & Miller, 2015).

Each module includes homework sheets for each skill learned, in addition to keeping track of the skills the adolescent used throughout the week on his or her diary card. Diary cards are (like they sound) a journal that the client keeps and they can be customized to fit the needs of your client. We have included several versions that are different based on the setting and the diagnosis. They can include moods on any given day, any skills they have previously learned, and any target behaviors the adolescent is working to increase or decrease (Miller et al., 2007). See Handouts 1.2–1.5 for several diary card examples.

Parents and caregivers may also take part in skills groups training, as this helps increase skills acquisition in different settings. Increasing the skills of the parents also serves to decrease any invalidation the adolescent may be experiencing (Rathus & Miller, 2015). Clinicians can initiate skills groups in many different ways, depending on the setting in which they are working. We will discuss different options for implementation further in each specific chapter. A short description of each skills training module, including the adolescent specific module, Walking the Middle Path, is below.

Mindfulness

The practice of mindfulness is considered a foundation of DBT—it is the first skill taught, and is practiced in every session (often several times). Mindfulness is based in Eastern traditions; however, mindfulness from a DBT perspective is not considered meditation. Instead, it is considered a skill to increase awareness in the moment and the ability to manage one's emotions and thoughts. The premise of mindfulness for adolescents is that they often struggle with racing thoughts, or have difficulty focusing on one thing at a time. By being mindful, they become better at controlling their thoughts instead of letting them be controlled *by* them (Linehan, 1993). Adolescents who regularly practice mindfulness are more aware of what is going on in their body, their mind, and are able to put it in context to any given situation. They become better at using skills effectively in difficult situations. The basic mindfulness skills include *what* (what you do when you practice mindfulness) skills: observe, describe, participate; and *how* (how you practice mindfulness) skills: one-mindfully, nonjudgmentally, and effectively (Linehan, 2015).

Interpersonal Effectiveness

The focus of this module is relationships, which can be extremely important considering how often adolescents struggle with volatile relationships. The skills in this module focus specifically on keeping one's own self-respect in a relationship, respecting others, getting needs met in an assertive fashion, and successfully evaluating and managing healthy relationships. Skills in this module (as with most modules) are often formulated in the form of acronyms, and include aspects of problem-solving related to interpersonal effectiveness, myths regarding relationships, self-esteem in relationships, and vulnerabilities that may affect how we interact in relationships (Linehan, 2015).

Distress Tolerance

The distress tolerance module includes skills related to coping with the current situation, especially when the adolescent cannot change it immediately. These could also be referred to as crises, in which the adolescent is struggling to manage emotions effectively and is more likely to engage in life-threatening behaviors. Distress tolerance skills include problem-solving, for example, considering which action to take to cope with the situation, as well as numerous acronyms regarding activities the client can engage in to cope with the situation when he or she cannot "fix" it right away. My favorite DBT skill, radical acceptance, is also included in the module, and involves the act of mentally accepting reality, over and over, as needed to reduce suffering (Linehan, 2015).

Emotion Regulation

This module not only deals with effective ways to cope with emotions, it teaches clients the biology of emotions, including primary and secondary emotions, and their purpose. Clients also learn about myths involving emotions, and how to be aware of emotions both physically and mentally. Skills in this module focus on helping clients engage in healthy coping activities and not only increase personal awareness of their emotions, but awareness of others' emotions as well (Linehan, 2015).

Walking the Middle Path

This module focuses on adolescent-specific dialectical dilemmas (see Table 1.2). It also helps adolescents learn the concept of dialectics and how it can be helpful to approach situations dialectically. Clients can learn skills to validate themselves and others, and regulate their emotions effectively without vacillating between behavioral extremes. This module also includes a basic section on behavioral principles including reinforcement, punishment, and shaping behaviors (Miller et al., 2007).

Table 1.2 DBT Dialectical Dilemmas

Common Dialectical Dilemmas	Adolescent Specific Dialectical Dilemmas
Emotional Vulnerability vs. Self-Invalidation	Excessive Leniency vs. Authoritarian Control
Active Passivity vs. Apparent Competence	Normalizing Pathological Behaviors vs. Pathologizing Normative Behaviors
Unrelenting Crises vs. Inhibited Experiencing	Forcing Autonomy vs. Fostering Dependence

Source: Adapted by permission from Miller et al., 2007.

Intersession Skills Coaching

Another standard mode of DBT treatment is 24-hour skills coaching. This mode is possibly the most intimidating for clinicians, and as result, they may not include it for fear of being accosted by after-hours calls. However, Linehan has stated she believes that clients should not have to be suicidal to receive extra attention from their therapists (Linehan, 1993). By allowing clients to call the clinician in between sessions as needed, specifically for skills coaching, the client is reinforced for using these skills. There are several rules that go along with phone coaching in DBT. Foremost, the client must call his or her therapist before he or she engages in a life-threatening behavior. This prevents the reinforcement clients often receive for engaging in that behavior (e.g., extra attention and love from parents and peers). Instead, the clinician reinforces the client for calling for phone coaching, and seeking help before life-threatening behaviors occur.

If the client abuses the privilege to call for coaching (e.g., calls but is resistant to coaching or insists on discussing other topics) the clinician addresses this extensively in the next individual session. By using time in session to focus on this therapy-interfering behavior, the clinician discourages the client from engaging in this behavior in the future. Most DBT therapists report that although they may initially receive frequent calls for skills coaching, as the client develops his or her own skills, these calls diminish and eventually cease. Per Linehan and colleagues, most skills coaching calls last about ten minutes.

When working with adolescents, clinicians make phone coaching available to parents and family members as well. This helps family members increase their own skills, reduce vacillating between behavioral extremes, and increase skills generalization for the adolescent. Though this may seem overwhelming, this mode of treatment can be adapted to fit the needs of the treatment team and setting. For example, instead of the primary clinician always being available for calls, team members can alternate this responsibility. Others limit the times that they are available for coaching (however this can limit the reinforcement of skills use and be less effective than full availability). Finally, if the setting is residential or inpatient, intersession coaching can be conducted by other trained staff members (e.g., nurses or social workers) who have been adequately trained (Linehan, 2015).

Individual Sessions

Individual counseling sessions are an important facet of standard DBT. Individual meetings often consist of evaluating commitment to treatment as well as interventions to manage therapy-interfering, life-threatening, and quality-of-life-interfering behaviors. Although clients review diary cards and other homework assignments in skills group, in individual sessions the clinician and the client discuss the diary card in more detail, in the context of their agreed-upon treatment targets. They also might conduct behavior chain analyses to decrease reinforcement of any problem behaviors.

It is also important for the clinician to engage the adolescent's parents in family counseling sessions. These sessions can be scheduled regularly, or on an as needed basis. The clinician can also schedule to meet with the parents individually. Again, the goal of these sessions is to help the adolescent learn and use new skills, enhance his or her ability to learn new behaviors (and extinction of unwanted behaviors), and maintain commitment to treatment (Miller et al., 2007).

Consultation Group

One of the most important facets of standard DBT is the clinician consultation group. From the beginning, Linehan has said that clinicians treating clients with emotional dysregulation and/or engaging in life-threatening behaviors need their own support. This is especially true for clinicians working with adolescents. The consultation group should consist of any clinicians engaged in the DBT program, as well as any nurses, doctors, case managers, and other staff members involved. Although it changes depending on the setting, the consultation team should be as comprehensive as possible. If you are a clinician working in private practice, you may find this treatment mode challenging—there may not be enough people in your practice who are involved in DBT to create a consultation group. However, you can also engage in consultation groups outside of your office. When I first started offering skills groups in a community mental health center, I attended a DBT consultation team that consisted of clinicians in community mental health centers throughout the city, as there were not enough clinicians in each individual center to create a consultation group. Similarly, I have known other clinicians in private practice who emailed other DBT teams in the community and asked to join their consultation team, or even joined a consultation team that met via online video conferencing.

Team meetings usually include case consultation with a focus on maintaining the fidelity of DBT treatment. Consultation groups often meet weekly but this can vary based on need. Meetings are set up a lot like DBT psychoeducational skills groups—they usually include mindfulness, DBT-related activities and skills, and behavioral interventions for "consultation"-interfering behaviors (e.g., repeated tardiness or lack of preparation) (Linehan, 1993).

Ancillary Modes

In addition to the standard modes of treatment, there are several other modes that may or may not be included in DBT treatment—for example, case management and pharmacotherapy. These modes should complement DBT treatment though they may not always be DBT based (e.g., treatment is provided from a provider that does not adhere to DBT principles). However, at the very least, clinicians should be able to work with other treatment providers to ensure they are on the same page with regard to reinforcing (or not reinforcing) behaviors the client and family use to manage emotion dysregulation (Linehan, 1993).

TREATMENT STRATEGIES

Treatment strategies in DBT encompass any approaches or techniques the clinician uses to achieve treatment goals. These techniques include commitment strategies, dialectical strategies, validation strategies, problem-solving strategies, stylistic strategies, and case management strategies. A brief overview is provided here; however if you are interested in learning about these in more detail, I highly encourage you to read about them in Linehan's (1993) text *Cognitive-Behavioral Treatment of Borderline Personality Disorder*.

Orientation and Commitment Strategies

Orientation and commitment strategies are essential to help the client understand the process of DBT, the expectations for both the client and clinician, and finally to engage the client in a commitment to certain parameters (length and frequency) of treatment. The importance of orienting and committing the client to treatment cannot be understated. In fact, I believe that most of the problems I have experienced with treatment compliance in DBT were related to the fact that I did not engage in enough orientation and commitment to treatment in the beginning, or I did not revert back to commitment strategies when they were needed mid-treatment. These strategies will be discussed fully in Chapter 2.

Dialectical Strategies

In both adolescent and adult DBT, dialectical strategies include three aspects: balancing treatment strategies, teaching dialectical behaviors to the client, and specific dialectical strategies. Balancing treatment strategies is one of the core themes throughout DBT treatment—and it involves constantly balancing acceptance and change. As Linehan stated "The primary therapy dialectic is that of change in the context of acceptance of reality as it is" (1993, p. 201). By focusing on validation *and* change, the clinician is able to provide support as needed while also helping the client to work towards change.

Teaching dialectical behaviors to the client is also important because it can help the adolescent see where he or she (or his or her family) is maintaining an either/or stance in any given situation. By learning about dialectics, clients can take on a dialectical worldview in their current life, which will increase their ability to be flexible and understand the viewpoint of others. Again, it should be noted that by teaching dialectical strategies you are not invalidating either side of the polarities that may arise for your client—instead, you are validating both (Miller et al., 2007).

Finally, there are several specific dialectical strategies that DBT clinicians employ to attain treatment goals with adolescents and their families. These include: entering the paradox, using metaphors, playing devil's advocate, extending, activating wise mind, making lemonade out of lemons, allowing natural change, and conducting a dialectical assessment. To learn more about these strategies in detail, refer back to the Linehan (1993) text or Miller et al. (2007).

Validation and Problem-Solving Strategies

Validation and problem-solving are considered core strategies in DBT, which means they are present in all interactions between the clinician and the client. As Miller et al. (2007) noted, when a clinician feels "stuck" with a client in treatment, often it is because he or she is focusing too much on either validation or change (problem-solving). Therefore, it is always important to utilize both, often simultaneously.

In DBT, validation strategies have six different levels, and four different types. This probably seems complex and overwhelming to simply read about, much less try to implement! However, you will likely find that you are engaging in the majority of these strategies already, especially since many of them have a foundation in person-centered therapy. For example, using basic reflections of feelings and thoughts, and providing encouragement, praise, and reassurance are all activities most clinicians use in all counseling sessions, DBT or otherwise.

Problem-solving strategies involve two steps—first the clinician and the client must fully understand the problem at hand, and second, they work together to address the problem and generate solutions. This is best done using a Behavior Chain Analysis (BCA) and can be conducted in a variety of formats. See Handout 1.6 for a BCA worksheet we created that may be helpful specifically for working with adolescents. There are several steps included in creating a BCA. First, define the problem—whether it is a life-threatening behavior, quality-of-life-interfering behavior, or a therapy-interfering behavior. Then identify the vulnerabilities the client may have that would pre-dispose him or her to engaging in the behavior, and lastly, the consequences of the problem behavior. The client then will work (with the help of the clinician) to identify the thoughts, feelings, and behaviors that led to the problem behavior. Finally, they work to identify a new chain with different behaviors, thoughts, and feelings that will lead to a new, more acceptable behavior. I teach my clients to be aware of the alphabet in this regard. For example, "A" always comes before "B," "M" before "N," and so on. If the problem behavior is "Z," we must identify the behaviors and thoughts that represent A–Y. If they can avoid preceding behaviors and thoughts, they are much more likely to avoid the problem behavior altogether. Remember, problem-solving strategies go hand in hand with validation strategies, and therefore when engaging in problem-solving, it is important for the clinician to engage in validation throughout. In other words, continue to approach treatment dialectically.

Stylistic Strategies

Stylistic strategies speak less to the *what* a clinician is going to do, and more to the *how* he or she will engage the client in treatment (Miller et al., 2007). There are two stylistic strategies—reciprocal strategies and irreverent strategies. Reciprocal strategies include being genuine and open to what the client is saying, and also at times using self-involving statements (e.g., expression of personal feelings regarding the client in the moment). This could also be considered using immediacy in session. For example, the clinician may make comments on his or her own feelings in session or on the client's thoughts, feelings, and behaviors related to the counseling process (Linehan, 1993). Irreverent strategies can be especially helpful with adolescents, and can include using humor, a different vocal tone, or some well-placed sarcasm. Though you will obviously want to be careful when using this skill, the main idea is that by using this strategy you will change the effect of the conversation or get the client's attention by putting him or her off balance, so to speak. This will help take the client out of his or her normal behavioral patterns that maintain emotion dysregulation, and helps him or her stop and use skills to effectively manage emotions. One example of this might be if a client reports a desire to sneak out of the house that evening to use drugs with his or her friends, and the clinician responds (in a light, non-accusatory tone, perhaps with a smile) "you're right, that's an excellent idea. I'm sure your parents won't mind that at all." Reciprocal strategies (as with most things in DBT) should be balanced with irreverent strategies (Miller et al., 2007).

Case Management Strategies

A clinician may incorporate case management strategies when there are issues with the client's environment that are preventing his or her ability to be successful in treatment. The foremost strategy in this section is called therapist-to-patient consultation. The main goal of this is for the clinician to help the client solve his or her own problems, instead of intervening on his or her behalf. By doing this, the clinician can help the client build mastery of his or her skills, while also minimizing splitting that sometimes happens with professionals and clients (when a client consciously or unconsciously divides counselors and staff against each other). The other strategies in this section including environmental interventions (considered as a last resort, when potential harm could come to the client and he or she does not have the skills or resources to solve the problem at hand) and consultation team meetings, where the consultation team actually applies DBT strategies and interventions to the clinician, when needed (for example, which the clinician's commitment is wavering, or he or she is engaging in therapy-interfering behaviors) (Linehan, 1993).

STAGES OF TREATMENT

There are four stages in DBT treatment. Each of these stages has specific treatment targets. Though the stages are numbered based on symptom severity from one to four, the client may not move through the stages linearly and may even meet criteria for two stages at the same time. When a client is initially admitted to treatment, the clinician, along with the consultation team, will make a decision regarding which stage fits the client's needs for the best treatment outcomes (Linehan, 1993).

Pretreatment Stage

Commitment strategies are essential during the pretreatment phase (see Chapter 2). The length of the pretreatment phase varies, depending on the setting and diagnosis.

The goal of pretreatment is for the clinician and the client to reach mutually agreed-upon expectations and a commitment to treatment. As we are sure you know, premature termination in counseling is common, especially for adolescents struggling with labile emotions. By taking the time needed to commit the client to treatment, hopefully you can avoid attrition. If at all possible the client should be given the choice between DBT and another form of treatment, as this will also increase his or her commitment. The pretreatment tasks in DBT with adolescents include: 1) Inform and orient the client and the family to DBT, 2) Secure the adolescent and the family's commitment to treatment, and 3) Secure the therapist's commitment to treatment (Miller et al., 2007).

Stage One

This stage is by far the most studied stage of DBT treatment. In this stage, the treatment targets are (in order of importance): decreasing life-threatening behaviors, decreasing therapy-interfering behaviors, decreasing quality-of-life-interfering behaviors, and increasing behavioral skills. Psychoeducational skills groups are usually implemented during stage one to address these treatment targets. The client can spend up to a year in this stage, as Linehan posits that clients should complete all skills training modules twice, to ensure mastery (1993). However, this model may be adjusted based on the needs of the client and the setting (Rathus & Miller, 2015). Although clients usually begin in this stage, and then move on to other stages, if they experience a relapse into previous life-threatening or therapy-interfering behaviors, they may move back a stage in order to refresh these skills. Clients remain in stage one until they are no longer engaging in life-threatening behaviors.

Stage Two

The major treatment target of stage two is decreasing post-traumatic stress. A client can either begin treatment in stage two (if he or she has previously learned to manage the aforementioned behaviors), or he or she can move on to stage two after successfully completing stage one. As Linehan (1993) warns, the client's ability to cope with the current situation, or with post-traumatic stress responses, should not be mistaken as a time to end treatment. Terminating treatment too early may lead to a relapse in stage one problematic behaviors. Instead, adolescents should engage in individual counseling (along with, possibly, a stage one graduate support group) and focus on accepting the facts of their trauma; reducing stigmatization, self-invalidation, and self-blame; reducing denial and intrusive stress-response patterns; and reducing dichotomous thinking about the traumatic situation (Linehan, 1993).

Stage Three

In this stage, the client works on individual goals and increasing self-respect. As Linehan noted, once clients are at this stage in treatment, they are likely to be struggling with self-blame and self-hatred that limit their ability to achieve happiness. This stage is centered on helping the client conceptualize his or her past, and process this with others. However, at this stage, though the client has moved past some of the life threatening, therapy-interfering, and quality-of-life-interfering behaviors of the previous stages, he or she may experience a relapse in life-threatening or quality-of-life-interfering behaviors. If this happens, the clinician should avoid shaming the client and instead focus on helping the client engage in more learning and previous coping skills (Linehan, 1993).

Stage Four

In stage four, the client focuses on resolving a sense of incompleteness, and finding freedom and joy. Essentially, in this stage the client works toward self-actualization, and may be more spiritually based, in which the client explores meaning and purpose. It is important to note that there is not much published on stage four in the DBT literature, likely due to the fact the clients with most urgent needs are in stage one.

STAGE ONE TREATMENT TARGETS

As stage one is the most common, we will spend some time describing the treatment targets in this stage. Once you have identified that your client meets criteria for stage one treatment, you will need to identify all of his or her reported problem behaviors. Then, you will need to decide which category the behavior falls under—life threatening, therapy interfering, or quality of life interfering. This is a judgment call that you will make on an individual basis—and this is one of the reasons the consultation group is so important! Remember that Linehan and colleagues consider life-threatening behaviors *any* behavior that puts the individual or others in imminent harm—other behaviors that may lead to negative consequences (e.g., risky sexual behavior) are more likely to be considered quality-of-life-threatening behaviors.

Decreasing Life-Threatening Behaviors

Many adolescents, regardless of their diagnosis, struggle with pervasive emotion dysregulation, and in an attempt to manage their emotions, they may engage in life-threatening behaviors. Even if they are ultimately ineffective at assuaging their feelings long-term, these behaviors act as an immediate relief to an otherwise tumultuous situation. This usually is experienced through non-suicidal self-injury, but can also include suicide threats/attempts, thoughts or threats of harming others, or failing to take life-sustaining medications. Life-threatening behaviors are addressed in stage one via skills training, individual treatment, intersession phone coaching, and the clinician consultation team (Linehan, 2015). See more on addressing life-threatening behaviors in Chapter 11.

Decreasing Therapy-Interfering Behaviors

Not surprisingly, there are *a lot* of actions under this umbrella. These activities can be any behavior engaged in by the client, the clinician, and/or family members that can limit the effectiveness of treatment. Therapy-interfering behaviors are further organized by activities that interfere with receiving therapy, with other clients, and/or burn out the counselor. The skills trainer and/or individual clinician can address these behaviors as needed.

Behaviors That Interfere With Receiving Therapy

There are numerous actions that can prevent the client from properly receiving therapeutic interventions from the clinician. These behaviors may include circumstances that prevent the client from attending therapy (e.g., tardiness, cancellations, repeated hospitalizations), inattentiveness in therapy (e.g., drug or alcohol use, disruptiveness in group sessions, emotional outbursts), non-collaboration (e.g., not responding, responding repeatedly with "I don't know"), combativeness (e.g., lying/arguing/challenging), and lastly, noncompliance (e.g., not completing homework or diary cards, not participating) (Miller et al., 2007).

Behaviors That Interfere With Other Clients

Adolescents interact with each other frequently during the psychoeducational skills group. These interactions are often extremely beneficial, as they can learn from one another and model appropriate responses and behaviors. However, some adolescents may engage in behaviors that interfere with others' success in treatment. Examples of these activities include engaging other clients in destructive behaviors, being openly judgmental of others (or the DBT process), or being loud and disruptive to other clients outside of session. Adolescents can be susceptible to peer pressure, which can increase the likelihood of these behaviors (Rathus & Miller, 2015).

Behaviors That Burnout the Clinician

As aforementioned, clinicians engaging in DBT need support, and the intensity of the treatment can have a negative impact on the clinician. Clients may contribute to this by challenging the clinician's limits and boundaries, being aggressive, or interfering with the motivation of other staff members through similar behaviors (Linehan, 1993).

Family Therapy-Interfering Behaviors

Family members can be a significant influence on the success of DBT treatment for adolescents. Similarly, family members can derail treatment by engaging in interfering behaviors. Examples may include not providing transportation for the client, or not allowing the adolescent to use the phone to engage in phone coaching. The clinician will often address these behaviors with the client, and facilitate the client's ability to use his or her skills to communicate his or her needs is the situation while also respecting relationships (Miller et al., 2007).

Clinician Interfering Behaviors

Lastly, the clinician may unwittingly disrupt the therapeutic process. He or she can become too non-dialectical (e.g., pushing too hard for change, or being overly validating without focusing enough on change) or being disrespectful to the client (e.g., being condescending, approaching a situation emotionally). The clinician can limit these behaviors by engaging in the consultation team, and being open to feedback from clinicians and clients regarding these behaviors (Linehan, 1993).

Decreasing Quality-of-Life-Interfering Behaviors

Due to the fact that their brains (specifically, frontal lobes) are still developing, all adolescents struggle with impulsivity and poor decision-making. When this stage of development is combined with pervasive emotion dysregulation, the list of activities that they may engage in that negatively impact quality of life are innumerable. These behaviors may include impulsivity, drug use, promiscuous sexual behavior, and engaging in abusive relationships. It may be difficult for adolescents and parents to discern which behaviors and activities may be considered normative. Regardless, you may spend time in consultation with the client, the family, and other clinicians on the team to determine what the agreed-on treatment targets will be during this stage. Quality-of-life-interfering behaviors are typically addressed after therapy-interfering behaviors. Linehan posited that if therapy is unproductive, the clinician and the client would be unable to address the quality-of-life-interfering behaviors as well.

Increasing Behavioral Skills

Finally, one of the most important facets of stage one is helping clients develop skills to combat previous dysfunctional coping strategies. This is where the weekly skills group (or learning skills in individual therapy) is important to incorporate interpersonal effectiveness, emotion regulation, mindfulness, and distress tolerance. Behavioral skills replace the previous problem behaviors, and help the client effectively manage his or her emotions. Clients learn these skills through weekly homework assignments, and keep track of when/how they use them via diary cards (Rathus & Miller, 2015).

STAGE ONE SECONDARY TREATMENT TARGETS—
DIALECTICAL DILEMMAS

Referring back to Table 1.2, Linehan noted that clients struggling with emotion dysregulation often fall into behavioral patterns that vacillate between two extremes, which she calls dialectical dilemmas. Basically, the problem behaviors you identified as primary treatment targets (above) become patterns, based on the client under-regulating or over-regulating their emotions (Miller et al., 2007). As result, the goal is to even out emotion regulation and bring the client back to the synthesis of both polarities.

Emotional Vulnerability vs. Self-Invalidation: The client will either experience extreme emotions with little or no effort to effectively manage them, or completely invalidate his or her emotions.
Active Passivity vs. Apparent Competence: The client will vacillate between doing little to help him or herself (and looking to others for help), or will seem like he or she has the skills and ability to manage a situation, when in reality, he or she does not.
Unrelenting Crises vs. Inhibited Experiencing: In this dilemma, the client vacillates between constant emotional crises (in an attempt to cope with emotions) and avoiding situations that trigger any difficult emotions.

In addition to the behavioral patterns delineated by Linehan (1993), Miller et al. (2007) noted that there were several dialectical dilemmas they noticed that occurred among parents, adolescents, and therapists. Not only do the adolescents fall into these behavioral patterns, but parents and therapists do as well, often in reaction to the adolescents' extreme vacillations.

Excessive Leniency vs. Authoritarian Control: This refers the vacillation between either letting the adolescent do as he or she pleases at any given time, or imposing extreme discipline and punishments.
Normalizing Pathological Behaviors vs. Pathologizing Normative Behaviors: The parents (or adolescent) either think that extreme, harmful behaviors are normal, or think and treat normal adolescent behaviors as extremely dangerous or abnormal.
Forcing Autonomy vs. Fostering Dependence: Parents or adolescents vacillate between cutting off ties, with the expectation of the adolescent to be self-sufficient too quickly, and the adolescent not having any freedom or autonomy at all.

Why should we care about these dialectical dilemmas? These patterns can actually perpetuate related problem behaviors. It is also worth noting that in several adaptations of DBT, researchers have added dialectical dilemmas specific to the population they are treating, so keep an eye out for that in the other chapters.

CONCLUSION

This chapter reviewed the biosocial theory of emotion dysregulation, treatment modes and targets, stages of DBT treatment, and various treatment strategies. If you are feeling overwhelmed, no worries—I have found that once I became familiar with the material (and with the help of the DBT consultation team), this information became second nature, and easily flowed with the implementation of skills and strategies in group and individual sessions. I think you will also find this material easy to approach once you have had time to digest and begin to apply it.

REFERENCES

Fleischhaker, C., Böhme, R., Sixt, B., Brück, C., Schneider, C., & Schulz, E. (2011). Dialectical behavioral therapy for adolescents (DBT-A): A clinical trial for patients with suicidal and self-injurious behavior and borderline symptoms with a one-year follow-up. *Child and Adolescent Psychiatry and Mental Health*, *5*(1), 1–10. doi:10.1186/1753-2000-5-3

Goldstein, T. R., Axelson, D. A., Birmaher, B., & Brent, D. A. (2007). Dialectical behavior therapy for adolescents with bipolar disorder: A 1-year open trial. *Journal of the American Academy of Child & Adolescent Psychiatry*, *46*(7), 820–830. doi:10.1097/chi.0b013e31805c1613

Katz, L. Y., Cox, B. J., Gunasekara, S., & Miller, A. L. (2004). Feasibility of dialectical behavior therapy for suicidal adolescent inpatients. *Journal of the American Academy of Child & Adolescent Psychiatry*, *43*(3), 276–282.

Koerner, K. (2012). *Doing dialectical behavior therapy: A practical guide*. New York, NY: Guilford Press.

Linehan, M. M. (1993). *Cognitive-behavioral treatment of borderline personality disorder*. New York, NY: Guilford Press.

Linehan, M. M. (2015). *DBT® skills training manual* (2nd ed.). New York, NY: Guilford Press.

Linehan, M. M. & Wilks, C. R. (2015). The course and evolution of dialectical behavior therapy. *American Journal of Psychotherapy*, *69*(2), 97–110.

Miller, A. L., Rathus, J. H., & Linehan, M. M. (2007). *Dialectical behavior therapy with suicidal adolescents*. New York, NY: Guilford Press.

Rathus, J. H. & Miller, A. L. (2015). *DBT® skills manual for adolescents*. New York, NY: Guilford Press.

Ricard, R. J., Lerma, E., Heard, C. C. (2013). Piloting a Dialectical Behavioral Therapy (DBT) infused skills group in a Disciplinary Alternative Education Program (DAEP). *Journal For Specialists in Group Work*, *38*(4), 285–306.

Salbach-Andrae, H., Bohnekamp, I., Pfeiffer, E., Lehmkuhl, U., & Miller, A. L. (2008). Dialectical behavior therapy of anorexia and bulimia nervosa among adolescents: A case series. *Cognitive and Behavioral Practice*, *15*(4), 415–425. doi:10.1016/j.cbpra.2008.04.001

The Grove Street Adolescent Residence of the Bridge of Central Massachusetts, Inc. (2004). Using dialectical behavior therapy to help troubled adolescents return safely to their families and communities. *Psychiatric Services*, *55*(10), 1168–1170. doi:10.1176/appi.ps.55.10.1168

Treatment Delivery and Implementation
K. Michelle Hunnicutt Hollenbaugh

This chapter will explore key components of treatment delivery in DBT. This includes committing the client to treatment, considerations for implementing your DBT program, and assessment. We will also explore the pros and cons of using standard DBT as opposed to an adapted form of DBT (DBT informed). Additionally, multicultural considerations will be discussed.

IMPLEMENTATION

Standard DBT vs. DBT Informed

As mentioned in the previous chapter, standard DBT is an intensive treatment with multiple modes of treatment to address all treatment targets. These modes include individual therapy, group skills training, between-session skills coaching, and the clinician consultation team (details on these are provided in Chapter 1). In DBT informed, only some modes of DBT are implemented, or adaptations are made to the original DBT model.

There are pros and cons on both sides of implementing standard DBT and DBT informed treatment. The benefits of implementing standard DBT are that this method of treatment is the most intensive, and has the most research behind it. Each mode addresses specific treatment functions and it is a highly structured intervention. There are clear expectations for the clinician and client alike. Conversely, the cons of implementing standard DBT are that it is very time intensive, and because there are so many modes of treatment, it may be costly for clients and insurance companies may be unwilling to reimburse for all services.

Similarly, there are pros and cons to implementing DBT informed treatment. The pros are that the treatment is tailored to the needs of the setting—that can include tailoring the time frame of the treatment, only implementing some modes of treatment, or adapting the material to fit specific needs and populations. There is research available on DBT informed approaches (albeit, not as much as with standard DBT), with promising preliminary results and positive outcomes for certain populations, including adolescents. The cons of DBT informed implementations are that they may include less structure, there are fewer resources available for specific populations, and

Table 2.1 Pros and Cons of Implementing Standard DBT vs. DBT Informed

Pros of Standard DBT	Pros of DBT Informed
Standardized implementation clarifies expectations for all stakeholders	The skills are adaptable for several different populations and settings
Evidence-based treatment can increase ability to attain funding	There is research that supports the effectiveness of using only some modes of DBT
Each mode of DBT addresses specific treatment targets	Can be more cost effective
Standard DBT has the most research supporting its effectiveness	Increases flexibility of the treatment
Cons of Standard DBT	*Cons of DBT Informed*
Implementing all modes can be costly, as well as training all clinicians and staff involved in the treatment	Research is limited on effectiveness
Standard DBT requires full commitment by practitioners	Difficulty in structuring the treatment, fewer resources available

less research base for adapted interventions (Hunnicutt Hollenbaugh, Klein, & Lewis, 2015). See Table 2.1.

Training

Training is a major consideration with implementing DBT in your setting. The gold standard in DBT training is the ten-week, intensive training offered by Behavioral Tech. This training is only offered to DBT teams, and, in my opinion, is fairly expensive ($10,000 for teams up to four, prices increase from there). However, as noted in the title, it is intensive and provides a lot of feedback and guidance for teams working to set up their DBT program. There are several other training options in addition to this—Behavioral Tech (www.behavioraltech.org) also provides an advanced, intensive training for individual clinicians, and trainings for specific applications of the treatment. Most recently, the procedures for becoming a Certified DBT Therapist have been put in place by Linehan and colleagues, and it is a lengthy process, including passing an exam and engaging in case consultation. Per the certification website (www.dbt-lbc.org), it costs a total of $845 from start to finish, with a $95 yearly recertification fee. However, certification is not required for you to use DBT in your practice and is only one of many options you have for training.

Different Settings

Implementing DBT in different settings can require adaptations based on the needs of your clients and the setting. These changes may include which modes you employ, and who is involved in your treatment team. Miller, Rathus, & Linehan (2007) wrote that at a bare minimum, you should have two clinicians involved in the treatment team when working with adolescents. This will allow adequate support for co-leading groups and engaging in consultation. Other professionals can (and ideally should) be involved as well—for example, psychiatrists, nurses, and school counselors, just to name a few. The hope is that all members of the team will have some training in DBT, be familiar with the underlying principles, and grasp their particular role in the treatment.

It is also important to consider what modes will be provided, how treatment targets will be addressed, and how the overall program will adhere to the various treatment functions. Skills group is the most common mode and the most easily provided. However, it may be difficult to address all treatment targets in the psychoeducational skills group, which is why you may want to consider including other modes, including individual sessions. The intersession skills coaching may not be possible in some settings; however, by being creative, you can still achieve the treatment goals—some programs are designed so clients can seek coaching from other professionals (e.g., technicians, nurses) between group and individual sessions to help generalize skill use.

Structural/Financial Considerations

Obviously, standard DBT can be expensive, and, as mentioned, insurance may not necessarily cover all modes. For example, clinicians have reported difficulties getting reimbursed for between session skills coaching in addition to weekly individual and group sessions. From a financial perspective, it simply may not be feasible for every organization to provide all modes of DBT treatment. An additional concern for many clinicians is physical space. It may not be structurally reasonable to implement full DBT in an inpatient or intensive outpatient unit. In schools, you may only be able to offer DBT in a group format. It is also important to consider how you will implement DBT into the existing infrastructure—will you only offer DBT, or will it be one of many treatment interventions you provide? In depth discussions with administrators and stakeholders in the planning stages can help streamline the implementation process and reduce any problems that may come up in the future.

Different Populations

As you likely have noticed, there are several chapters in this text that address the use of DBT with different populations. This is due to the fact there are several populations that struggle with emotion dysregulation, and could therefore benefit from a DBT approach. Since DBT is a flexible treatment, you can easily adapt DBT interventions to the needs of the population you are treating. Adaptations can be made to the material, how it is presented, and how much is presented at one time. Just as the original DBT material has been adapted for adolescents, clinicians should engage in thoughtful consideration regarding which adaptations will be appropriate, while also being mindful of maintaining the fidelity of the treatment.

COMMITMENT STRATEGIES

There are several commitment strategies DBT clinicians use to engage the client in treatment. As we mentioned before, spending time committing the client to treatment is essential and can predict overall success in treatment. If you begin treatment, but do not have at least partial commitment to treatment, you may be engaging in a therapy-interfering behavior yourself! At best, lack of commitment can reduce the effectiveness of the treatment and at worst, lead to premature termination. Though these strategies are especially important in the beginning, you may need to default back to these strategies throughout the treatment, essentially recommitting the client to treatment. Commitment strategies in DBT include: foot in the door/door in the face, playing the devil's advocate, evaluating pros and cons, connecting present commitments to prior commitments, highlighting freedom to choose and absence of alternatives, and cheerleading (Miller et al., 2007). See Handout 2.1 for a handout that will help you remember the DBT commitment strategies.

Foot in the Door/Door in the Face

You may be familiar with these terms, and you may have even used them in other treatment approaches. With foot in the door, the clinician asks for an initial small commitment from the client—hence, the clinician is getting his or her foot in the door. Then, once the client has agreed to make this small commitment, the clinician requests a larger commitment. With the door in the face technique, the clinician makes a very large or seemingly impossible request, and then, when the client balks at the idea, the clinician reduces this request significantly. In my experience, although both techniques have worked effectively, I have found door in the face to be more effective with adolescents, as they are usually resistant to agreeing to small requests at first, but are more likely to agree after comparing it to something much larger. For example, you could start by asking the client to complete a full diary card, but then reduce it to just a small portion of the diary card.

Playing Devil's Advocate

I have to admit, when I first heard about this technique, I was skeptical. Again, as it sounds, the clinician takes the opposite side of what he or she might normally take in the counseling relationship. This throws off the balance (remember the metaphor Linehan uses—the client and clinician are on either sides of a teeter-totter) the adolescent is familiar with and can lead him or her to switch sides with you completely. So, instead of arguing for full commitment to treatment, you might instead suggest the client isn't ready for this, or it isn't a good idea. Sounds crazy, right? Once I was working to engage an adolescent in treatment, and she was giving reason after reason as to why she couldn't do the work, couldn't use her skills, and basically was a hopeless case. Finally, admittedly, with a little frustration, I stated "Maybe you're right. Obviously this isn't working, and it sounds like you've tried everything." The client blinked, and stopped for a second. Then she said "But I can't give up." I couldn't believe it! It worked! We then engaged in a discussion about that piece of her that didn't believe she should give up. She then started convincing me why she needed to keep trying.

Evaluating Pros and Cons

The main objective of this technique is to evaluate the pros and cons of engaging in DBT treatment with the client in a realistic and nonjudgmental manner. Not only does this highlight the fact that there will be cons (e.g., homework, time commitment), it is also an opportunity to emphasize the benefits (e.g., building a life worth living). Your job will be to find a way to emphasize the fact the pros outweigh the cons. This not only helps the client view the situation objectively, it will help him or her consider possible obstacles that may come up later in treatment.

Connecting Present Commitments to Prior Commitments

There are times when your client will need to be reminded of the previous commitment he or she made in order to reinforce a current commitment. Connecting current commitments to prior commitments is a strategy that is especially important in recommitment. One of the major examples used in DBT is when a client begins to threaten to use behaviors that he or she had committed not to use when treatment began. For example, if your client committed to not using alcohol, but then, after a fight with his mother, states he plans to go out that night and drink, you could ask (in a nonjudgmental tone) "But I thought you were going to try your best not to do that? That was what you committed to when we started treatment" (Miller et al., 2007, p. 147). This technique helps reaffirm the client's positive choices while also reminding him of his obligations in the treatment process.

Highlighting Freedom to Choose and Absence of Alternatives

This technique can seem a little manipulative (though really, to an extent, these are all a little manipulative). Highlighting the freedom to choose and absence of alternatives involves pointing out the fact that the client has a choice whether to stay in treatment, however the choices are highly stacked towards staying. Basically, on one side, the option is to try to manage things as he or she had been previously (which was unsuccessful) or, he or she could try the DBT program, which could ultimately lead to a life that includes all of the things that are important to the client. When presented that way, the client sees that leaving treatment is not really a viable option, but this provides the control to make that decision independently.

Cheerleading

As we've said, in DBT, the clinician is constantly vacillating between acceptance and change. Cheerleading is the acceptance piece of the commitment strategies. Throughout treatment, it is important to praise your clients and emphasize your belief that they can be successful in this treatment. With every commitment strategy used, a validating, cheerleading statement can help increase the client's commitment. This highlights two of the dialectical assumptions in DBT—the client is doing the best he or she can, and, he or she can do better, and try harder.

ASSESSMENT

There are several aspects of assessment in DBT: initial diagnostic assessment of the client, valuation of treatment outcomes, and overall appraisal of the program.

Initial Diagnostic Assessment

You likely already have procedures for conducting an initial biopsychosocial assessment that helps you gather ample information regarding symptoms, history of the presenting problem, and any other contributing factors. However, you may wish to add some questions specifically related to DBT treatment targets such as life-threatening behaviors, therapy-interfering behaviors, and quality-of-life-interfering behaviors (see Chapter 1 for more detailed descriptions). These treatment targets are a major facet of DBT treatment planning; therefore it is important to attain a full picture of what these behaviors look like during the assessment period. You will also want to include aspects to assess the fit of the program for the client. This can include time commitment, program inclusion criteria (to be discussed later in this chapter), and adolescent/parent willingness to commit to the program (Miller et al., 2007).

Assessment of Treatment Outcomes

The treatment targets in your program may be the same as traditional DBT programs (e.g., increase emotion regulation, decrease suicidal ideation/attempts and self-harm behaviors), or they may be different based on your population. For example, if you are working with adolescents who struggle with depression and anxiety, your targets will likely include the reduction of panic attacks and depression-related symptoms. Regardless, utilizing a formalized assessment can be helpful for creating measured progress.

There are several instruments that are traditionally used in DBT, and many of these are discussed in subsequent chapters in this book. It is important to ascertain which assessment best fits the needs of your program. As with all assessments, be sure that you (or whoever will be administering the assessment) fully review the instructions for administration and scoring, as well as the reliability, validity, and norming group information.

Overall Program Evaluation

Though you likely will use assessments to measure client progress, it is also important to engage in an overall evaluation of your program. There are several ways to approach this process. First, a collective analysis of your clients' assessments can give you an overall sense of whether your program is effective. You can also use satisfaction surveys, individual interviews, and focus groups, as they may provide further insight directly from the clients. Taking these steps will help you make adjustments to increase positive outcomes in your program. It will also help you show positive progress to administrators and other stakeholders, which will hopefully increase support and investment.

MULTICULTURAL CONSIDERATIONS

Unfortunately, there is very little published on using DBT with different cultures. However, DBT is a flexible approach, and adaptations for diversity can be done intentionally, as long as you are mindful of your cultural worldview, knowledge, and skills, as well as those of your client (Ratts, Singh, Nassar-McMillan, Butler, & McCullough, 2016).

The majority of research on DBT with diverse cultures is related to clients of Hispanic descent. For example, one adaptation described two new parent-adolescent dialectical dilemmas that can occur between the parents and children in Latino families (Germán et al., 2015). The first dialectical dilemma, *old school vs. new school*, discusses the polarization between the parents' traditional beliefs from their own country (children should be obedient and not question their parents) and the adolescent's beliefs based on the culture they currently reside in (I should have the freedom and responsibilities that my friends have). The second dialectical dilemma, *over-protection vs. under-protection*, describes the juxtaposition between parents who do not give their children any freedom (due to fear and beliefs that the world is unsafe, often because they came from a country that was not safe) and the parents who expect their children to take on too many responsibilities (for example, being required to watch younger siblings every day). For both of these dilemmas, it is important to validate the experiences of both parents and adolescents, and work to help them find the middle path via compromise and empathy (Germán et al., 2015). Other researchers used *loteria* cards for contingency management, and common Latino idioms and fables to help clients understand the DBT skills and aspects (McFarr et al., 2014). They also treated each client with respect and warmth common in Latino interpersonal interactions.

Another study adapted DBT for Native American adolescents. They implemented traditional DBT; however they also included a local spiritual counselor to regularly conduct traditional Native American spiritual practices, including sweat lodge ceremonies and talking circles (Beckstead, Lambert, DuBose, & Linehan, 2015). This study supports other research that suggests that by incorporating a culture's traditional spiritual healers into mental health treatment, you can increase clients' acceptance and compliance with treatment (Bledsoe, 2008). For example, if there is a church that largely serves Hispanic constituents, you may be able to work in collaboration with their pastor to promote the benefits of DBT treatment, as well as provide support and education to the community.

Multicultural considerations are not limited to race and ethnicity. Adolescents' gender identity, disability status, and socioeconomic status (SES) may also warrant treatment adaptations. For example, in one study, lower SES adolescents did not experience any differences in treatment outcomes compared to their higher SES counterparts; however, they did experience more problems with treatment compliance (James et al., 2015). Providing resources when possible (for example, bus passes), conducting reminder phone calls, and planning in the beginning for any possible barriers to treatment can help combat this. Communicating with parents and guardians may also be important, as they may often have additional stressors with work and finances that may affect compliance. Depending on your setting, the ability to provide food and/or childcare as needed could increase treatment compliance. Gender identity may be an important consideration if you offer single gender groups, as transgender clients may be in the process of transitioning, or simply not ready to solidify themselves as one gender or another. This can limit their ability to take part in DBT groups if they are aligned by gender; however if you offer mixed gender groups, this problem can be avoided. You also may need to make accommodations for clients with disabilities such as visual and hearing impairments. This can include providing a sign language interpreter, seeking out resources in braille, or providing skills teaching in individual sessions to increase comprehension. Regardless of the adaptations you make for diversity purposes, be sure to elicit feedback from clients, collaborate with your consultation team to maintain the fidelity of the treatment, and conduct program evaluation and assessment to be sure your program continues to meet identified treatment targets.

CONCLUSION

There is a lot of groundwork to cover before implementing a DBT program. In eagerness to get started, many clinicians may wish to jump in and start providing services ASAP. However, it is first important to consider how DBT will be applied, with consideration to the setting and population, as well as the modes, functions, and stages of treatment (see Chapter 1). Once you have made these choices, and decided how you will evaluate individual progress as well as programmatic progress, then remember obtaining at least partial commitment from the client and his or her family to treatment is important. Spending this time in the pretreatment phase will increase compliance, as will engaging in recommitment as necessary throughout treatment. Finally, remember that after implementation you can continue to make adaptations as needed to ensure the success of your program and your clients.

REFERENCES

Beckstead, D. J., Lambert, M. J., DuBose, A. P., & Linehan, M. (2015). Dialectical behavior therapy with American Indian/Alaska Native adolescents diagnosed with substance use disorders: Combining an evidence based treatment with cultural, traditional, and spiritual beliefs. *Addictive Behaviors*, *51*, 84–87. doi:10.1016/j.addbeh.2015.07.018

Bledsoe, S. E. (2008). Barriers and promoters of mental health services utilization in a Latino context: A literature review and recommendations from an ecosystems perspective. *Journal of Human Behavior in the Social Environment*, *18*(2), 151–183. doi:10.1080/10911350802285870

Germán, M., Smith, H. L., Rivera-Morales, C., González, G., Haliczer, L. A., Haaz, C., & Miller, A. L. (2015). Dialectical behavior therapy for suicidal Latina adolescents: Supplemental dialectical corollaries and treatment targets. *American Journal of Psychotherapy*, *69*(2), 179–197.

Hunnicutt Hollenbaugh, K. M., Klein, J. M., & Lewis, M. S. (2015). Implementing dialectical behavior therapy (DBT) in your practice—standard DBT vs. DBT informed. *Counseling Today*, *58*(2), 40–45.

James, S., Freeman, K. R., Mayo, D., Riggs, M. L., Morgan, J. P., Schaepper, M. A., & Montgomery, S. B. (2015). Does insurance matter? Implementing dialectical behavior therapy with two groups of youth engaged in deliberate self-harm. *Administration and Policy In Mental Health and Mental Health Services Research*, *42*(4), 449–461. doi:10.1007/s10488-014-0588-7

McFarr, L., Gaona, L., Barr, N., Ramirez, U., Henriquez, S., Farias, A., & Flores, D. (2014). Cultural considerations in dialectical behavior therapy. In A. Masuda (Ed.), *Mindfulness and acceptance in multicultural competency: A contextual approach to sociocultural diversity in theory and practice* (pp. 75–92). Oakland, CA: Context Press/New Harbinger Publications.

Miller, A. L., Rathus, J. H., & Linehan, M. M. (2007). *Dialectical behavior therapy with suicidal adolescents*. New York, NY: Guilford Press.

Ratts, M. J., Singh, A. A., Nassar-McMillan, S., Butler, S. K., & McCullough, J. R. (2016). Multicultural and social justice counseling competencies: Guidelines for the counseling profession. *Journal of Multicultural Counseling and Development*, *44*(1), 28–48. doi:10.1002/jmcd.12035

Treatment Team and Continuity of Care

K. Michelle Hunnicutt Hollenbaugh
and Jacob M. Klein

DBT includes a range of services provided by a team of professionals. In this chapter we will focus on the roles of various DBT team members, and outline their unique contributions to the client's success in treatment. The composition of your treatment team will vary based on the setting you work in, and the population with whom you are working. You may also find that one individual on the treatment team fulfills more than one role. Regardless, there are a lot of factors to consider, including training, availability, and commitment to the DBT model. As the setting and team members may change over the course of treatment, we will also address best practices for continuity of care in this chapter.

TREATMENT TEAM MEMBERS AND ROLES

Your treatment team will comprise of anyone who is involved in providing any mode of DBT to the adolescent. This can include counselors, psychologists, psychiatrists, and mental health technicians. Remember, the goal is to work collaboratively as a team and meet weekly for consultation. Everyone on the team should have received some sort of training in DBT, though there are a lot of different ways to provide this. In general, it is best practice for at least the treatment team leader to have received intensive (40–80 hours) training (Miller, Rathus, & Linehan, 2007).

Other providers in the community can also be considered ancillary team members. A team member can be anyone who is aware of the client's treatment goals, and also has an understanding of the basic fundamentals of DBT (Linehan, 1993). Many of your clients may be receiving other services—for example, medication management by a psychiatrist or licensed nurse practitioner, or case management through a local nonprofit agency. Regardless, these other providers are only considered treatment team members if they are committed to fulfilling DBT treatment goals, and are working collaboratively with other team members. For example, a case manager who refers a client for hospitalization every time he or she expresses thoughts of suicide would not be working in alignment with the DBT model to reinforce positive coping skills use. Instead, by hospitalizing the client immediately, the case manager has reinforced the use of inpatient hospitalization as a method of coping with emotion dysregulation.

See Table 3.1 for a list of possible treatment team members, including ancillary team members. We will review the most pertinent in this chapter; however other team members that may be specifically related to a setting or diagnosis will be reviewed in the corresponding chapter.

Your client should be aware of all the professionals involved in his or her treatment, and the role of each of these members, regardless of the setting. We have included handouts (Handout 3.1 and Handout 3.2) that may be helpful, and can include information on team members, how they will be working with the client, and how to contact them if needed.

Table 3.1 Treatment Team Members and Roles

Team Member	Role
Primary Team Members	
Team Leader	This person likely serves more than one role, but as the team leader he or she maintains the fidelity of the treatment, manages consultation team meetings, and any other administrative concerns related to providing DBT.
Primary Clinician	Addresses treatment targets, behavioral problem-solving. Intersession skills coaching.
Skills Trainer	Teaches skills and enhances use.
Case Manager	Addresses secondary treatment targets and advocacy for the client, consultation to the client.
Ancillary Team Members	
School Counselor	Assists in skills generalization, consultation to client, intersession skills coaching.
Psychiatrist	Provides medication management, assists in skills generalization, and reinforcement of skills use.
Probation Officer	Assists in generalization and reinforcement of skills use, monitoring and extinction of problem behaviors. Intersession skills coaching.
Nurse	Provides medication management, consultation to client, intersession skills coaching.
Mental Health Technician	The rest of these members may assist in generalization and reinforcement of skills use, extinction of problem behaviors, and intersession skills coaching.
Sports Coach	
Pastor	
Dietician	
Physician or Other Medical Specialist	

Team Leader

The team leader has a lot of responsibility, and may also have several different roles. As the team leader, he or she will be expected to have the most training, and be sure the other team members have adequate training as well. He or she will also be in charge of maintaining the fidelity of the treatment, ensuring consultation team meetings take place, and that the team stays on task during meetings. Finally, the team leader manages any other administrative duties or concerns regarding the DBT treatment. For example, as the team leader for my DBT treatment team, I regularly need to make in-the-moment decisions about concerns that might arise. This can include client concerns that cannot wait until consultation team meetings, logistics of program evaluation, and contact with members of the community.

Skills Trainer

The primary role of the skills trainer is to help the client learn new skills, and use them in all areas of his or her life. The skills trainer is usually a different person than the primary clinician that meets with the adolescent and family for individual and family sessions. Linehan (2015) noted that it might be more difficult for the primary counselor to switch to skills trainer mode and vice versa. By having a different individual in each role, it makes it easier for them to focus on their specific treatment targets. Skills trainers facilitate the psychoeducational skills group, and monitor homework and diary card completion. They may address therapy-interfering behaviors that are specifically related to group attendance and participation. They may also be available for intersession phone coaching. If there are additional therapy-interfering behaviors, or concerns regarding the client, the skills trainer will consult with the primary clinician, who will address these concerns in the next individual or family session (Linehan, 2015).

Primary Clinician

The primary clinician is responsible for decreasing problem behaviors, and generalization of new skills. He or she conducts the individual (traditionally held weekly) and family sessions (as needed) (Miller et al., 2007). During individual sessions the primary clinician will begin by reviewing the diary card, then work with the client to conduct behavior chain analyses related to problem behaviors they engaged in that week. For example, if one of the client's identified treatment targets is to decrease self-harm, and the client indicated on his or her diary card that he or she engaged in self-harm on two days that week, two separate chain analyses will be conducted for each separate incident. Linehan emphasizes the point that diary cards and problem behaviors should be addressed first, before you can move on to topics the client wishes to discuss. This approach can help you extinguish problem behaviors via negative reinforcement. Throughout, be sure to use DBT treatment strategies and regularly balance validation and change.

Case Manager

Though case management is not a service provided in all settings, it is fairly common, especially in community mental health centers. If your organization does provide case management, optimally, the case manager will be a fully trained member of the DBT team and attend regular consultation meetings. It is also possible that the adolescent may be receiving case management at a different agency. In this situation, the case manager would become an ancillary team member, but hopefully would at least have a basic knowledge of the DBT model and the client's treatment goals.

Case managers are in charge of many aspects of care, but primarily they focus on coordinating and linking the client to resources (housing, adjunct services, food, clothing) and treatment. They also may help with scheduling meetings, acting as a liaison between treatment providers, and providing assistance in crisis situations. However, it is essential for the case manager to be aware of the importance of providing consultation to the client. This refers to the process of coaching and empowering the adolescent to advocate for him or herself, instead of doing it for him or her. For example, if the adolescent tells the case manager he or she would like to change the next appointment time with the primary clinician, instead of calling the primary clinician for the client, the case manager should help the adolescent identify skills that he or she can use to make this call him or herself. Truthfully, all team members should be aware of and use consultation to client; however, it's particularly salient for case managers, as their main role is facilitating services and advocating for the client. If the case manager has concerns or questions about the adolescent's ability to advocate for him or herself in a given situation, this should be presented and discussed in consultation team meetings.

Physician

Though it may be rare that the client's medical doctor is actively involved in treatment, this might occur if the adolescent has a chronic health condition that needs regular monitoring, or perhaps receives psychiatric medications via a primary care physician. In either case, it is important the doctor is aware the adolescent is receiving DBT treatment, and aware of his or her treatment targets. This can be especially true if some of the client's problem behaviors are medically related. This can include medication noncompliance (not taking medications as prescribed, or taking too much or too little), dietary noncompliance (for example, a client who is diabetic not adhering to a prescribed diet), or use of medication as a form of self-injury (this can also be exhibited in the form of taking more or less than prescribed). See Handout 3.3 for a worksheet that can help parents and adolescents keep track of their medication compliance.

It may also be the case that the client is not actively involved with a doctor when he or she begins DBT, but it then becomes clear that he or she would benefit from medical attention. Hopefully then you will be able to make an appropriate referral to a physician who is aware of DBT and will work closely with the treatment team.

Psychiatrist

Depending on the setting you work in, you may or may not provide in-house psychiatric services. If there is a psychiatrist on site, optimally, he or she will attend DBT consultation team meetings and be actively involved in providing DBT treatment. If a psychiatrist within a different organization provides pharmacological services, you will want to facilitate regular communication with the treatment team. In some ways, communication with the psychiatrist is more important than communication with other ancillary team members, as treatment goals and medication can be strongly interrelated. For example, your client may only have an appointment with his or her psychiatrist once every few months. As result, the primary clinician and other consultation team members may be first to notice any adverse side effects or problems related to medication. In addition, the adolescent's weekly diary card may be important information for the psychiatrist to have access to, as it will contain a daily rating of the adolescent's emotions, symptoms, and medication compliance.

Other Ancillary Team Members

Other individuals who may be involved in the DBT are listed in Table 3.1, and will be covered in corresponding chapters. Please be aware that this list is not exhaustive—depending on the population you work with, there may be any number of adults and professionals who can be involved in helping the client reach his or her treatment goals. You can ascertain who these individuals are through the initial biopsychosocial assessment. Ask the client and his or her parents about mentors, extra-curricular activities, and any other family members that may serve an important role in the client's life. For example, even though grandparents may not necessarily be a part of family sessions and skills training, if the adolescent has a close relationship with one or both of them, it is still important that they are involved in facilitating the adolescent's success.

CONTINUITY OF CARE

It is possible (or, depending on your setting, likely) that the needs of your client may change during the course of treatment, and as result, he or she may be transitioned to more intensive or less intensive care. Continuity of care refers to providing a smooth transition for clients when moving through different levels (higher or lower intensity) of care related to his or her treatment needs (Guiford, Naithani, & Morgan, 2006). This can be especially important when providing DBT treatment, due to the interdisciplinary nature of the treatment team.

Decisions regarding changes in the level of care the client receives can be difficult to make, and should be made collaboratively with your consultation team, the adolescent, and his or her parents. As the goal of DBT is to facilitate the client's ability to engage in positive skills use instead of engaging in problem behaviors (which are often life threatening), facilitating the client's ability to continue to use and learn those skills should be a primary consideration. For example, if the client is transitioning from an inpatient setting to a partial hospital, intensive outpatient, or even outpatient setting, you and your team will want to do your best to find a provider that provides DBT treatment. This could include a referral to outpatient DBT treatment while simultaneously referring to a partial hospital or intensive outpatient setting that either provides DBT or is aware of the DBT and can continue to support the adolescent's treatment goals.

Similarly, if the team decides the client is in need of a higher level of care—for example, from outpatient treatment to inpatient hospitalization—you will need to be able to communicate the client's treatment goals to inpatient providers, as well as behavioral targets. If a client is hospitalized, traditionally the client should not have any contact with the clinician until he or she is discharged. The goal of this limitation of contact is to reduce the reinforcement (often increased love and attention) the client might receive from being hospitalized. It can be especially difficult to facilitate communication when the client is transitioning between levels of care, and this is a time that Handout 3.5, which discusses the basics of DBT and the client's treatment targets, may come in handy.

CHALLENGES AND SOLUTIONS

Confidentiality and Releases of Information

One challenge you will undoubtedly face is attaining the proper documentation to communicate with other professionals and relevant family members. We're sure you're familiar with the Health Insurance Portability and Accountability Act (HIPAA, hhs.gov, 2016), which makes it illegal to disclose any health or treatment information without written consent by the adolescent's parents. Though many of your clients may be more than happy to sign a release of information for you or other providers to disclose information to each other, others may be more reluctant to do so. This could be for a variety of reasons, including concerns about who will be able to see their records, and what will be done with those records. These concerns can often be alleviated by taking the time to explain to the client's parents what they will be signing, why it is important, and their rights to rescind the written release of information at any time (see Handout 3.4 for a form explaining confidentiality). If the client's parents are willing to sign a release, it will often include an expiration date. Therefore, a team member should be charged with ensuring that all necessary documentation is updated regularly.

In the event that the client's parents are still unwilling to sign a release of information, you can ask them to personally communicate the necessary information. If they are willing, you can work together to complete a brief form that describes the basics of DBT, the client's treatment goals, and the skills he or she is working on (see

Handout 3.5). Similarly, if they are willing, you could give them a blank form for the other professional to complete and send back to you via the client and his or her guardians. This form could include anything the other professional would want the DBT team to know, or any questions the other professional has (see Handout 3.6 for an example). In the event the client is willing to facilitate this communication, it is imperative that any information shared between the professionals is directly provided via the client, as without a written release of information, it would be illegal for you to communicate or send this documentation directly.

Therapy-Interfering Behaviors by Ancillary Team Members

Though all team members can fall prey to therapy-interfering behaviors, ancillary team members may be especially susceptible, as they may have limited experience and training related to DBT. These therapy-interfering behaviors will likely come in the form of reinforcing behaviors the client has been working to extinguish. For example, let's say your client is working to decrease self-harm behaviors, and she voices that she is having thoughts of harming herself to her psychiatrist. You would hope that her psychiatrist would either engage her in skills coaching, or encourage her to call her therapist for skills coaching over the phone. However, what may happen instead is that the psychiatrist immediately starts the process to have the client hospitalized. This unintentionally reinforces the problem behavior, and the client may be less likely to focus on using her skills in the future.

Therapy-interfering behaviors can also occur when an ancillary team member fails to engage in consultation to the client (see above under case manager). As another example, say your client tells his school counselor that he is having a problem with his therapist. Again, your hope would be that the school counselor would coach the client through addressing the problem directly with the therapist. However, instead the school counselor may contact the therapist herself to discuss the issue. When this happens, the client misses an opportunity to use his skills to advocate for himself. Instead, he is reinforced for going to others for advocacy, and this also can cause rifts between team members, as the school counselor will then seem aligned with the client against the therapist.

Most therapy-interfering behaviors can be prevented (or extinguished) by clearly communicating to the team member the adolescent's treatment targets, and how they can help the client increase skills use. However, regardless of the amount of information you share, there may be treatment providers who are simply unwilling or unable to align with the DBT approach. If this happens, the consultation team will want to work with the adolescent and his or her parents to discuss the issue and any possible solutions.

(Mis)Communication

Perhaps one of the most difficult challenges in DBT is maintaining communication between team members, the client, and the client's parents. Part of the informed consent the adolescent and his or her parents complete should explain the role of the consultation team and the communication that will take place between members of the DBT team at your site. This should also include the basics of confidentiality, and the limits to that confidentiality. Once this has been clarified as an important aspect of DBT treatment, it will be your responsibility to be sure that the communication between team members is done effectively and confidentially. This can be done via a form that is completed and placed in the client's file. Then, anyone involved in the client's treatment will be able to see this note and be aware of any concerns (see Handout 3.7). Similarly, any major concerns should be brought up and addressed during consultation team meetings.

Miscommunications can arise when information or issues regarding a client are not shared with everyone on the team. For example, if the skills trainer has a concern about the client's possible substance use, and shares his or her concerns with the primary clinician, but not the case manager, the case manager then may not know to watch for warning signs of substance use. Similarly, if the concern is communicated from one team member to another without the original team member writing out the concerns, some of the information may be inadvertently changed or left out much like the game *telephone* (a game played with a group of children—one child starts a message that is whispered into the next child's ear, and once each child has passed the message on, the last child says the message out loud. Usually, by the time the last child states the message, it has significantly changed from the original message!).

Training

Training is an important consideration for the DBT treatment team (see Chapter 2). Members who will be directly implementing treatment need to be fully trained in the model in order to ensure fidelity and best practices (Miller et al., 2007). However, you may be conflicted as to the best way to provide this. The amount of training team members who are not providing direct care should have to maintain the fidelity of the treatment will vary based on the population, the setting, and also the resources you have for training. If your site does not have a lot of funding for training, there are many options for self-study. There may also be concerns about providing training for new team members that join after the DBT program has started. Though it can be challenging, setting a formalized structure for all team members to receive adequate training will save you problems later on.

SUMMARY

There are a number of professionals that can be involved in your adolescent's treatment team. As always, this will vary based on your site and the population with which you work. Not only is it important that each team member knows his or her roles, but it is also important that adolescents and their parents are aware of the role each professional plays. Communication with ancillary treatment providers can be tricky, but it is necessary for the adolescent to generalize skills use. Problems can arise when ancillary team members are not properly informed of the DBT approach and the client's treatment goals. Our hope is that the handouts provided in the Handouts section will facilitate your ability to effectively and efficiently communicate with other providers.

REFERENCES

Guiford, M., Naithani, S., & Morgan, M. (2006). What is 'continuity of care'? *Journal of Health Services Research & Policy*, *11*(4), 248–250. doi: 10.1258/135581906778476490

hhs.gov (2016). *Health information privacy*. Retrieved from www.hhs.gov/hipaa/

Linehan, M. M. (2015). *DBT® skills training manual* (2nd ed.). New York, NY: Guilford Press.

Miller, A. L., Rathus, J. H., & Linehan, M. M. (2007). *Dialectical behavior therapy with suicidal adolescents*. New York, NY: Guilford Press.

Outpatient Settings
K. Michelle Hunnicutt Hollenbaugh

In this chapter we will discuss implementing DBT for adolescents in outpatient settings, including community mental health agencies and private practice settings. The majority of research on DBT is related to outpatient settings (MacPherson, Cheavens, & Fristad, 2013). However, there are so many differences based on setting, you will still have to consider what DBT will look like for your clients, and program evaluation will be essential to verifying that your clients are reaching their treatment goals.

CONSIDERATIONS BEFORE IMPLEMENTING DBT

As we've already discussed in Chapters 1–3, there are a lot of factors to consider when implementing DBT. Outpatient settings require less adaptations; however, you're going to need to make a lot of decisions. For example, will you be implementing standard DBT or adapted DBT? What population will you be targeting, and what will the goal of DBT be? If you decide to adapt, remember to review the first couple chapters so you are sure you are covering all of the treatment targets, even if you are only offering one or two modes of treatment (for example, only individual treatment or only skills group).

Private Practice

Clinicians implementing DBT in their private practice face unique challenges. It may be difficult to implement standard DBT, especially with limited team members to provide the multimodal treatment. Some independent clinicians in private practice offer individual and group DBT treatment, and then offer phone coaching during limited hours. If you do not have enough clinicians to form a DBT consultation team within your private practice, remember you can form or join a team in the community, with other clinicians in their private practice or community mental health settings (see Chapter 3 for more on forming consultation teams).

Community Mental Health

In some ways, implementation of DBT in community mental health (CMH) settings is easier than private practice because there are often fewer limitations with regard to billing. Often clients receiving treatment in CMH have Medicare or Medicaid, and these programs do not have limits on services the way other third-party insurance companies often do (Ben-Porath, Peterson, & Smee, 2004). On the other hand, it can be more difficult to fit the program into an existing system, especially when administrators do not understand the behavioral principles of DBT and the benefits of the multimodal approach. If you find yourself in a situation in which your administrators are not supportive of developing a DBT program, you may need to conduct a needs assessment ahead of time. By doing this, you can show your administrators the importance of the program, and the match between DBT and the needs of the population you serve (Carmel, Rose, & Fruzzetti, 2014).

Traditional Treatment Targets With Adolescents

See Table 4.1 for the hierarchy of treatment targets in DBT and examples for standard DBT. We will include this table in the majority of the other chapters in this book, and give different examples based on the setting and population.

You can use the *My Target Behaviors* handout with your client to identify and address specific treatment targets (see Handout 4.1). It can be completed by the client during individual sessions and should be focused on both the introduction of new behaviors or specific DBT skills, and reducing problematic behaviors. This handout can be completed in conjunction with the behavior chain analysis to help you and your

Table 4.1 Traditional DBT Treatment Targets and Hierarchy

Treatment Targets	Examples
Primary Treatment Targets	
Life-Threatening Behaviors	Urges, thoughts, or behaviors that harm self or others
Therapy-Interfering Behaviors	Not completing homework Arriving late to session Not attending session Angry or irritable mood Argumentative or defiant behavior **Parents:** Not providing transportation to treatment Not attending treatment Not engaging in or attempting to practice skills Interfering with others in group
Quality-of-Life-Interfering Behaviors	Substance use Risky sex Impulsivity Academic issues **Parents:** Being punitive

Treatment Targets	Examples
Increasing Behavioral Skills	Mindfulness Emotion Regulation Interpersonal Effectiveness Distress Tolerance Walking the Middle Path
Secondary Treatment Targets	
Dialectical Dilemmas Excessive Leniency vs. Authoritarian Control	Parents allowing the adolescent to not return home several nights of the week, then suddenly grounding the adolescent for six months.
Active Passivity vs. Apparent Competence	The adolescent will not use skills at all vs. attempting to manage crisis situations when he or she actually needs guidance.
Unrelenting Crises vs. Inhibited Experiencing	Client vacillates from either constantly experiencing emotional crises (discord with parents and friends, problems in school) to cutting him- or herself off from all emotions completely (suppressing).

clients work together to identify problem behaviors, and find ways to reinforce new positive coping skills.

Diary Cards

In addition to the behavior chain and the treatment targets handouts, see Handouts 1.2–1.5 for several adapted versions of the DBT diary card. The diary card is essentially a journal the client completes daily and brings to session every week. It includes a list of skills the client has learned, emotions the client has experienced, any target problem behaviors, and related treatment targets. The client then indicates the day he or she engaged in the skill or behavior, or rates how much he or she experienced an emotion or urge. We have included an adaptation of the diary card for some of the chapters in this book or you can adapt these cards with your specific needs. It is essential that the client understands the importance of the diary card, and commits to completing it. At first, the diary card can look overwhelming, so instead I usually have the client start small, and track one or two things for the week. Once the client has become accustomed to the process, we begin to slowly add more skills/behaviors to track. In traditional DBT, the client brings the diary card to individual sessions, and then you will discuss any problem behaviors that the client engaged in over the week—and then complete a behavior chain for each of those behaviors. The client may also bring the diary card to skills group; however, this will only be to discuss skills use from the previous week, not problem behaviors (Linehan, 2015).

If the client has not completed the diary card, then he or she must take time in session to complete it, and you should not give the client attention during this time—instead work on paperwork or keep yourself busy doing something else. The goal is to be sure that you are not reinforcing the client for not completing the diary card. I have a colleague who will actually sit and read a magazine while clients complete unfinished diary cards! Conversely, when the client does complete the diary card and bring it in, it is important to positively reinforce this with praise and celebration.

It's usually best if the client finds a regular place to keep the diary card—for example, beside his or her bed. The adolescent should then set a time that he or she will complete the card daily—usually right before bed works well, but any time is fine, as long as it is completed. There are also smart phone apps that have DBT diary cards that are customizable—this may be more appealing to adolescents, and therefore they may be more likely to complete them.

STANDARD SKILLS MODULES FOR ADOLESCENTS

As we mentioned in Chapter 1, there are five standard skills modules in DBT for adolescents (Miller, Rathus, & Linehan, 2007). You can decide which skills to teach your clients, and in what order you wish to teach them in. This will vary based on your clients' treatment targets—for example, if you have a lot of clients who engage in very serious life-threatening behaviors, you may want to focus on distress tolerance skills, so they can start using those skills to reduce those behaviors. We will cover a few of the skills from each module that we believe can be the most helpful for adolescents, and are easily adapted for a variety of treatment targets.

Mindfulness

Mindfulness is by far the most important skill in DBT, as it underlies all of the other skills. There are mindfulness exercises throughout all of the skills modules, and the majority of DBT skills include some aspect of awareness in the present moment. It's important that you teach this skill early, and encourage adolescents to practice it often. See Handout 4.2 for a list of some of our favorite mindfulness exercises. What I love about mindfulness in DBT is that it is not limited to the traditional mindfulness meditation of sitting quietly and focusing on breathing. Literally any activity can be considered practicing mindfulness, as long as the adolescent is focused on that one thing, in the moment, and nothing else. I encourage my clients to find an activity they do every day, and be mindful during that activity. That can be showering, doing chores, or driving (an optimal one!). You also can have fun with mindfulness in session. Linehan (2015) and Rathus and Miller (2015) highlight some interactive mindfulness activities that are frequently used in DBT—for example, singing *Row, Row, Row Your Boat* in a round (with hand movements) or "mirroring" a partner's movements silently. I've also found that a lot of activities involved in improvisation (improv) acting can be used as interactive mindfulness practice—as well as games that test adolescents' ability to think quickly.

Interpersonal Effectiveness

DEAR MAN

Linehan (2015) developed this acronym to help clients assertively ask for something they want, or say no to a request. This can be an important skill for adolescents, who may not have been taught how to communicate assertively, or may be struggling with emotion dysregulation and therefore not be able to think objectively in the moment (see Handout 4.3 for a worksheet on interpersonal effectiveness myths). The acronym stands for Describe, Express, Assert, Reinforce, stay Mindful, Appear confident, and Negotiate (see Handout 4.4). When you teach this skill, your goal will be to help your clients remember the acronym, identify situations in which they might use DEAR MAN, and help them practice in session (group or individual, depending on the format of your DBT program) so they get a feel for going through the steps. When I have had clients practice in group sessions, I usually have them pair up and work together, and then switch, so each client has the opportunity to role-play the person using the acronym, and role-play the person listening. I usually allow them to choose a situation they want to role-play, or I will give them one if they have trouble thinking of one. For example, a friend consistently borrows clothes but doesn't return them, and the client needs to request that the friend return the clothes. They usually have a lot of fun with it, and if the "receiving" person is difficult, it is a good opportunity for the adolescent to use a broken record technique, and practice maintaining an assertive approach. I also remind them that DEAR MAN can also be used via email and text message, which can be helpful as they would have more time to think through each step.

The part of this skill that my clients struggle the most with is the fact that they can use the acronym perfectly; however, they still cannot control the other person. So, even though they are assertive in an attempt to get their needs met, this does not mean that the other person will receive it well, or comply with the request. You will want to discuss this with your clients, and discuss distress tolerance skills they can use in the event that this does happen (Linehan, 2015).

Emotion Regulation

What Emotions Do for You

There are a lot of skills in the emotion regulation module. However, I have found that my clients have the most insight when we discuss what emotions are, and why we have them (see Handouts 4.5, 4.6, and 4.7). This sounds simplistic, but I am always surprised at how many people aren't aware of this basic information—and how absolutely empowering it can be. It can be really helpful for clients to know that their emotions aren't bad—even anger or sadness. What can be harmful and/or have consequences are the behaviors we engage in as result of those emotions. We also discuss the difference between primary and secondary emotions, which can also be surprising for adolescents to realize that anger can be a secondary emotion to hurt or sadness. In this discussion, I usually have the clients give examples of times that emotions have been helpful for them, and compare the differences between those times and the times when they were not helpful. We can then go on and talk about the skills they can use to decrease their vulnerability to emotions, and increase positive emotions.

Acting Opposite

This skill is extremely flexible, and we have adapted it (and highlighted others' adaptations) in a few of the other chapters for specific treatment targets. The premise of this skill is that adolescents will identify the action they wish to engage in that is related to their current emotion (anger, sadness, jealousy) and do the exact opposite. So, for example, watching a funny movie when sad, or doing something nice and caring for someone else when angry. Adolescents can work together in group sessions to generate ideas for activities that are the opposite action of a few emotions. This can be fun (and can get silly) and then after they have generated the list together (for example, on a whiteboard), they can take a picture of it on their phones so they have it when they need it (see Handout 4.8).

Cope Ahead

This is another skill you will see in some of the other chapters in this book. In this skill, adolescents are encouraged to imagine situations that may come up in the future that they will need to use coping skills instead of engaging in a problem behavior. Then they actually practice imagery and imagine themselves in the situation, using their skills (see Handout 4.9). I like this skill because it helps adolescents actually use the skills when they need it. I have often found that we talk about skills, and clients are very receptive to them in session, but then forget to use them in the moment. With this skill, they identify the specific situation in which they will use skills, and then actually imagine it happening, which increases the likelihood of skills use.

Distress Tolerance

Radical Acceptance

This is my favorite distress tolerance skill. It's especially useful for adolescents because there are a lot of things in their life that they cannot control. In this skill, adolescents are encouraged to accept reality to reduce suffering associated with something painful (see Handout 4.10). You will want to emphasize that acceptance does not equal approval—there are a lot of situations we do not approve of, but we still need to accept reality. Not only do we suffer when we refuse to accept pain, but we also can't do anything to change what we can control until we accept the situation. Sometimes this skill is difficult for adolescents to grasp, due to the nuances in the wording (it is difficult to let go of the association between the words accept and approve). However, I like it because it can align with some spiritual beliefs—for example, the belief that "God has a plan" can go along with acceptance. Regardless, there are some situations that are extremely difficult to accept—for example, the death of a loved one. In this case, it will be important for you to emphasize that radical acceptance is acceptance of every aspect of that situation—including the part of the adolescent that does not wish to accept the situation at all.

STOP

This skill is perfect for adolescents—I like to think of it as thought stopping for behaviors (behavior stopping!). The goal is for the adolescent to be able to imagine a stop sign and stop in the moment, before engaging in a problem behavior. This can especially be helpful for clients who have problems with anger and fighting (see Chapter 7). After stopping themselves in the moment, they then use mindfulness to increase awareness of the situation, and make a decision regarding how to go forward. This is another skill that can be fun to practice in session—either having the client role-play the situation and use the STOP skill, or some other activity to emphasize the point of stopping suddenly in the moment. For example, a colleague of mine will have group members walk around the room in a circle and then yell "Stop!" (they stop), "Take a step back!" (they take a step back), "Observe!" (they mindfully observe in the moment), and then "Proceed mindfully!" (they continue to walk in the circle, and then do this once or twice more).

Walking the Middle Path

Miller et al. (2007) developed Walking the Middle Path as a skills module to specifically address the parent–child relationship. There are three main skills taught in this module: dialectics, validation, and behaviorism. These skills can definitely be helpful for adolescents individually; however, they are most effective when taught to parents and adolescents together, as then they are able to work together to use the skills outside of session.

Dialectics and Dialectical Dilemmas

We have already discussed dialectics and dialectical dilemmas in detail in Chapter 2, so refer back to that section as needed. However, in the Walking the Middle Path module, the focus is on teaching adolescents and parents about dialectics, and how they can fall into patterns related to the dialectical dilemmas. This may be a more difficult task. See our handouts on Dialectical Dilemmas and Walking the Middle Path in Handout 4.11 and Handout 4.12, respectively. The main idea to communicate to your clients is that two seemingly opposite points of view can both be correct. Once they have grasped that idea, they can work together to see each other's point of view, which will improve their relationship tremendously. Sometimes what has been helpful for me is to have them give examples of their point of view in conflicts they have had: for example, if the adolescent's point of view is "I believe I should be able to stay out later because I am old enough to take care of myself" and the parent's point of view is "I do not believe you should stay out later because I am concerned about you and you still aren't an adult," you can help them see the truth in both of those statements, and hopefully by understanding each other further, they can reach a mutual agreement.

Validation

Once you have taught your clients about dialectics and seeing the truth in both sides, you will want to teach them how to validate each other. This is a skill that clinicians in helping professions often take for granted. We do this all the time, so it often becomes second nature. I sometimes forget that a lot of people aren't even familiar with the term! It will be important for you to spend some time teaching your clients and their parents not only about self-validation, but validating others as well (see Handout 4.13 in the back of the text). In addition to teaching them why it is important to validate, and how to do it, you also want to be clear about what NOT to validate (namely, the problem behavior itself). Finally, you can always find something to validate, even if you do not want to validate behavior, you can validate emotions, or you can validate their past experiences that may have led them to engage in thinking errors and the resulting problem behaviors.

Behaviorism

It probably doesn't occur to you to actually teach your clients behaviorism—though we often use it in our interventions, rarely do we actually discuss the concept with our clients. This may be especially true for adolescents, as at first, it may be a difficult concept to understand. However, by teaching adolescents and their parents these concepts, we empower them to analyze their own behaviors and interactions, and make changes to decrease problem behaviors. It can also be helpful because many adults and adolescents are very familiar with one aspect of behaviorism—punishment. However, one of the things I really like about the discussion of behaviorism in Walking the Middle Path is how much they emphasize the importance of *reinforcement*—which is an aspect of behaviorism we often overlook. Parents may get into the habit of implementing punishment without considering how much more effective reinforcement can be, and because of this, making sure that both the adolescent and parents understand reinforcement can be extremely helpful in reducing and eliminating problem behaviors (Miller et al., 2007). See Handout 4.14 for a handout on changing behaviors.

SAMPLE GROUP SESSION FORMATS

In many of the chapters in this book, we have included a sample group session format for all five DBT modules for adolescents. See Handouts 4.15 and 4.16 for sample handouts that review the group process and group rules. See Table 4.2 for the standard version of this—in many chapters this format remains the same; however, we have included adapted and new skills as applicable for the population we discuss in that chapter. The format below is structured for six weeks in each module. This can be altered easily, and you will notice different formats in the chapter on DBT with families, in schools, and in a partial hospital setting. Typically, DBT skills groups are open at the beginning of each module, and then closed until the next module commences.

Table 4.2 Sample Skills Training Schedule

Module/Session	Skills, Activities, and Handouts
Mindfulness: Module 1	
Session 1	Orientation to DBT and Skills Training Group Rules Biosocial Theory
Session 2	Reasonable, Emotion, and Wise Mind Mindfulness Practice—What Is Mindfulness?
Session 3	Mindfulness What Skills (Observe, Describe, Participate)
Session 4	Mindfulness How Skills (One-Mindfully Effectively, Nonjudgmentally)
Session 5	Loving Kindness
Session 6	Review
Distress Tolerance: Module 2	
Session 1	Review of Group Rules and DBT Skills Training, the Biosocial Theory, and Emotion Dysregulation Introduction to Distress Tolerance
Session 2	STOP Skill
Session 3	Distract With Wise Mind ACCEPTS, Self Soothe With the Six Senses
Session 4	IMPROVE the Moment
Session 5	Pros and Cons, TIPP
Session 6	Acceptance Skills, Willingness, and Willfulness
Walking the Middle Path: Module 3	
Session 1	Review of Group Rules and DBT Skills Training, the Biosocial Theory, and Emotion Dysregulation as needed Introduction to the Walking the Middle Path Module
Session 2	Dialectics
Session 3	Dialectical Dilemmas

(Continued)

Table 4.2 (Continued)

Module/Session	Skills, Activities, and Handouts
Session 4	Validation
Session 5	Behaviorism
Session 6	Problem-Solving and Behavior Chain Analysis
Emotion Regulation: Module 4	
Session 1	Review of Group Rules and DBT Skills Training, the Biosocial Theory, and Emotion Dysregulation as needed Introduction to Emotion Regulation
Session 2	ABC—Accumulating positive experiences, Build mastery, Cope ahead
Session 3	PLEASE—treat Physical illness, balance Eating, Avoid drugs, balance Sleep, get Exercise
Session 4	Mindfulness of Current Emotions
Session 5	Check the Facts
Session 6	Opposite Action
Interpersonal Effectiveness: Module 5	
Session 1	Review of Group Rules and DBT Skills Training, the Biosocial Theory, and Emotion Dysregulation as needed Introduction to Interpersonal Effectiveness
Session 2	GIVE—Gentle, Interested, Validate, Easy manner
Session 3	DEAR MAN—Describe, Express, Assert, Reinforce, be Mindful, Appear confident, Negotiate
Session 4	FAST—be Fair, no Apologies, Stick to values, be Truthful
Session 5	Factors to consider when asking for something or saying no
Session 6	THINK—Think, Have empathy, Interpretations, Notice, Kindness

OUTCOME EVALUATION

As we mentioned briefly in Chapter 2, outcome evaluation is an important facet of implementing a DBT program. We have included a few common methods of measuring outcomes in DBT programs here, and then will include any specific assessments for adaptations in the corresponding chapters.

Diary Cards

As we mentioned earlier in this chapter, diary cards are a versatile tool to measure progress. Not only can you use it to check in with your clients weekly, but you can also use it to monitor the frequency of skills use and problem behaviors to see if there are any changes over time. You could also aggregate this data across clients, to see if there are any overall trends in frequency of skills use and problem behaviors.

The Difficulties in Emotional Regulation Scale (DERS)

The DERS (Gratz & Roemer, 2004) is very common in DBT outcome research and was developed specifically to measure emotion regulation. It includes six scales: non-acceptance of emotions, difficulties engaging in goal directive behavior, impulse control difficulties, lack of emotional awareness, limited access to emotion regulation strategies, and lack of emotional clarity. The DERS is a flexible tool and can be administered frequently, as it only has 36 Likert-scale items and therefore your clients should be able to complete it relatively quickly.

The DBT Ways of Coping Checklist (WCCL)

The WCCL (Neacsiu, Rizvi, Vitaliano, Lynch, & Linehan, 2010) is another very common formal assessment in DBT, and includes scales on skills use, general dysfunctional coping, and blaming others. Clients are asked to rate skills use on 59 Likert-scaled items. The WCCL is also an instrument that you could administer to your clients frequently—however, it is longer than the DERS and therefore may take the client a little bit longer to complete.

CHALLENGES AND SOLUTIONS IN OUTPATIENT DBT COUNSELING

Attrition

One of the benefits of DBT is that clients who engage in a DBT program are usually less likely to drop out than clients receiving other services at the same site (Ben-Porath et al., 2004). Regardless, dropout is still a concern, but working with parents and adolescents to commit them both to treatment in the beginning can help combat this. As we discussed in Chapter 2, this can be difficult, especially when parents are reluctant to participate. One of the ways to get clients to commit to treatment is to offer a shorter treatment length (also, see commitment strategies in Chapter 2). You'll notice the sample format we have includes six-week modules. You may decide to have longer or shorter modules—this will depend on how long you believe is reasonable for the adolescents and parents with whom you will be working. Another approach that may work in a community mental health center is presenting DBT as a program that is difficult to qualify for, with only certain clients being included in treatment (Fruzzetti et al., 2007). Clients may then be more invested in the treatment and feel good about being part of something special. Recommitment to treatment is essential at times, and commitment strategies can be revisited as necessary to prevent attrition. Usually, clinicians set up a certain number of sessions the client can miss before being considered "on a break" or "on a vacation" from treatment. (Remember, clients can't fail

DBT treatment.) Again, you will want to make this decision based on what you think is appropriate for you and your clients.

Staff Turnover

Some researchers have found that engaging in DBT training can actually reduce levels of burnout. Therefore, by teaching clinicians DBT you may be able to reduce the amount of staff turnover your agency normally experiences (Carmel, Fruzzetti, & Rose, 2014). Regardless, especially if you work in a community mental health center, you may experience a fair amount of turnover, and this may be challenging with regard to maintaining an acceptable level of training in consultation team members. New staff members can be trained by the team leader, or other team members who have had an extensive amount of DBT training and experience. You may also wish to send new staff members to training. For example, Behavioral Tech offers a one-week intensive training for new team members who are joining teams that have already attended the DBT intensive training (see Chapter 2 for more about training in DBT).

Treatment Fidelity

In addition to training, you will also need to pay attention to treatment fidelity—you will want to find a way to measure how much your program adheres to the DBT model on a regular basis. The easiest way to do this is through the consultation team—you can have team members listen to or watch tapes of each other, in order to ascertain that they are adhering to DBT practices. This can include using dialectical strategies and a behavioral approach to treatment targets. By doing this, you will not only maintain the quality of your program, but also be sure that you are delivering the best treatment possible for your clients.

Billing

Billing may be an issue as insurance companies rarely reimburse for all modes of DBT. There are many ways to approach payment. For example, some experts have posited that clinicians apply a flat DBT treatment rate that would be billed weekly, regardless of the number of sessions or between-session phone coaching (Comtois, Koons, Kim, Manning, Bellows, & Dimeff, 2007). The authors also suggested that clinicians could bill insurance for individual sessions, and have the client pay out of pocket for the cheaper, group sessions. This could also be applicable if you wish to implement a family-members-only skills group, which can be offered at the same time as the adolescent skills group. This group could be an out-of-pocket expense for parents, but at very low cost. Other clinicians have actually measured treatment outcomes and then provided that data to insurers. By doing this, as well as meeting with insurers to discuss the importance of maintaining the fidelity of the treatment, they were able to receive increased compensation for the services they provided (Koons, O'Rourke, Carter, & Erhardt, 2013). That being said, many clinicians do not take insurance, and another option is to simply bill the client and let them submit to their insurance for out-of-network reimbursement.

SUMMARY AND CONCLUSIONS

The take away from this chapter is that DBT is very flexible and versatile. Feel free to be intentionally creative in how you implement modes of treatment, and how you teach different skills to your clients. There can be a lot of factors to consider, and some of your main problems may be related to the logistics of billing, administration, and implementation. Though we don't include all of the skills in our discussion here (or even in the text) our hope is that the skills we have highlighted and adapted will be helpful for your DBT program.

REFERENCES

Ben-Porath, D. D., Peterson, G. A., & Smee, J. (2004). Treatment of individuals with borderline personality disorder using dialectical behavior therapy in a community mental health setting: Clinical application and a preliminary investigation. *Cognitive and Behavioral Practice*, *11*(4), 424–434. doi:10.1016/S1077-7229(04)80059-2

Carmel, A., Fruzzetti, A. E., & Rose, M. L. (2014). Dialectical behavior therapy training to reduce clinical burnout in a public behavioral health system. *Community Mental Health Journal*, *50*(1), 25–30. doi:10.1007/s10597-013-9679-2

Carmel, A., Rose, M. L., & Fruzzetti, A. E. (2014). Barriers and solutions to implementing dialectical behavior therapy in a public behavioral health system. *Administration and Policy in Mental Health and Mental Health Services Research*, *41*(5), 608–614. doi:10.1007/s10488-013-0504-6

Comtois, K. A., Koons, C. R., Kim, S. A., Manning, S. Y., Bellows, E., & Dimeff, L. A. (2007). Implementing standard dialectical behavior therapy in an outpatient setting. In L. A. Dimeff & K. Koerner (Eds.), *Dialectical behavior therapy in clinical practice: Applications across disorders and settings* (pp. 37–68). New York, NY: Guilford Press.

Fruzzetti, A. E., Santisteban, D. A., & Hoffman, P. D. (2007). Dialectical behavior therapy with families. In L. A. Dimeff, K. Koerner (Eds.), *Dialectical behavior therapy in clinical practice: Applications across disorders and settings* (pp. 222–244). New York, NY: Guilford Press.

Gratz, K. L. & Roemer, L. (2004). Multidimensional assessment of emotion regulation and dysregulation: Development, factor structure, and initial validation of the difficulties in emotion regulation scale. *Journal of Psychopathology and Behavioral Assessment*, *26*, 41–54.

Koons, C. R., O'Rourke, B., Carter, B., & Erhardt, E. B. (2013). Negotiating for improved reimbursement for dialectical behavior therapy: A successful project. *Cognitive and Behavioral Practice*, *20*(3), 314–324. doi:10.1016/j.cbpra.2013.01.003

Linehan, M. M. (1993). *Cognitive-behavioral treatment of borderline personality disorder*. New York, NY: Guilford Press.

Linehan, M. M. (2015). *DBT® skills training manual* (2nd ed.). New York, NY: Guilford Press.

MacPherson, H. A., Cheavens, J. S., & Fristad, M. A. (2013). Dialectical behavior therapy for adolescents: Theory, treatment adaptations, and empirical outcomes. *Clinical Child and Family Psychology Review*, *16*(1), 59–80. doi:10.1007/s10567-012-0126-7

Miller, A. L., Rathus, J. H., & Linehan, M. M. (2007). *Dialectical behavior therapy with suicidal adolescents*. New York, NY: Guilford Press.

Neacsiu, A., Rizvi, S., Vitaliano, P., Lynch, T., & Linehan, M. M. (2010). The dialectical behavior therapy ways of coping checklist: Development and psychometric properties. *Journal of Clinical Psychology*, 66, 1–20. doi:10.1002/jclp.20685

Rathus, J. H. & Miller, A. L. (2015). *DBT® skills manual for adolescents*. New York, NY: Guilford Press.

Family Counseling
K. Michelle Hunnicutt Hollenbaugh

Although traditional DBT for adolescents includes a mode of treatment that involves family members, other researchers have focused specifically on adapting DBT skills to treat the whole family (Fruzzetti, Santisteban, & Hoffman, 2007). This approach is logical—if you remember, one of the major facets of the biosocial theory of emotion dysregulation is the invalidating environment (see Chapter 1). However, in family DBT counseling, family members are not blamed for contributing to the invalidating environment. Instead, the focus is on the system, and the idea that in the face of a family member who experiences emotion dysregulation, and subsequently engages in impulsive or life-threatening behaviors, family members may unknowingly respond in an invalidating manner, in an effort to cope with the distress those behaviors put on the system (Miller, Glinksi, Woodeberry, Mitchell, & Indik, 2002). Though this adaptation is still being developed and studied, preliminary studies have shown that treating the family in skills group is related to a decrease in problem behaviors in adolescents (Uliaszek, Wilson, Mayberry, Cox, & Maslar, 2014).

CONSIDERATIONS FOR IMPLEMENTING DBT FOR FAMILIES

Family counseling can be implemented in several ways, and you will need to decide ahead of time what will work best for you and your clients. See Table 5.1 for a list of different ways to incorporate family counseling with DBT. Your foremost consideration will be the purpose of the intervention and your treatment goals. In general, implementing skills training via group format is easier and cheaper than working with each family individually. Multifamily groups that include several clients and their parents are useful if the goal is to facilitate the client's generalization of skills and stop problem behaviors (Fruzzetti et al., 2007). Hoffman, Fruzzetti, and Swenson (1999) also report that by using multifamily groups, group members experience cross-validation from other group members, see behaviors modeled by others, and experience dialectics. However, if the treatment goal is to assist the parents and increase parenting skills, you may instead wish to have the family members engage in a group separate from the adolescent. If you decide against implementing skills groups with the inclusion of family members, you can always implement family counseling on an as-needed basis, and engage in family sessions when there are specific issues that need to be addressed. In any of these scenarios, you might consider whether family

Table 5.1 Options for Implementing Family Counseling in DBT

Format	Benefits
Multifamily skills groups that include several families and adolescents	Help adolescent generalize skills, stop problem behaviors. Group members can validate each other, model skills use, and experience the dialectic of different viewpoints.
Skills teaching sessions for just the adolescent and his or her family	Can spend more time on problem-solving in a personalized approach for the family.
Separate skills groups for families and adolescents that run concurrently	Can focus on skills acquisition for parents specifically, including skills related to discipline and parenting.
Adjunct family counseling sessions that include the client as needed	Less involvement of family members may increase commitment by family members; this amount may be sufficient.
Adjunct family counseling sessions that do not include the client as needed	Intermittent skills training for parents can address specific problem behaviors in the system and/or inadvertent validation of problem behaviors.

members other than parents or guardians should be a part of the groups (e.g., siblings, grandparents). Fruzzetti et al. (2007) emphasize that no matter what format you decide to implement family counseling, it is important that the counseling environment be a *no-blame zone*, in which both parents and adolescents can feel safe and work together to increase skills and focus on treatment goals.

ADAPTATIONS TO TREATMENT TARGETS IN FAMILY COUNSELING

If you decide to adapt DBT skills to address the family specifically, Miller et al. (2002) addressed how treatment targets can be changed accordingly. See Table 5.2 for a list of these treatment targets and some examples of what the problem behaviors might look like. Basically, the treatment targets change from the traditional individual hierarchical targets, and instead are focused on the family system, and problems that involve all family members. These treatment targets will not replace the individual treatment targets, and instead will support the treatment targets developed with the adolescent individually.

SKILLS ADAPTATIONS IN FAMILY COUNSELING

A few researchers have developed a family counseling curriculum that includes adaptations to DBT skills, as well as some new skills to enhance communication and

Table 5.2 Treatment Targets in DBT Family Interventions

Treatment Targets	Examples
Primary Treatment Targets	
Family Interactions That Contribute to Adolescent Life-Threatening Behaviors	Validation and/or reinforcement of life-threatening behaviors Invalidation and/or punishment of healthy skills use
Family/Parent Therapy-Interfering Behaviors	Not providing transportation to treatment Not attending treatment Not engaging in or attempting to practice skills Not completing family homework assignments Not seeking out intersession phone coaching when needed
Family/Parent Quality-of-Life-Interfering Behaviors	Being punitive Being willful
Increasing Behavioral Skills of All Family Members	Relationship Mindfulness Walking the Middle Path Validation Problem-Solving Parenting Skills Psychoeducation
Secondary Treatment Targets	
Dialectical Dilemmas—Excessive Leniency vs. Authoritarian Control	Parents allowing the adolescent to not return home several nights of the week, then suddenly grounding the adolescent for six months
Normalizing Pathological Behaviors vs. Pathologizing Normative Behaviors	Vacillating between treating harmful and extreme behaviors as normal, and typical adolescent developmental behaviors as pathological
Forcing Autonomy vs. Fostering Dependence	Expecting the adolescent to be able to care for him or herself vs. doing too much for the adolescent

cohesion (Fruzzetti et al., 2007). The format developed by Fruzzetti (1997), which is for a multifamily skills group, takes place weekly for one and a half hours, for six months (this can be adjusted as needed). The first hour is used for learning new skills, and the last 30 minutes is allotted for consultation regarding family interactions and problem-solving, with an emphasis on validation and behaviorism in a systems approach (Fruzzetti et al., 2007). Hoffman et al. (1999) delineated four basic assumptions in DBT family counseling, which are adaptions from Linehan's (1993, p. 7) original assumptions in DBT:

1. There is no one truth nor any absolute truth.
2. Everyone is doing the best he or she can.
3. Everyone needs to try harder.
4. Everyone needs to (try to) interpret things in a mindful/nonjudgmental way.

The following skills have been adapted for use specifically with families in DBT. Though only a few are highlighted here, the majority of the skills taught in DBT can be adjusted to address family relationships—this can be as easy as changing the examples you use in session to make them applicable for family members, and highlighting how use of individual skills benefits everyone in the family.

Genograms

Though using a genogram may seem cliché, Miller et al. (2002) actually suggest using it as a form of assessment when you begin working with a family. The focus during this activity is on the system, and the pattern of invalidating behaviors in the family system (for example, if the parents experienced invalidation as children). This also helps the family see the adolescent's behavior in the context of the system, and enhances the *no-blame* stance in DBT family therapy. See Handout 5.1 for a worksheet on using genograms with families in DBT.

Psychoeducation on Relevant Diagnoses

One aspect researchers have suggested is educating family members on mental illness and emotion dysregulation (Fruzzetti et al., 2007). Psychoeducation may be especially helpful for parents and family members who do not understand the cause of emotion dysregulation, the function of the behaviors the adolescent engages in, and/or how they relate to his or her symptoms. This can also include educating parents on adolescent development, and specifically how they learn how to regulate emotions.

Relationship Mindfulness

Fruzzetti (2006) took all of the skills in the mindfulness module (observe, describe, participate, one-mindfully, effectively, and nonjudgmentally) and applied them specifically to focusing on others and relationships. See Handout 5.2 for a related homework sheet on using relational mindfulness skills. Relationship mindfulness is based on specifically being aware of relationships and other people. Not only does this help increase emotional intelligence, but also it can facilitate the ability of the adolescents and their family members in validating each other and reducing conflict. Fruzzetti et al. (2007) also highlight the importance of families spending time together engaging in interactive activities. By assigning this as homework, you can help parents and adolescents recognize the difference between simply spending time together (e.g., watching TV together but focusing on other things) and actually interacting by playing a game, talking, or sitting down for a meal.

Problem Management and Validation

This module doesn't vary much from the Walking the Middle Path, so we won't spend a lot of time discussing it here (see Chapter 4 to read more about the Walking the Middle Path module). However, Fruzzetti et al. (2007) did create a really neat double chain analysis for parents and adolescents to work on together to gain understanding into conflict. See Handout 5.3 for an adapted worksheet. Basically, each person shares his or her initial thoughts and emotions, and then discusses their interacting responses, thoughts, and emotions that took place during the conflict. This helps them not only have empathy and validate each other, but to problem solve to prevent conflict in the future. Teaching parents and adolescents how to reinforce each other will also help decrease maladaptive behaviors on both sides.

Miller et al. (2002) also encourage the development of a family crisis plan after engaging in the chain analysis. This plan will be clear on what each family member needs to do in the case of the adolescent thinking about or engaging in life-threatening behaviors. This is especially important because often in crisis situations, parents (and adolescents) automatically revert back to previous behaviors without even thinking about it. By clearly writing out a plan, family members will be more likely to use the skills they have learned to reduce life-threatening behaviors.

Radical Acceptance in Relationships

Fruzzetti (1997) adapted the distress tolerance skill radical acceptance to fit the needs of families who regularly find themselves in the same pattern of conflicts. This skill is also referred to as *closeness*, because the goal is to help the parent and adolescent build connection. He delineates three steps: first, the client (or parent) must stop trying to change the other person, and instead accept any disappointment or sadness via the use of mindful tolerance. He or she can then grieve the loss of not being able to change the other individual. The second step is to look at the negative consequences that were related to trying to change the other person. These can be personal consequences, consequences for the relationship, and consequences for the other individual. The final step is to participate fully in the relationship, accepting the other person as he or she is, and letting go of anger and disappointment through validation and empathy.

This skill may be difficult to grasp for parents and adolescents. Your job will be to help them see the difference between behaviors (especially harmful ones, that really do need to stop) and personality traits. For example, if an adolescent tends to be forgetful (personality trait) and as result frequently forgets to check in with his parents when he is out with friends (problem behavior), the focus should be on radically accepting the fact that the adolescent is forgetful. By accepting this, it will be easier for the parent to validate the adolescent, and then they can work together to stop the problem behavior (acceptance in the context of change!).

Emotion Regulation in Relationships

The focus of emotion regulation in family counseling is to help all family members be aware of their emotions, and specifically use skills to lower emotional reactivity during conflict. Fruzzetti et al. (2007) also focuses on teaching family members the difference between primary and secondary emotions, and how this can affect their thinking and their behavior during a conflict.

Making Repairs

Fruzzetti (1997) highlights this skill briefly in the interpersonal effectiveness module he developed for families. What I like about this skill is the focus on the meaning and purpose of an apology. We have become so accustomed to saying the words "I'm sorry," that we often forget that the goal of an apology is to acknowledge wrongdoing and repair the relationship. By focusing on this skill, parents and adolescents can be more intentional in their apologies, which can increase communication and decrease conflict. I personally have primarily used the making repairs skill in groups—for example, if clients were late, they would make repairs with the other members. They would state what they were making repairs for (being late) and communicate why they needed to make repairs (e.g., disruptive and disrespectful to others to be late to group) and then state what they will do to make sure it will not happen again (e.g., set an alarm to be sure to leave home on time. If it became a continued problem, they would be prompted to complete a behavior chain related to the problem behavior of being late repeatedly). This can be a helpful exercise for parents and adolescents to practice, and it is also an important skill for the clinician to model when necessary.

Family Diary Card

Just like individual DBT skills training, family members can complete a weekly family diary card to keep track of skills use and problem behaviors that occur within the system. This diary card should be personalized to each family, and all family members should commit to completing the diary card daily (if the adolescent is also engaged in individual skills training, this diary card will be *in addition* to the individual diary card he or she completes weekly). By keeping track of the skills they use and the problem behaviors that arise, they will be able to acknowledge any positive or negative behavioral patterns, and work to make changes accordingly.

Parenting

Some researchers have developed a whole module based on parenting skills (Fruzzetti et al., 2007). This module may be especially helpful if you plan on implementing parents-only skills groups. The skills taught include validation and problem-solving, education about developmental stages of adolescents, setting boundaries, and interpersonal effectiveness skills tailored to parenting. Relational mindfulness and radical acceptance in relationships can also be interwoven in this module (Fruzzetti et al., 2007).

SAMPLE FAMILY SKILLS GROUP FORMAT

In Table 5.3 we have developed a sample format for a six-week multifamily DBT skills group based on the adaptations we described above. Though the structure and content of each session can definitely be changed to fit the needs of your setting, you will want to be sure to describe each skill in detail, give a lot of examples, and elicit questions from group members. You will also want to emphasize the importance of completion of the family diary card and homework assignments to increase their mastery of the skills.

Table 5.3 Sample Format of Multifamily Skills Group (Six Weeks)

Session 1	Introduction Group Rules Biosocial Theory Overview of DBT Psychoeducation on Adolescent Development and Relevant Diagnoses Review and assign family diary card
Session 2	*Review family diary card* Validation of Self and Others Problem Management Crisis Planning Identifying Family Problem Behaviors/Interactions *Assign homework*
Session 3	*Review family diary card* Relational Mindfulness Awareness of Others, Interactive Time Together *Assign homework*
Session 4	*Review family diary card* Emotion Regulation/Decreasing Emotional Reactivity *Assign homework*
Session 5	*Review family diary card* Interpersonal Effectiveness—Radical Acceptance in Relationships Making Repairs *Assign homework*
Session 6	*Review family diary card* Conclusions, Review, Problem-Solving, and Planning

CHALLENGES AND SOLUTIONS IN DBT WITH FAMILIES

Unsurprisingly, commitment to treatment is a focal point in working with families in DBT. In Chapter 2 we emphasized the importance of committing adolescents *and* parents to treatment, regardless of family involvement in actual sessions. However, in family DBT skills training it is essential that all family members are aware of the goals and purpose of the treatment, and make a decision to engage in treatment. This may take some time (refer back to the commitment strategies discussed in Chapter 2). In addition to using DBT commitment strategies, you can nonjudgmentally educate parents on the biosocial theory and how their involvement in treatment can be essential in helping the adolescent learn healthy coping skills.

As with any counseling intervention for families, when several individuals are involved, treatment can get more complicated. You may find it more difficult to manage the session, especially when there is a high level of emotion dysregulation and conflict in the family. Your best defense against problems in session is setting the structure and rules beforehand, and enforcing them when necessary by reminding participants of their previous commitments. In addition, use the support of the consultation team when needed, and practice radical acceptance and a nonjudgmental stance, not only of your clients, but yourself.

OUTCOME EVALUATION

Along with the traditional assessments used to measure progress in DBT (see Chapter 2) and other assessments listed throughout this text, you may have treatment targets related specifically to family relationships that you wish to measure. Consider the goals of your program, as well as the cost and length of the assessment when choosing any form of formalized evaluation for families.

Diary Cards and Frequency of Problem Behaviors

As we've mentioned, this is the easiest way to measure progress in DBT. By monitoring family diary cards, you have the ability to track use of skills, and problem behaviors. Analyzing the adolescent's individual diary card in addition to the family diary card can give you a full picture, and can help you connect patterns between the two. If you aggregate this data over time, you will be able to measure the overall effectiveness of your program in reducing problem behaviors.

Validating and Invalidating Behaviors Coding Scale

This scale was developed by Fruzzetti (2001) and is actually a coding manual that you can use to observe parents and rate their behaviors as validating or invalidating on a seven-point scale. Though more research is needed to validate this scale further (it was originally developed and validated for couples), preliminary research did show high inter-rater reliability when observing parent behaviors in a clinical setting (Shenk & Fruzzetti, 2014). Though this assessment is easily administered, as it can be done simply through observation, it is possible that the rater could be biased, and since the ratings are subjective, it may be helpful to have a blind reviewer conduct the observation and coding.

Adolescent Family Life Satisfaction Index

This 13-item questionnaire measures how positively adolescents rate their families. The adolescents respond to items on a Likert scale and rate their satisfaction with interactions with their parents and their siblings (Henry & Plunkett, 1995). Rizvi, Monroe-DeVita, and Dimeff (2007) suggest the use of the scale because it is short, and easy for adolescents to complete. It can also be administered as frequently as every session, so you can gain an accurate picture of your client's progress (Rizvi et al., 2007).

Family Adaptability and Cohesion Evaluation Scale (FACES) IV

This assessment is by far the most popular and most validated of the assessments listed here (though, as a result, it will likely be more expensive to administer than the others). It can be completed by any family member, and includes 42 Likert-scale items (Olson, 2011). This scale was developed to measure family flexibility and cohesion, which may or may not be an outcome you are aiming for in your program. However, the use of DBT skills, including validation and coping, is likely to be related to a family's cohesiveness and flexibility. There is an extensive amount of research on the development of this assessment, which may be a very good reason to choose this assessment on its own, or along with other tests.

KEY POINTS TO CONSIDER/CONCLUSIONS

The amount you are able to involve family members in treatment may vary based on your setting and the population with which you work. Regardless, remember that DBT is extremely flexible, and you can use a lot of different methods to incorporate the family in skills acquisition. You will also want to emphasize the *no-blame* stance in session, and remain nonjudgmental to facilitate family members' ability to work together to identify problem behaviors in the system, and most importantly identify solutions for all of them to live a life worth living (Linehan, 1993).

REFERENCES

Fruzzetti, A. E. (1997). *Family DBT skills*. Reno: University of Nevada.
Fruzzetti, A. E. (2001). *Validating and invalidating behaviors coding scale*. Reno: University of Nevada.

Fruzzetti, A. E. (2006). *The high conflict couple: A dialectical behavior therapy guide to finding peace, intimacy, and validation*. Oakland, CA: New Harbinger.

Fruzzetti, A. E., Santisteban, D. A., & Hoffman, P. D. (2007). Dialectical behavior therapy with families. In L. A. Dimeff & K. Koerner (Eds.), *Dialectical behavior therapy in clinical practice: Applications across disorders and settings* (pp. 222–244). New York, NY: Guilford Press.

Henry, C. S. & Plunkett, S. W. (1995). Validation of the adolescent family life satisfaction index: An update. *Psychological Reports, 76*, 672–674. doi:10.2466/pr0.1995.76.2.672

Hoffman, P. D., Fruzzetti, A. E., & Swenson, C. R. (1999). Dialectical behavior therapy—family skills training. *Family Process, 38*, 399–414. doi:10.1111/j.1545–5300.1999.00399.x

Linehan, M. M. (1993). *Cognitive-behavioral treatment of borderline personality disorder*. New York, NY: Guilford Press.

Miller, A. L., Glinski, J., Woodberry, K. A., Mitchell, A. G., & Indik, J. (2002). Family therapy and dialectical behavior therapy with adolescents: Part I: Proposing a clinical synthesis. *American Journal of Psychotherapy, 56*(4), 568–584.

Olson, D. (2011). FACES IV and the circumplex model: Validation study. *Journal of Marital And Family Therapy, 37*(1), 64–80. doi:10.1111/j.1752–0606.2009.00175.x

Rizvi, S. L., Monroe-DeVita, M., & Dimeff, L. A. (2007). Evaluating your dialectical behavior therapy program. In L. A. Dimeff & K. Koerner (Eds.), *Dialectical behavior therapy in clinical practice: Applications across disorders and settings* (pp. 326–350). New York, NY: Guilford Press.

Shenk, C. E. & Fruzzetti, A. E. (2014). Parental validating and invalidating responses and adolescent psychological functioning: An observational study. *The Family Journal, 22*(1), 43–48. doi:10.1177/1066480713490900

Uliaszek, A. A., Wilson, S., Mayberry, M., Cox, K., & Maslar, M. (2014). A pilot intervention of multifamily dialectical behavior group therapy in a treatment-seeking adolescent population: Effects on teens and their family members. *The Family Journal, 22*, 206–215. doi:10.1177/1066480713513554

Partial Hospital Programs and Settings

Garry S. Del Conte

This chapter describes the application of dialectical behavior therapy (DBT) for adolescents in a partial hospital program (PHP) setting. This approach has shown promise as an alternative to hospitalization in treating a transdiagnostic group of adolescents with severe emotional health problems (Del Conte, Lenz, & Hollenbaugh, 2016; Lenz & Del Conte, 2016; Lenz, Del Conte, Hollenbaugh, & Callender, 2016). I will review the advantages of partial hospitalization programs as an alternative to inpatient care, and provide an overview of milieu treatment incorporating a dialectical philosophy. I will also describe Daybreak Treatment Center, a clinician-run PHP where I serve as the clinical director, as an example of one such program, and provide a detailed picture to help you finesse existing programs or to build new ones. Handouts 6.1–6.9 include sample worksheets helpful for program implementation.

A 2015 report indicated that hospitalization rates had increased 79.45% for 10- to 14-year-olds and 54.8% for 15- to 17-year-olds between 2006 and 2011 (Torio, Encinosa, Berdahl, McCormick, & Simpson, 2015). The authors also reported disproportionate increases in the number of hospitalizations for suicide attempt, suicidal ideation, and non-suicidal self-injury of 151% for 10- to 14-year-olds and 81.6% for 15- to 17-year-olds, trends that the authors characterized as alarming. When presented with a young patient with a severe mental health disorder, particularly if suicidal ideation or self-injury is present, a community-based clinician would understandably recommend hospitalization in the absence of readily available alternatives. However, inpatient psychiatric care is expensive and evidence for its long-term effectiveness in reducing mental health symptoms is lacking (Sheldow et al., 2004). The application of DBT in a PHP program may represent a clinically promising and cost-sensitive way to address the needs of adolescent patients.

The American Association for Ambulatory Behavioral Healthcare (AAABH, n.d.) defines partial hospitalization as

a time-limited, ambulatory, active treatment program that offers therapeutically intensive, coordinated, and structured clinical services within a stable therapeutic milieu. This modality, or method of treatment, is an alternative to hospitalization and offers the flexibility to deal with a very wide range of conditions.

(para. 1)

Many researchers (e.g., Hoge, Davidson, Hill, Turner, & Ameli, 1992; Hoge, Davidson, & Sledge, 1997; Kiser, King, & Lefkovitz, 1999; Kiser & Pruitt, 1991; Luber, 1979) have described partial hospitalization as having multiple benefits as an alternative to inpatient hospitalization. These benefits include cost effectiveness, improved treatment acceptability, maintaining the patient in their community, and avoiding the stigmatization associated with psychiatric hospitalization. Compared with hospitalization, PHPs are inherently cost effective. For example, a study by Grizenko and Papineau (1992) showed that 6.6 days of PHP treatment could be provided for the same cost as only one day of hospitalization. Lower costs have the potential clinical benefit of increasing treatment duration without increasing overall cost per treatment episode.

Lastly, my 20-plus years of experience in managing a clinician-owned and -operated private sector partial program demonstrates the viability of a business model for outpatient providers. Clinician-owned and -administered facilities are cost effective and facilitate provision of evidenced-based treatment free of the potential impediments associated with larger institutions.

CONSIDERATIONS BEFORE IMPLEMENTING DBT

Dialectical Milieu

Researchers have advanced the application of DBT principles and protocols by bringing a dialectical philosophy to our understanding of milieu functioning. However, it may be helpful for you to have some background information on the concept of milieu management. The French word milieu translates to "surroundings," and in mental health treatment, it is used to describe the physical and social environment of patient care in hospital, residential, or partial hospital settings. Gunderson (1979, 1983) defined five therapeutic activities and their associated therapeutic functions within a milieu, regardless of the underlying theoretical model of care. The specific treatment functions are containment, support, structure, involvement, and validation (Gunderson, 1979).

Containment represents safety and encompasses both the physical and interpersonal safety of each patient. This includes policies and procedures that govern fire safety, disaster plans, contraband items, staff response to any crisis that presents a potential risk of patient injury, and the level of staff supervision and patient movement in the facility. Support refers to the ability of the staff to foster a feeling of hope in the patient. Staff members are trained to help patients develop adaptive, growth-oriented attitudes and behaviors. Nurturance, warmth, and encouragement, together with compassion and sensitivity are hallmarks of supportive staff actions that encourage patients' participation in treatment and improve their self-esteem. The third milieu treatment function, structure, indicates the degree of choice each patient has in the program of scheduled activities within the milieu. Structure is defined by the program's schedule, its rules and the associated consequences of breaking them, and the phases or levels of care that mark movement through the program from admission to discharge. The structure of the program provides the scaffolding for the various modalities of treatment, and creates a sense of routine that fosters self-management skills. Involvement encompasses the transactional features of milieu that encourage patients and family members to value their treatment and membership in the therapeutic community, which is defined by the interactions between the patient and staff. Patients are regarded as partners for achieving positive treatment outcomes, and treatment staff interacts with patients in a manner that promotes a positive treatment ethic. Activities of involvement may include community meetings, forms of patient governance, and team-building exercises. Finally, validation refers to milieu activities that are individualized to each patient's unique needs and circumstances. It includes collaboration on an individual's plan of care and staff-patient interactions based on understanding and acceptance of each patient's personal narrative. The term validation is used similarly in DBT, but it is not synonymous—in DBT, validation requires the therapist to identify the inherent truth or wisdom in behaviors, even those that are maladaptive, and to communicate this understanding to the patient. In contrast to the DBT meaning, Gunderson (1979) defines validation as a function that is the end point of therapeutic milieu, and is balanced atop the four preceding functions. A safe, supportive environment that is appropriately structured and valued results in personal confirmation, an outcome that Gunderson describes as providing "a greater capacity for closeness and a more consolidated identity" (1979, p. 332).

In addition, Zeldow (1979) described two divergent models of milieu therapy, the rational model and the dynamic model. The rational model aligns with Gunderson's (1979) functions of containment and structure, and the milieu is understood as the organizational structure that supports the administration of independent treatment modalities. The dynamic model aligns with Gunderson's (1979) functions of support and involvement, and an emphasis is placed on relationships that both bolster and facilitate change. In the dynamic model, the milieu is viewed as a modality in its own right: a super modality that supersedes the others.

Zeldow's (1979) divergent milieu models and Gunderson's (1979) milieu therapeutic functions form a foundation to apply a dialectical philosophy to milieu treatment. The concept of dialectics defines a worldview that incorporates the following assumptions: 1) all things are connected to all other things, 2) change is the only constant, and 3) seeming opposites can be integrated to form ever-closer approximations to ever-evolving truths (see Chapter 2). Discerning the truth that lies on both sides of a polarity and honoring the value in apparent opposites deepen our understanding of milieu functioning in a manner that enhances program administration as well as patient care.

Figure 6.1 illustrates the features and structure of a dialectically organized milieu. It is adapted from Linehan's (1993) description of therapist skills and characteristics and from Zeldow's (1979) distinction of divergent milieu models. Despite polar opposites being present, the effective dialectical stance balances each dimension and meshes seeming opposites together. That synthesis gives rise to a new understanding, one that honors the truth in each pole. The central dialectic of DBT is the continuous joining of acceptance and change. Linehan (1993, p. 110) states, "DBT represents a balance between behavioral approaches, which are primarily technologies of change,

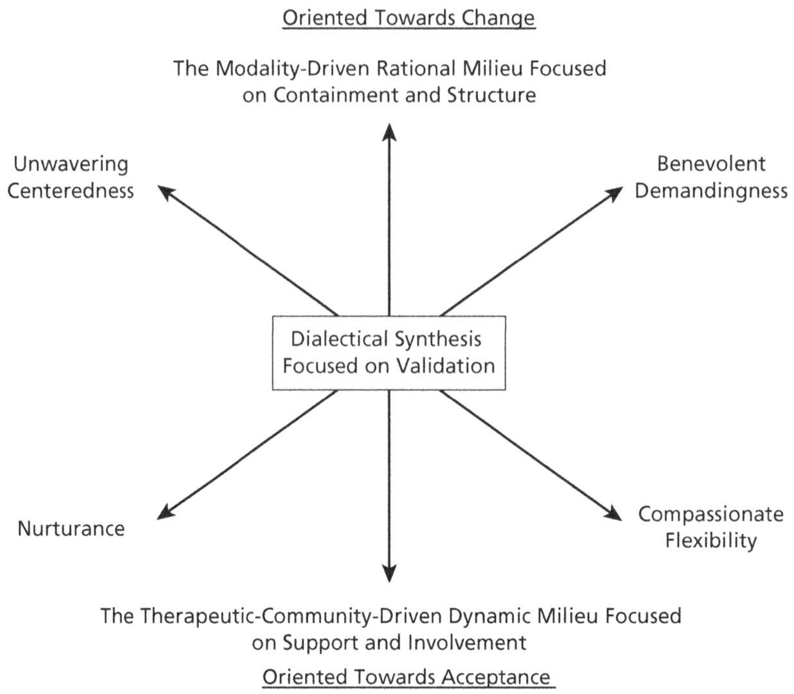

```
                    Oriented Towards Change

          The Modality-Driven Rational Milieu Focused
                  on Containment and Structure

                              ↑
  Unwavering    ↖                              ↗    Benevolent
  Centeredness                                       Demandingness

                    ┌─────────────────────┐
                    │ Dialectical Synthesis │
                    │ Focused on Validation │
                    └─────────────────────┘

  Nurturance    ↙                              ↘    Compassionate
                                                    Flexibility
                              ↓

         The Therapeutic-Community-Driven Dynamic Milieu Focused
                   on Support and Involvement
                    Oriented Towards Acceptance
```

Figure 6.1 Model of a Dialectical Milieu

Source: Adapted by permission from Linehan (1993) *Cognitive-Behavioral Treatment of Borderline Personality Disorder*. New York: Guilford Press.

and humanistic and client-centered approaches, which can be thought of as technologies of acceptance."

Nurturance vs. Benevolent Demandingness

Linehan (1993) describes the dialectic of nurturance vs. benevolent demandingness as an essential characteristic of the DBT therapist, and we find it to be a component of an effectively operating DBT milieu. For example, consider adolescents who struggle with school refusal, and have failed to respond to outpatient interventions. These adolescents and their families become extremely distraught in response to requirements for mandatory attendance, even when the environment is understood to be warm and supportive.

From a position of benevolent demandingness, the program views admission and attendance as all-or-nothing propositions. The program includes contingencies for attendance, which becomes a prerequisite for obtaining desired outcomes. Via benevolent demandingness, the program upholds a belief in both patient and family capabilities, and they are encouraged to weather the emotional storm of an initial intense extinction burst of problem behaviors. In the beginning, the patient and family believe that things are getting worse.

The nurturance pole upholds a different attitude and behaviors. Staff members are predominately sensitive and compassionate. Teaching, coaching, and cheerleading are used to foster learning how to change and let go of avoidance in favor of approach and attendance. Unfortunately, in isolation, we have rarely seen either stance consistently produce the desired results.

Joining a nurturing stance with one of benevolent demandingness has yielded a protocol that honors both sides of this polarity. Admission is an extended process that includes partial day attendance, and occurs over a few days, which allows for both exposure and shaping. During this time, the primary therapist weaves together psychoeducation and lessons on selected skills and coaches the family and patient to restructure the home environment to decrease avoidance and increase attendance. This process unfolds against a backdrop that holds firm on the end point of the admission process: regular, daily, full-time, and on-time attendance. This synthesis results in improved treatment efficacy and enhanced treatment acceptability.

Unwavering Centeredness vs. Compassionate Flexibility

The polarity of unwavering centeredness vs. compassionate flexibility is a second dialectical dimension (Linehan, 1993) used in DBT milieu management. The milieu reflects unwavering centeredness on a set schedule and reasonable rules. The value of a consistent schedule and consensus on which behaviors are encouraged (or discouraged) creates cohesion among the staff, and a predictable, safe setting for patients and family. However, an overly rigid focus on consistency or rule compliance can restrict the milieu from modeling a synthesis that permits the simultaneous expression of compassion and control. In this regard, Linehan states, "Neither arbitrary boundaries or consistency is particularly valued in DBT" (1993, p. 110). The capacity to remain open to new information, to modify expectations when necessary, and to exhibit flexibility without sacrificing control form the blueprint for reaching a dialectical synthesis.

For example, consider our milieu rule on subgrouping. This rule prohibits communication between patients outside of regular program hours. This rule is not popular among adolescent patients because it runs against the grain of normative adolescent experience. However, without this prohibition, the problems that flow from extra-program interactions between patients are manifold. The fundamental difficulty is that once a subgroup is established between two or more patients, their open, honest participation in key treatment modalities is compromised. Specifically, self-disclosure is diminished, and the potential for positive peer pressure to reinforce change in problem behavior is often lost. This rule and the manner in which we describe the benefit to patient and families have stood the test of time; however, exceptions are occasionally made. Such exceptions most frequently occur with socially isolated, avoidant patients who reap a significant therapeutic benefit from post-program hour socialization. The ability to make exceptions requires remaining open to new and relevant information that leads to flexible, creative rule modification. A dialectical synthesis of compassion and control is achieved when exceptions are implemented in a time-limited, adult-supervised manner with the collaboration of staff, patients, and parents. In sum, effective exceptions are enhanced by being aware of the polarity, including its dialectical tensions and the need for solutions that honor the truth on both sides.

Rational vs. Dynamic Milieu Models

The rational milieu is designed to efficiently deliver treatment modalities. Functions of containment and structure are reflected in milieu features such as a precisely executed schedule and clear, simple rules. In the PHP setting this model intensifies the treatment effect, not only by providing for a high treatment dose, but also by encouraging coordination and collaboration among treatment modality providers. Viewing modalities as independently efficacious also promotes maintaining treatment adherence within modalities. In this model, the combined effect of modalities is synergistic (Abroms, 1969).

In contrast, the dynamic milieu model is interpersonally driven and based on the values and principles of therapeutic community movement (Jones, 1983; De Leon, 1994). Functions of support and involvement yield what Silvan, Matzner, and Silva (1999) term a "super group." In the super group, patients are a meaningful force in reaching positive treatment outcomes. Treatment staff models a pro-treatment ethic and maintains a milieu culture that promotes the assumptions of the underlying model of care. This approach has particular utility in adolescent treatment because it incorporates important developmental processes associated with peer group influence. Prinstein and Dodge (2008) report that the developmental literature consistently supports the strong effect of peer influence among adolescents. Allen and Antonishak (2008) add that peer group influence can have a powerful and positive effect on acquiring and transmitting adaptive values. The authors also note that the experience of helping one another in this context has the added benefit of producing strong positive feelings and enhancing self-esteem.

We cultivated a hybrid form of milieu group therapy termed *problem-solving group* as a means of achieving a dialectical synthesis between the rational, modality-driven model (with its value on structure and efficient scheduling), and the dynamic model (with its values on social process, interpersonal connection, and positive peer pressure). The structure and application of this problem-solving group is detailed in the concluding section of this chapter.

ADAPTATIONS TO DBT FOR PHP SETTINGS—THE DBT MILIEU APPLIED

Treatment Context

Daybreak Treatment Center was founded in 1992 by two health care providers with past experience in hospital-based child and adolescent mental health care. The facility is accredited by the Joint Commission and holds state licensure to provide partial hospitalization treatment and state approval to provide transitional educational services. The physical plant is a detached one-story structure of approximately

Table 6.1 DBT Treatment Assumptions in an Adolescent Partial Hospitalization Program

1.	Everyone is doing the best they can.
2.	Everyone wants to improve.
3.	Everyone wants to do better, try harder, and be more motivated to change.
4.	You may not have caused all of your problems, but you still have to solve them.
5.	Life is painful as it is currently being lived.
6.	New, more skillful behavior must be learned and applied in all important situations.
7.	Dialectics means two things that seem like opposites but can both be true.
8.	It's always better to take things as well-meaning instead of assuming the worst.
9.	You cannot fail in this therapy.
10.	All behaviors (actions, thoughts, and emotions) are caused.
11.	Figuring out and changing the causes of behavior are more effective ways to change than judging and blaming.

Adapted with permission from: Miller et al., 2007.

5,500 square feet located on a one-acre property in a suburb of a large southeastern city.

More than half of the patient care space is available for independent outpatient mental health services. The interior space is designed to enhance the engagement of patients, families, and staff in DBT treatment principles and to create an atmosphere infused with the DBT skills curriculum. Artwork throughout the facility is visually pleasing and conveys a DBT theme, and DBT vocabulary, idioms, and mnemonics are prominently displayed. Additionally, whiteboards with markers and the list of DBT treatment assumptions are placed throughout the facility with an open, ongoing invitation to staff, patients, and families to write and endorse treatment assumptions they find helpful or appealing (see Table 6.1). Interactive bulletin boards dedicated to different DBT skill modules serve as an additional engagement and teaching tool and are included in two classroom spaces and three group rooms. Group rooms also have audio-visual equipment and whiteboard space available for teaching DBT skills and for other group modalities.

Patient Characteristics

The adolescent patients range in age from 13 to 18 years. All admissions are voluntary, and costs are paid directly by the family or their insurance carrier. The average length of stay for the most recently completed year (2015) was 31.5 days or just over six weeks. In a recent sampling (Lenz et al., 2016) of 66 consecutive community-referred admissions, the majority were Caucasian females, with an average age of 15. Most patients were diagnosed with depressive disorder, bipolar disorder, or mood disorder not otherwise specified.

Table 6.2 Curriculum Template for a DBT Partial Hospital Program

Time	Monday to Friday
7:45 am	Arrival and preparation for morning meeting
8:00 am	Morning meeting and goal sheet review
8:30 am	Educational therapy and academic preparation
11:00 am	Problem-solving group
12:00 am	Lunch and community assignments
12:30 am	DBT skills group
1:45 pm	Closure group and evening/family time goal setting
2:00 pm	Dismissal

Morning Meeting and Mindfulness

See Table 6.2 for the typical daily schedule at Daybreak Treatment Center. Morning meeting occurs daily for 30 minutes and opens the program day. The meeting begins with each patient reading from the prior evening's daily goal sheet (Handout 6.1). The daily goal sheet, which differs from the patient diary card, is a group monitoring device that provides feedback from self, family, and staff for the previous 24 hours. Patient self-monitoring includes personal ratings on DBT homework and diary card completion. Parents provide comments on the previous night's activity with a focus on description rather than judgment. The group leader and members use information reported from the daily goal sheet to highlight potential agenda items for the remainder of the days' scheduled modalities, which could include individual or family therapy or problem-solving group therapy. This review process thereby strengthens the pertinence of upcoming modalities with information and collaboration across providers and modalities. Morning meeting always closes with a brief mindfulness activity that is chosen by either patients or the staff.

Educational Therapy and Academic Preparation

Educational therapy and academic preparation occur daily and account for 15 hours a week on average. Every patient is enrolled in a state-approved transitional educational program and is provided with an individualized course of study that mirrors the curriculum of the school to which they will return. To maintain therapeutic intensity, the educational space is adjacent to patient care areas. Educational staff members use DBT strategies and coach skills in addressing behaviors that manifest in the learning environment. In addition to teaching self-management skills, the educational specialist also uses missing-links analysis when homework completion is a target (see Handout 6.2—Missing Links Assessments).

Problem-Solving Group

The problem-solving group meets daily for an hour. The group leader teaches and guides group members in the use of behavioral assessment (chain and missing-links analysis) and solution analysis. The group balances social process components (associated with the dynamic milieu model) with the structure of a DBT individual session (associated with the rational, modality-driven milieu model). Group members are encouraged to invite other members to address problematic behavior revealed during the morning meeting. Avoidance is addressed through the transparency afforded by parental report discussed in the morning meeting. Group members also consult their own diary cards and are expected to bring problematic behaviors to the group following the targeting hierarchy of stage one DBT (see Chapter 1). For example, if a patient was absent the prior day and also reported a serious peer conflict related to a relationship target, the absence, which interferes with therapy, would be addressed before the peer conflict, which is a quality-of-life issue.

The group, coached by the leader, strives to maintain a dialectical stance, balancing acceptance and change while collectively completing chain and solution analysis. The members work together on troubleshooting solutions and following up on agreed solution analysis. Group process elements may include members devising programmatic contingencies for patients who are willing to collaborate on having their environment prompt them towards more effective behavior. The group process also teaches and reinforces skills. Senior group members can experience a sense of mastery and competence by teaching skills to newer members. Teaching skills to others helps patients see themselves as positive role models and assists in peer maintenance of a pro-treatment community ethic. The problem-solving group also provides members with opportunities to validate one another, to reinforce effective behavior, and to provide cheerleading as needed.

Lunch and Community Responsibilities

A 30-minute period for lunch and community responsibilities is used strategically to manage social interactions with assigned seating and to provide the experience of helping with common family-friendly household tasks. The *Lunch Time Tasks* worksheet (see Handout 6.3) will help you facilitate organizing the lunch period. Lunchtime is also used as an opportunity for informal practice of mindful eating and to encourage healthful nutrition with reference to reducing vulnerability as taught in the PLEASE skill.

DBT Skills Group

The DBT skills group meets daily for 90 minutes. It is staffed with co-leaders and structured as recommended by Linehan (1993, 2015) and Rathus and Miller (2015). An initial period focuses on homework review, and after a brief break, new skill(s) and a subsequent homework assignment are covered.

Homework is assigned daily, and homework tasks have been modified in two ways. First, worksheets that require weekly reporting now accommodate daily or weekend-long time frames. Second, patients are routinely assigned the home task of teaching skills to their parents (Handout 6.4), which has multiple objectives. Teaching skills to parents creates a pro-treatment atmosphere in the home. It reinforces the adolescent's learning and allows them to demonstrate skillful behavior in the presence of their parents. Further, the parents benefit by knowing which skills are currently being taught and by having the opportunity to learn and practice skillful means on their own.

Daily skills learning over multiple weeks can become stale and stagnate. To remain faithful to the content of the published skills curriculums (Linehan, 2015; Rathus & Miller, 2015), supplemental teaching activities designed to create greater patient interest and learning through action-oriented individual and group activities have been added to our schedule of skills (Del Conte & Olsen, 2016).

One important way skills teaching is facilitated is through the use of what Andolfi, Angelo, Menghi, and Nicholò-Corigliano (1983) described as the concrete metaphor. The concrete metaphor, created by the therapist (or skills trainers), uses play and a tangible metaphor to strengthen skill acquisition. For example, one way to reinforce the lesson of opposite action is to play the game of Sardines, which flips the concept of classic Hide-and-Seek. In Sardines, one person hides while all other players close their eyes and count (usually to about 25). When the counting is completed, the search for the hider begins. When a seeker finds the hider, he or she doesn't say anything, but in the spirit of opposite action, quietly crawls into the hiding spot with the hider. The person who finds the hider must wait until no one is nearby before crawling into the same space to prevent others from finding the spot. In Sardines the seekers slowly disappear, and the hiding place becomes increasingly cramped as the hiders become packed in like sardines. The game ends when the last of the seekers finds the "sardines." When the participants discuss the game experience, the trainer can make teaching points about the opposite action skill and make analogies between the game and their real-life experiences using the skill. This alteration is supported by results from a recent study in this PHP-based application of DBT, which found that the adolescent population appears to learn and apply skills more effectively when the learning includes action and concrete exercises (Lenz et al., 2016).

A final teaching tool is contained in our DBT@Daybreak YouTube channel (www.youtube.com/channel/UCAVlvlYOig-2OuC9Shc-dlg). This channel includes a collection of entertaining video clips that teach skills and are organized according to the lessons that make up our DBT milieu skills curriculum. An example might include watching the online video the "Sad Cat Diaries," and discussing common thinking mistakes (see Handout 6.5—*Top 10 Thinking Errors*).

Closure Group

The 15-minute closure group activity is the briefest of the program day and often merges with the end of DBT skills group. Each patient receives their program goal sheet for the program day and briefly interacts with staff regarding their functioning during the current day and their behavioral objective for the coming evening.

Parent DBT Skills Class

A once weekly group for parents includes the three components of the Middle Path module (Miller et al., 2006; Rathus & Miller, 2015), and the format is modeled after that provided by Perepletchikova and colleagues (2011). The content is suitable for a six-week sequence, and the format allows rotating staff instructors to facilitate scheduling (see Table 6.3). The topic listing and handouts are organized as a Skills Manual for Families, and they are provided at the time of admission and family orientation.

Table 6.3 Curriculum for Six-Week Parent Middle Path Skills

Date	Lesson	Topic	Description
	1	Introduction to Dialectical Reasoning and Problem-Solving Dialectics Handout I	Guiding principles of dialectics (i.e., there is no absolute nor relative truth, opposite things can both be true, change is the only constant, and change is transactional), how these principles apply to parenting and ways to practice dialectics.
	2	Three Common Dialectical Dilemmas of Adolescence Thinking Mistakes Dialectics Handout II	Dialectical dilemmas that apply to parenting adolescents (excessive leniency vs. authoritarian control; forcing autonomy vs. fostering dependence; and pathologizing normative behaviors vs. normalizing pathological behaviors). Reviewing common thinking mistakes that impact ability to remain dialectical.
	3	Mindfulness of Relationships/Validation Five Ways Parents Ignore Underlying Feelings Handout Validation Handout I	Defining validation, why we validate, roadblocks to validation, ways parents inadvertently invalidate underlying feelings, important things to validate. Defining teen and adolescent stages that can reduce ability to understand and relate.
	4	Creating a Validating Environment Validation Handout II	Nonverbal (e.g., active listening and being mindful of invalidating reactions, such as rolling eyes and turning back) and verbal validation (e.g., observing and reflecting feelings back without judgment, looking for kernel of truth).

(Continued)

Table 6.3 (Continued)

Date	Lesson	Topic	Description
	5	Introduction to Behavior Change Techniques Behaviorism Handout I	Defining behavior and determining the functions of the behavior, vulnerability factors, replacement behaviors, and incompatible behaviors.
	6	Ways to Increase and Decrease Behavior Behaviorism Handout II	Setting behavioral goals, reinforcement, punishment, extinction, and differential reinforcement.

TREATMENT ADHERENCE IN THE DBT MILIEU

See Table 6.4 for a list of the modes and treatment team members in the DBT milieu with corresponding behavioral targets. In addition to addressing treatment targets via several modes of treatment, we also maintain the treatment fidelity through several different venues.

Therapist Supervision/Consultation Group

A supervision/consultation group for primary therapists meets weekly for 90 minutes and is organized as recommended in the original treatment manual (Linehan, 1993). This group is distinct from traditional team staffing. In a standard team staff meeting, all treatment team members report on treatment progress and modify goals and interventions for each patient's individualized treatment plan. In contrast, the DBT supervision/consultation group is a provider-centered group required for all primary therapists and may include therapists providing DBT skills and leading the problem-solving group. The primary goal of the supervision/consultation group is to enhance clinician competence and motivation to deliver DBT in a manner consistent with standard treatment principles (Linehan, 1993) and accepted adaptations applicable to adolescents (Miller et al., 2006).

Monthly Staff Supervision/Consultation Group

A monthly supervision consultation group for all staff members supplements the ongoing staff training, consultation, and cheerleading that occurs on a nearly daily basis through constantly unfolding and changing milieu events. This meeting has a broader scope and more flexible format than the weekly meeting, but it retains a focus on staff motivation and adherence to the treatment model. An opening mindfulness exercise and a review and discussion of one or two commitments from among the staff and therapist commitments begin these meetings. Activities vary and are based on staff requests or perceived needs. Activities might include didactic teaching, role-plays, and problem-solving with challenging cases.

Table 6.4 Hierarchy of DBT PHP Behavioral Targets by Role and Mode

Mode or Treatment Team Role	Behavioral Target Hierarchy
Admission Process	Pretreatment orientation/commitment of patient and family Pretreatment assessment of patient goals and problems
Primary Therapist	Continued orientation/commitment of patient and family Overall coordination of modes and behavioral targets
Individual Therapy	Decrease life-threatening behaviors Decrease therapy-interfering behaviors Decrease quality-of-life problems Increase skill acquisition, application, and generalization
Medication Management	Enhance capability to acquire skills Decrease quality-of-life problems associated with DSM-V diagnosis (e.g., symptoms of Bipolar Disorder)
Phone Coaching (after program hours)	Eliminate suicide crisis behaviors Increase skill application and generalization Therapy relationship repair
Skills Coaching in the Milieu	Stop behaviors that destroy therapy Increase skill application and generalization Decrease therapy-interfering behaviors
Morning Meeting	Decrease therapy-interfering behaviors Increase treatment commitment Increase problem-solving and planning skills
Educational Specialist/ Educational Therapy	Decrease therapy-interfering behaviors Decrease academic-related quality-of-life problems Increase self-management skills
DBT Problem-Solving Group	Decrease therapy-interfering behaviors Increase interpersonal skills Increase problem-solving and dialectical reasoning skills Decrease quality-of-life problems
DBT Skills Group	Stop behaviors that destroy therapy Increase acquisition and application of DBT skills Decrease therapy-interfering behaviors
Parent Skills Class	Strengthen treatment commitment Increase Middle Path skills acquisition, application, and generalization

Phases of Care

Features of the milieu structure inspired by DBT principles include a system of treatment phases that honor the principle that DBT is a voluntary process. Patient commitment is required for treatment to be effective. Our phase system is inspired by and modeled after the phases of treatment for DBT in adult inpatient settings (Swenson, Witterholt, & Bohus, 2007). Patient movement from admission through treatment and discharge is marked by the treatment phases of 1) Entering, 2) Working, and 3) Exiting.

The Entering Phase blends orientation and strengthening commitment with assessment, goal formulation, and the creation of a crisp, behaviorally specific set of targets related to goal attainment. Handout 6.6 includes an overview of an acronym to help the adolescents understand treatment (Behavioral, Educational, Action Oriented, Teamwork), and Handout 6.7 is an identification worksheet. Both of these devices provide a foundation for the work in the Entering phase. New patients and family members also view a creative and highly informative eight-minute YouTube video by Esme Shaller titled "What the Heck Is DBT?" (www.dbtcenteroc.com/what-the-heck-is-dbt-by-dr-esme-shaller-ucsf/).

The first family meeting occurs after the patient has made a commitment to participate. The patient has identified personally meaningful goals and commits to using skillful means in lieu of problem behaviors. In that first family meeting, the patient presents goals and discusses problem behaviors. The patient is also encouraged to ask for parental help in carrying out the plan. All standard DBT commitment strategies (see Chapter 2) may be used as needed during this phase. Programmatically, advancing from Entering to Working is encouraged by contingencies in the milieu, staff cheerleading, positive peer pressure, and when indicated, problem-solving in the problem-solving group. These strategies in combination usually keep the time spent in the Entering Phase under two weeks. A congratulatory group announcement publically marks movement from the Entering to the Working Phase.

The Working Phase focuses on learning and practicing new skills in all relevant contexts. Targets in the Working Phase are personalized and, as one would expect in a transdiagnostic group, specific targets in the quality-of-life domain vary widely among group members (see Table 6.5). What remains invariant is adherence to the DBT target hierarchy, which places reduction of life-threatening behaviors before all other considerations. Also consistent with standard stage one DBT, the second class of behavioral targets comprises behaviors that interfere with or threaten the ability to receive or continue in care.

The third phase, Exiting, begins in the last week of PHP treatment and runs concurrently with the Working Phase. Patients in this final phase are entitled to additional perks like leading morning meeting mindfulness, assisting with orientation of new patients, and most popularly, earning the privilege of exchanging accumulated stickers for cash value gift cards. Contingencies aside, the work of Exiting is to create patient commitment and involvement in a practical plan of continued care. See Handout 6.8 for a handout on the three phases of treatment.

Parents are always instrumental in supporting a continued care plan, and case management services are provided to assist with the process. Concurrently, this phase is implemented to embrace the consultation to the patient focus of DBT. Frequently, patients are returning to a community therapist who may not be trained in DBT. In those cases, patients are coached to ask for what they need. The usual request is

Table 6.5 Treatment Targets for a DBT PHP

Treatment Targets	Examples
Primary Treatment Targets	
Life-Threatening Behaviors	Harm to self or others Urges to harm self or others Thoughts of harming self or others Voicing a desire to harm self or others
Milieu-Interfering Behaviors	Being disruptive in group sessions Not practicing skills or completing diary card Sleeping in group sessions
Quality-of-Life-Interfering Behaviors	Substance use Risky sex/impulsive behavior Vandalism Lying to parents Breaking rules at home Academic issues Skipping school
Increasing Behavioral Skills	Mindfulness Distress Tolerance Walking the Middle Path Emotion Regulation Interpersonal Effectiveness

to continue the features of DBT that are typically compatible with the practice patterns of most outpatient providers. For example, asking to continue with a form for self-monitoring, retaining behaviorally specific goals, or beginning sessions with a collaborative agenda are all reasonable requests. It can also mean that the DBT program therapist is available to speak to the outpatient provider in support of, not in lieu of, the patient's request. The exact manner in which the consultation is implemented must take into account the patient's age, his or her capacities to interact with adults in powerful positions, and the importance of the task to be completed. As a DBT therapist, a good place to start the decision-making process might be with the question, "Am I robbing this adolescent of the opportunity to become more skillful if I step in and do this for him or her?"

Behavioral Contingencies and Expectations

If the phases of care provide an overview map of the treatment course from admission to discharge, then behavioral contingencies and expectations form the specific directions. Community rules and guidelines are grouped into categories consistent with DBT concepts of therapy-enhancing, therapy-interfering, and therapy-destroying behaviors (see Handout 6.9). Contingencies are weighted towards use of positive reinforcement. For example, patients can earn stickers for educational and DBT skills homework completion and program points for therapy-enhancing behaviors like on-time attendance and positive group participation. Points earn levels that translate into daily and weekly privileges. Aversive consequences apply, but they retain a problem-solving character. Worksheets termed TIBS (Therapy-Interfering Behavior Solutions) can double as a correction-overcorrection protocol for egregious rule violations. Worksheet elements consist of a mini chain analysis for acts of commission or, in the absence of an expected behavior, a mini missing-links assessment. In all cases, staff members who coach the patient towards more skillful future responses and making appropriate repairs when indicated oversee these processes.

Staff Use of Validation and Skills Coaching

The treatment staff cultivates a pro-treatment community ethic consistent with the assumptions and principles of DBT. The staff endeavors to create a skills-savvy atmosphere infused with the language and concepts of the DBT skills curriculum. The staff is versed in effective coaching including mini chain and solution analysis as needed throughout the program day. The staff is trained to create a no-fault, validating environment that forms the foundation for ongoing pursuit of change, moving the patient closer to their treatment goals. Staff members' understanding of validation and its effective use is important for two reasons. First, validation is generally accepted to be central to addressing the biological vulnerabilities of individuals who have deficient emotional modulation and who have been exposed to invalidating experiences in their families and in the community at large. Second, validation effectively addresses adolescent developmental vulnerabilities associated with normative tasks of self-definition and identity formation. A staff that conveys understanding decreases willfulness and increases willingness to participate in problem-solving.

TREATMENT TEAM ROLES IN THE DBT MILIEU

Administrator

The administrator is responsible for establishing and implementing a profitable business plan consistent with the clinical mission of the program. Administrators are in charge of all billing and accounts receivable procedures, all negotiations and contracts with third-party payers, and all policy and procedures related to census management including public relations, communication, and marketing.

Clinical Director

The clinical director is a Linehan Board-Certified DBT Clinician. The position requires supervising all aspects of patient care and program implementation. He or she is responsible for leading all facility staff to provide DBT in accordance to the standards

Table 6.6 Daybreak Treatment Center Staff Agreements

1. **Dialectical Agreement:** No one individual or viewpoint is the "right" one, everyone's viewpoint has validity, and the truth is arrived at by integrating differing, even opposing, points of view.

2. **Phenomenological Empathy/Nonpejorative Agreement:** Staff members will seek out the most empathic interpretation of the clients' and their colleagues' behavior, being guided by a nonjudgmental behaviorally descriptive approach to the empirical evidence.

3. **Consistency Agreement:** Although different staff members should be consistent in focusing on each patient's targets, on observing program rules and policies, and on implementing DBT principles and guidelines, they need not be consistent in matters of style or approach.

4. **Observing Limits Agreement:** Different staff members should honor their own natural personal limits in the program. These limits will, of course, be different from one staff member to the next and may differ within staff across time (as long as all staff members are also observing program-wide limits as articulated in rules and policies of the program).

5. **Fallibility Agreement:** All staff members are fallible, make mistakes, and therefore need not be defensive about this; we agree to use these moments as opportunities to better learn the treatment model.

6. **Consultation-to-the-Patient Agreement:** All staff members will consult to the patient, within the limits of their developmental capabilities, in managing his or her relationships with others, including family and other staff in the program, rather than trying to manage those things for the patient.

Adapted with permission from: Swenson, C. R., Witterholt, S., & Bohus, M. (2007). Dialectical behavior therapy on inpatient units. In L. A. Dimeff & K. Koerner (Eds.), *Dialectical behavior therapy in clinical practice* (p. 84). New York, NY: Guilford Press.

under which the empirical base was established. The clinical director is also responsible for modeling adherence to Staff Agreements (Table 6.6) and for being accessible to consult with all program staff throughout the program day. He or she is also responsible for all training and research activities occurring in the facility. Lastly the clinical director is responsible to the administrator to ensure that all services are provided in a cost-effective manner consistent with organizational budgetary goals and objectives.

Admissions Director

The admissions director is responsible for completing all pre-admission tasks including face-to-face assessment to determine appropriateness for admission in accordance with program admission criteria. The admissions director takes the lead in the initial orientation of patients and families to program requirements and in strengthening their commitment to care. The admission director coordinates with the administrator and clinical director to manage issues regarding finances or suitability for treatment.

Primary Therapist: Case Management, Individual Therapy, and Family Meetings

All primary therapists complete foundational training in DBT or are advanced doctoral students in clinical psychology working under the direct supervision of the clinical director. The primary therapist is responsible for case formulation and overall coordination of treatment interventions. The primary therapist also provides individual therapy and family meetings. Sessions are structured in keeping with standard outpatient DBT (Miller et al., 2006). The Entering phase is the pretreatment stage and includes orientation to DBT treatment assumptions, use of a daily diary card, and the role of chain analysis in problem-solving. Most importantly, the primary therapist is responsible for shaping a strong commitment to participate in DBT treatment that includes reaching a mutual agreement on goals and target problems. From the point of commitment, individual sessions follow the standard DBT target hierarchy that sequentially address decreases in 1) life-threatening behavior, 2) therapy-interfering behavior, and 3) quality-of-life-interfering behavior while seeking 4) increases in use of skills across all needed areas. This latter target is also addressed through DBT phone coaching after program hours and during weekends.

The family initially attends individual sessions to join in and support the treatment commitment made by the patient. Subsequent meetings are provided to address family transactional patterns that are increasing or decreasing problematic behaviors, to structure the patient's environment, and to create case management plans for post-discharge care.

Psychiatrist

A child and adolescent psychiatrist oversees all medical aspects of care. Each patient is evaluated, and psychotropic medications are used when indicated. Their effectiveness is monitored and managed by the physician with feedback from other team members. The psychiatrist operates from a DBT informed standpoint, which means that medication is prescribed to enable acquisition and use of skills. The physician is also aware of efforts to treat the patient in the home environment and supportive of them. When hospitalization is needed, the physician provides attending services and partners with the primary therapist and family towards a rapid transition back to the PHP level of care whenever feasible.

Director of Education and Educational Specialist Staff

The director of education provides or supervises educational specialists in providing educational assessments, interventions, and liaison with each patient's family and home school. The educational specialists approach the tasks of education from a DBT informed perspective. In class, use of DBT skills is frequent and specific to behavioral targets. Missing-links analysis seems particularly effective in increasing task completion and serving as a useful springboard for teaching self-management skills. Additionally, educational specialists serve as DBT skills trainers. Professional educators are often a good fit for teaching the skill modules of DBT and balance nicely with co-leaders who have a traditional mental health care background. This seemingly nontraditional role for educators is likely to become more commonplace with the introduction of DBT teaching materials specifically for educators in school settings (Mazza, Dexter-Mazza, Miller, Rathus, & Murphy, 2016).

Program Coordinator

The program coordinator is in charge of all milieu policies and procedures and serves as a facility manager responsible for the integrity of the physical plant. In collaboration with program therapists and the director of education, he or she is responsible for program implementation in the face of frequently complex and challenging patient and family presentations. Lastly, he or she is responsible for all staff scheduling, ensuring the efficient use of staff resources, continuously accounting for census fluctuations and other factors affecting staff availability and staffing needs.

OUTCOME EVALUATION

Whenever treatment is adapted from its original evidenced-based structure we assume an obligation to collect data to know whether or not we are achieving effective outcomes. Rizvi, Monroe-De Vita, and Dimeff (2007) provide additional reasons including gaining ongoing support from administrators, improving reimbursement rates with third-party payers, establishing credibility with patients and families to make a commitment to treatment and providing the treatment staff with evidence that their efforts are effective. In addition to the Difficulties in Emotion Regulation Scale (DERS; Gratz & Roemer, 2004) and the DBT Ways of Coping Checklist (WCCL; Neacsiu, Rizvi, Vitaliano, Lynch, & Linehan, 2010) described in Chapter 4, we have also used the assessments below to evaluate outcomes in our program.

Interpersonal Sensitivity (INT)

The INT (Derogatis, 1994) is actually a subscale from the Symptom Checklist-90-R (SCL) that focuses specifically on an individual's interactions with others and awareness of emotions in relationships. This subscale can be used to measure skills use related to the interpersonal effectiveness module, as well as the adolescent's ability to regulate emotions and manage stressful situations. This assessment can be helpful in conjunction with other methods of evaluation to gather information specifically on the adolescent's relationships.

The Frieburg Mindfulness Inventory (FMI)

The FMI (Walach, Buchheld, Buttenmuller, Kleinnecht, & Schmidt, 2006) is a 14-item self-report assessment that measures the adolescent's ability to be aware of the current moment. Items are Likert scaled, and questions are framed around the adolescent's ability to objectively notice emotions and experiences. This assessment is relatively short, and therefore it can be administered frequently to measure adolescents' mindfulness skill development.

SUMMARY AND CONCLUSIONS

I have endeavored to integrate theoretical and practical issues to demonstrate how DBT might be effectively applied in a PHP setting. If the essence of a "good idea" is doing something better and less expensively than previously possible, then this approach appears to qualify. The potential to provide evidence-based treatment safely and sufficiently while avoiding the costs and liabilities inherent in hospital care deserves our careful attention. From a practice standpoint, the PHP system of service delivery may be within the reach of many clinician-run organizations. Larger practices may already have sufficient resources in place and only require a carefully constructed business plan to determine the financial feasibility of offering this level of care for adolescent patients and their families.

REFERENCES

Abroms, G. M. (1969). Defining milieu therapy. *Archives of General Psychiatry*, *21*(5), 553–560.

Allen, J. P. & Antonishak, J. (2008). Adolescent peer influences: Beyond the dark side. In M. J. Prinstein & K. A. Dodge (Eds.), *Understanding peer influence in children and adolescents* (pp. 141–160). New York, NY: Guilford Press.

American Association of Ambulatory Behavioral Healthcare (AAABH). (n.d.). *An overview of the partial hospitalization modality*. Retrieved from www.aabh.org/partial-hospitalization-progra

Andolfi, M., Angelo, C., Menghi, P., & Nicholò-Corigliano, A. M. (1983). *Behind the family mask: Therapeutic change in rigid family systems*. New York, NY: Brunner/Mazel.

De Leon, G. (1994). The therapeutic community: Toward a general theory and model. In F. Tims, G. De Leon, & N. Jaincull (Eds.), *Therapeutic community: Advances in research and application. NIDA Research monograph Series, number 144* (pp. 16–53). Rockville, MD: National Institute on Drug Abuse.

Del Conte, G. S., Lenz, A. S., & Hollenbaugh, K. M. (2016). A pilot evaluation of dialectical behavior therapy for adolescents within a partial hospitalization treatment milieu. *Journal of Child and Adolescent Counseling*, *2*(1), 16–32.

Del Conte, G. S. & Olsen, E. (2016). *DBT in motion*. Unpublished manual.

Derogatis, L. R. (1994). *Symptom checklist-90-R. Administration, scoring, and procedures manual*. Minneapolis, MN: National Computer Systems, Inc.

Gratz, K. L. & Roemer, L. (2004). Multidimensional assessment of emotion regulation and dysregulation: Development, factor structure, and initial validation of the difficulties in emotion regulation scale. *Journal of Psychopathology and Behavioral Assessment*, *26*, 41–54.

Grizenko, N. & Papineau, D. (1992). A comparison of the cost-effectiveness of day treatment and residential treatment for children with severe behaviour problems. *The Canadian Journal of Psychiatry/La Revue canadienne de psychiatrie, 37*(6), 393–400.

Gunderson, J. G. (1979). Defining the therapeutic processes in psychiatric milieus. *Psychiatry, 41*, 327–335.

Gunderson, J. G. (1983). An overview of modern milieu therapy. In J. G. Gunderson, O. A. Will, Jr., & L. R. Mosher (Eds.), *Principles and practice of milieu therapy* (pp. 1–13). New York, NY: Jason Aronson.

Hoge, M. A., Davidson, L., Hill, W. L., Turner, V. E., & Ameli, R. (1992). The promise of partial hospitalization: A reassessment. *Psychiatric Services, 43*(4), 345–354.

Hoge, M. A., Davidson, L., & Sledge, W. H. (1997). Alternatives to acute hospitalization. In K. Minkoff & D. Pollack (Eds.), *Managed mental health care in the public sector* (pp. 191–204). The Netherlands: Harwood Academic Publishers.

Jones, M. (1983). Therapeutic community as a system for change. In J. G. Gunderson, O. A. Will & L. R. Mosher (Eds.), *Principles and practice of milieu therapy* (pp. 177–184). New York, NY: Jason Aronson.

Kiser, L. J., King, R., & Lefkovitz, P. M. (1999). Best practices: A comparison of practice patterns and a model continuum of ambulatory behavioral health services. *Psychiatric Services, 50*(5), 605–618.

Kiser, L. J. & Pruitt, D. B. (1991). Child and adolescent day treatment: A general systems theory perspective. In G. K. Farley & S. G. Zimet (Eds.), *Day treatment for children with emotional disorders* (pp. 85–96). New York, NY: Plenum Press.

Lenz, A. S. & Del Conte, G. S. (2016). *Efficacy of dialectical behavior therapy versus mixed model milieu among adolescents in a partial hospital program*. Manuscript in preparation.

Lenz, A. S., Del Conte, G., Hollenbaugh, K. M., & Callender, K. (2016). Emotional regulation and interpersonal effectiveness as mechanisms of change for treatment outcomes within a DBT program for adolescents. *Counseling Outcome Research and Evaluation, 7*(2), 73–85. doi:10.1177/2150137816642439

Linehan, M. (1993). *Cognitive-behavioral treatment of borderline personality disorder*. New York, NY: Guilford Press.

Linehan, M. M. (2015). *DBT® skills training manual*. New York, NY: Guilford Press.

Luber, R. F. (1979). *Partial hospitalization: A current perspective*. New York, NY: Plenum.

Mazza, J. J., Dexter-Mazza, E. T., Miller, A. L., Rathus, J. H., & Murphy, H. E. (2016). *DBT skills in schools: Skills training for emotional problem solving for adolescents (DBT STEPS-A)*. New York, NY: Guilford Press.

Miller, A. L., Rathus, J. H., & Linehan, M. M. (2006). *Dialectical behavior therapy with suicidal adolescents*. New York, NY: Guilford Press.

Neacsiu, A., Rizvi, S., Vitaliano, P., Lynch, T., & Linehan, M. M. (2010). The dialectical behavior therapy ways of coping checklist: Development and psychometric properties. *Journal of Clinical Psychology, 66*, 1–20. doi:10.1002/jclp.20685

Perepletchikova, F., Axelrod, S. R., Kaufman, J., Rounsaville, B. J., Douglas-Palumberi, H., & Miller, A. L. (2011). Adapting dialectical behaviour therapy for children: Towards a new research agenda for paediatric suicidal and non-suicidal self-injurious behaviours. *Child and Adolescent Mental Health, 16*(2), 116–121.

Prinstein, M. J. & Dodge, K. A. (2008). Current issues in peer influence research. In M. J. Prinstein & K. A. Dodge (Eds.), *Understanding peer influence in children and adolescents* (pp. 3–13). New York, NY: Guilford Press.

Rathus, J. H. & Miller, A. L. (2015). *DBT® skills manual for adolescents*. New York, NY: Guilford Press.

Rizvi, S. L., Monroe-DeVita, M., & Dimeff, L. A. (2007). Evaluating your dialectical behavior therapy program. In L. A. Dimeff & K. Koerner (Eds.), *Dialectical behavior therapy in clinical practice: Applications across disorders and settings* (pp. 326–350). New York, NY: Guilford Press.

Sheldow, A. J., Bradford, W. D., Henggeler, S. W., Rowland, M. D., Halliday-Boykins, C., Schoenwalk, S. K., & Ward, D. M. (2004). Treatment costs for youths receiving multisystemic therapy or hospitalization after a psychiatric crisis. *Psychiatric Services*, *55*(5), 548–554.

Silvan, M., Matzner, F. J., & Silva, R. R. (1999). A model for adolescent day treatment. *Bulletin of the Menninger Clinic*, *63*(4), 459–480.

Swenson, C. R., Witterholt, S., & Bohus, M. (2007). Dialectical behavior therapy on inpatient units. In L. A. Dimeff & K. Koerner (Eds.), *Dialectical behavior therapy in clinical practice* (pp. 69–113). New York, NY: Guilford Press.

Torio, C. E., Encinosa, W., Berdahl, T., McCormick, M. C., & Simpson, L. A. (2015). Annual report on health care for children and youth in the United States: National estimates of cost, utilization and expenditures for children with mental health conditions. *Academic Pediatrics*, *15*, 19–35.

Walach, H., Buchheld, N., Buttenmuller, V., Kleinnecht, N., & Schmidt, S. (2006). Measuring mindfulness—the Freiburg mindfulness inventory (FMI). *Personality and Individual Differences*, *40*, 1543–1555. doi:10.1016/j.paid.2005.11.025

Zeldow, P. B. (1979). Divergent approaches to milieu therapy. *Bulletin of the Menninger Clinic*, *43*(3), 217–232.

DBT in Inpatient Settings
K. Michelle Hunnicutt Hollenbaugh
and Jacob M. Klein

In this chapter, we will discuss adaptations for DBT in inpatient hospitalization settings. An inpatient unit is an ideal setting to implement DBT, as it provides a short-term, immersive experience for adolescents that specifically targets their life-threatening behaviors and the resulting hospitalizations. In fact, the underlying goal of an inpatient DBT program is to help the client use skills and reduce problem behaviors so he or she will not need to be hospitalized in the future (Swenson, Witterholt, & Bohus, 2007). Because being hospitalized is often unintentionally reinforcing for adolescents, having the program, or milieu (inpatient environment), structured around DBT will help reduce that reinforcement. In addition, the implementation of a DBT program may reduce staff burnout, as it provides them with the training and skills to work effectively with extremely dysregulated adolescents.

Preliminary research supports the use of DBT on inpatient units (Linehan, 2015). Studies have found that an inpatient DBT program can reduce behavioral problems (Katz, Cox, Gunasekara, & Miller, 2004), increase positive treatment outcomes and reduce non-suicidal self-injury (McDonell et al., 2010), and provide long-lasting remission of mental health symptoms (Kleindienst et al., 2008). Though these results are promising, they remain preliminary, and therefore you should be mindful of your population, and availability of other evidence-based treatments before implementing DBT.

CONSIDERATIONS BEFORE IMPLEMENTING DBT

Implementing DBT on an inpatient unit requires a significant amount of adaptation from the standard DBT model that was designed for outpatient settings. Basically, you will be taking a treatment intervention that was developed to be implemented over six months, and adapting it to be implemented over the course of several days. How you will adapt DBT will depend largely on the average length of stay in your program. This can vary greatly—you may be in a residential setting, where you have up to several months to implement standard DBT, or you may have only a few days. Regardless, you will need to spend a lot of time considering the best way to determine that the client receives the essential skills necessary for successful coping upon discharge.

You will also need to consider whether you are going to implement a full model that includes all DBT functions and modes (see Chapter 2), or only implement certain modes of treatment. For example, implementing the skills group only is common on inpatient units; however, there is a lack of research supporting the effectiveness of this approach (Swenson et al., 2007). This decision will be based on your population, the average length of stay on your unit, and your access to resources and training. For example, if you are working on a traditional acute care inpatient unit, full DBT may be warranted to help adolescents eliminate life-threatening behaviors and reduce the frequency of hospitalizations. However, if you do not have the resources or ability to engage all of the unit staff in training, it may be best to start with the skills group to acquaint staff and administration with the underlying tenants of DBT until you are able to attain the backing and assets to implement the full model.

The existing program may influence your decision regarding whether to adopt or adapt DBT. For example, if the current program has been in existence for a while, it may be more challenging for you to implement such an extreme paradigm shift from the current treatment approach. You may experience resistance from unit staff (nurses, psychologists, technicians, etc.), as DBT focuses less on punitive punishment for problem behaviors, and instead highlights the importance of behavioral reinforcement. In addition, staff availability to help clients generalize skills and reinforce skillful behavior in the moment is essential, which may be a major shift from the current approach in your program (Swenson, Sanderson, Dulit, & Linehan, 2001). To combat this, you will need to work hard to attain staff and administration commitment. Using the commitment strategies we discuss in Chapter 2 can be a useful strategy, as well as using available data and research to show them the possible benefits of making such a drastic clinical change (Miller, Rathus, & Linehan, 2007). You can also emphasize the potential for the program to reduce behavioral problems on the unit. For example, several years ago, I worked on an (non-DBT) inpatient unit for adolescents. One adolescent (who had already displayed a pattern of behavior problems) approached a staff member and stated, "I'm bored." The staff member, not unkindly, replied, "Group will be starting soon," and went back to what she was doing. The adolescent, still bored, proceeded to disrupt another group of adolescents across the room. When one of them asked her to leave them alone, the adolescent grabbed her by the hair, pulled her out of her seat, and proceeded to punch her repeatedly. As you can imagine, this caused a flurry of activity, restraint of the adolescent, and distress for the other adolescents on the unit. I often think of this incident and wonder if things would have been different if the staff member, instead of briefly responding to the adolescent, had coached the client to use her skills to find an activity to keep herself busy until group started. Perhaps the whole altercation could have been avoided. Regardless, by using DBT consistently to coach adolescents on an inpatient unit, staff may be able to reduce behavioral issues on the unit, thus making their jobs easier and more enjoyable.

One of the major facets of DBT is the client's ability to make a decision regarding whether to engage in DBT or not, as this drastically increases the client's commitment to treatment (Linehan, 1993). Optimally, the client should have the ability to choose regardless of the setting, and if at all possible the adolescent should be provided the option of engaging in either DBT program, or another non-DBT program. This may be difficult to achieve, unless the hospital you work in has more than one unit. Some researchers have altered which group sessions the patient will engage in based on whether or not he or she has committed to DBT treatment—those who have committed attend skills group, and those who do not attend a pre-commitment group, which has the goal of facilitating the client's commitment to DBT (Swenson et al., 2007). Regardless, if you are not able to find a way to offer an alternative treatment, you will need to work even harder upon admission to gain even a small amount of commitment from the client to engage in DBT, even if that is only for a day, or a couple hours.

Finally, you will need to consider parent and family participation. Again, this may depend on the average length of stay in your program. For example, some acute hospitalization settings have an average length of stay of three to five days. With this short time period, it may be difficult to fully engage adolescents, much less the parents, in treatment. However, family members should be included in one or two individual sessions with the primary therapist, so they can understand the behavioral reinforcement involved in the client's problem behaviors, and learn skills to help the adolescent generalize the use of those skills after discharge.

ADDITIONAL TREATMENT TEAM MEMBERS

There are a few additional treatment team members on an inpatient unit, and in an ideal situation, all staff involved in treatment will be fully trained in DBT and regularly engage in DBT consultation meetings. On an inpatient unit, staff members surround adolescents, who can provide positive reinforcement for skills use, and in-the-moment skills coaching when adolescents need guidance to handle emotion dysregulation effectively (Swenson et al., 2007). This is an excellent asset to DBT inpatient programs—the adolescent will consistently receive reminders to use skills and get intentional validation and reinforcement for engaging in skillful behavior. Due to the intensive and frequent nature of these interactions, consultation is essential for staff, although this can be complicated with variations in the days and times of their shifts. You can alter these meetings by providing brief consultation meetings several times a week, or providing consultation as needed in the moment, at the staff member's request (Swenson et al., 2007).

Outpatient Therapist

The outpatient therapist is an ancillary treatment team member in this adaptation, and has a unique role. The therapist should be aware the adolescent has been hospitalized, and hopefully has provided helpful information to the inpatient therapist regarding the adolescent's treatment. However, the outpatient therapist should have little to no contact with the adolescent during hospitalization. This is mainly to prevent reinforcement of life-threatening behaviors (see skills coaching in Chapter 1); however it can also help the client become immersed in the inpatient unit until discharge.

Though it would be ideal if the outpatient therapist were a DBT therapist, if they are not, they should at least be aware of the DBT approach and any behavioral reinforcement related to the client's life-threatening behaviors that have come to light during their time in your program (Swenson et al., 2001).

Primary Inpatient Therapist

The primary inpatient therapist has the traditional role of treatment planning, reviewing diary cards, and committing (and recommitting) the client to treatment. However, the inpatient therapist also works to help the client plan for discharge. This can include helping the client identify barriers to success upon discharge, facilitating family sessions to increase the likelihood of success, resolving any conflicts in the invalidating environment, and engaging the client in behavior chains when he or she engages in (or has the urge to engage in) life-threatening behaviors.

Nurses, Psychiatrists, and Other Unit Staff Members

As mentioned previously, all staff members on the unit will have an important role in helping the client learn and generalize DBT skills, as they will have frequent interactions with them throughout their stay. In addition to this role, they will also need to engage in consultation to the client. Due to the intensive nature of an inpatient unit, an adolescent may have a problem with one staff member, and then approach another staff member in an attempt to resolve the issue. In these types of situations, it is important that staff members help adolescents identify skills they can use to effectively approach the situation, and then help them practice using those skills. Not only does this facilitate the use of appropriate assertive behavior, but it also prevents the adolescent from causing conflict between staff members (Linehan, 1993).

ADAPTATIONS TO TREATMENT TARGETS FOR INPATIENT SETTINGS

The treatment targets for adolescents in inpatient settings are similar to those in standard outpatient DBT. However, researchers have highlighted a few differences—they identify unit/milieu interfering behaviors as well as outpatient therapy-interfering behaviors that led to hospitalization in the first place. They also target quality-of-life-interfering behaviors that occur on the unit, and in outpatient settings (Swenson et al., 2007). See Table 7.1 for examples of treatment targets in inpatient settings. Adolescents should work together with their primary clinician to identify the treatment targets on which they will work (with life-threatening behaviors at the top) and then start by engaging in a detailed behavior chain on the behavior that led them to be hospitalized. The goal of this is to notice any aspects of the chain that reinforced the adolescent for engaging in the life-threatening behavior—for example, feeling loved and cared about by others, when they didn't prior to the behavior (Swenson et al., 2001).

Table 7.1 Treatment Targets for Inpatient DBT

Treatment Targets	Examples
Primary Treatment Targets	
Life-Threatening Behaviors	Harm to self or others Urges to harm self or others Thoughts of harming self or others Voicing a desire to harm self or others Hoarding items in an attempt to harm self or others
Inpatient Therapy-Interfering Behaviors	Being disruptive in group sessions Not practicing skills or completing diary card Sleeping in group sessions Arguing and/or yelling at unit staff Refusing skills coaching
Outpatient Therapy-Interfering Behaviors	Not completing diary card or homework Arriving late to sessions or missing them completely Overstepping boundaries with the therapist (e.g., calling the therapist in crisis repeatedly) **Parents:** Not providing transportation to treatment Unintentionally reinforcing life-threatening behaviors
Inpatient Quality-of-Life-Interfering Behaviors	Arguing/yelling and/or fighting with other adolescents on the unit Destroying or vandalizing unit property Engaging in sexual relationships with other adolescents on the unit Not engaging in basic hygiene activities
Outpatient Quality-of-Life-Interfering Behaviors	Substance use Risky sex and other impulsive behaviors Arguing with parents/not completing chores
Increasing Behavioral Skills	Mindfulness Distress Tolerance Walking the Middle Path Emotion Regulation Interpersonal Effectiveness

SPECIFIC SKILLS AND ADAPTATIONS FOR INPATIENT SETTINGS

There are a few adaptations to DBT for inpatient settings. Foremost, similar to the format presented by Del Conte in Chapter 6, researchers have identified three stages in inpatient DBT treatment—*getting in*, *getting in control*, and *getting out* (Swenson et al., 2007). During the *getting in* phase, the client is oriented to the unit, formally commits to DBT, and works together with the primary therapist to identify treatment targets. During the *getting in control* phase, the client works to learn and generalize skills, and conducts behavior chains as needed to address problem behaviors. Finally, during the *getting out* phase, the client works together with the therapist to plan for discharge, and prepare for challenging situations once discharged so he or she will be less likely to engage in life-threatening behaviors and be hospitalized again. Swenson et al. (2007) recommend celebration and affirmation when the client successfully transitions from one phase to the next, which will culminate in a graduation ceremony when the client is discharged, to reinforce their progress and skillful behavior, and also as a model of treatment success for other adolescents on the unit.

Contingency Management

Contingency management on inpatient units is as standardized as possible, so that staff members can respond consistently to problem behaviors. In the event the client engages in a problem behavior, he or she is instructed by staff to complete a behavior chain regarding that behavior. Though, at first, the adolescent may need guidance and coaching from a staff member, after having practice, the adolescent should be able to complete this on his or her own. After completing the behavior chain, the adolescent will either process the behavior chain individually with a staff member or during group with peers and the group leader (this will vary based on the problem behavior and the set up for your program). Finally, if necessary, the adolescent will make repairs by identifying how he or she will keep from engaging in the problem behavior in the future (Swenson et al., 2001; Swenson et al., 2007; Katz et al., 2004).

Skills Adaptations

Due to the nature of the setting, you may have a very limited time to teach adolescents skills, and as result you may not be able to teach them all. As a result, you will need to focus on the most important skills for stabilization and preventing re-admission, which will likely be mindfulness skills, distress tolerance skills, and validation and behaviorism from the walking the middle path module (Swenson et al., 2001; Swenson et al., 2007; Katz et al., 2004; Miller et al., 2007).

The primary therapist can teach the adolescent the basics of mindfulness upon admission, and then he or she should be invited to engage in mindfulness activities frequently throughout the day—either as scheduled with others in the unit, or on his or her own. Though the focus will be on mindfulness, distress tolerance, and walking the middle path, skills from the other modules can be included, and should be chosen to specifically facilitate the client's coping in the moment as well as after discharge.

Mindfulness of Current Thoughts

This mindfulness exercise can be especially helpful for adolescents who are in an inpatient setting. There are often situations on an inpatient unit where the adolescent has little control, yet he or she still has to cope with a situation—for example, when another adolescent on the unit begins to act out aggressively, and staff need to intervene. By being aware of their thoughts in the moment, adolescents can differentiate between thoughts and emotions, and also notice if they are having thoughts or urges to engage in a life-threatening behavior (Linehan, 2015).

Self Soothe the Five Senses

This skill can be important for adolescents on an inpatient unit, as the milieu should be designed to be comfortable but not overly comforting, to reduce reinforcement of problem behaviors for hospitalization (Swenson et al., 2007). As a result, it can be helpful for the adolescent to identify things they can use to self soothe their senses. This can be done during group, and the group leader can facilitate the adolescents to build a 'self soothe' box where they can gather objects to soothe all of their senses, or they can do this on their own. Soothing all of the five senses may be difficult on an inpatient unit with few resources—however, with some creativity, he or she should be able to identify an item that can soothe each of his or her senses. For example, they can find a picture from a magazine or other source of a beautiful location that they would like to visit someday. They can seek out a soft craft item, if the unit has one available (for example, a puff ball or a feather), or use a stress ball, which are often common on inpatient units. They can also be creative in soothing taste and smell, and identify one object to use for both—for example, a granola bar that contains chocolate.

Pros and Cons

Pros and cons can be a great skill for planning for discharge. The client can identify one (or more than one) problem behavior, and identify what the pros and cons of engaging in that behavior vs. not engaging in that behavior after discharge. Hopefully you and other staff members worked with the client using behavior chains to identify and remove any aspects of the environment that previously reinforced the problem behavior (for example, his or her parents giving extra validation and attention when he or she voices suicidal thoughts). As result, there will be more pros to resisting the urge and using skills (parents will instead provide validation and attention when he or she acts skillfully). The client can then keep this list, either on an index card or on a sheet of paper, and keep it somewhere he or she will see it regularly, or carry it around in a pocket or purse (Linehan, 2015).

Willingness (vs. Willfulness)

This skill is in the distress tolerance module, and can be helpful for any adolescent, regardless of the setting or diagnosis (see Handout 7.1). By being *willing*, the client can choose to do what is needed in the situation, in an effective and mindful manner. When the client is *willful*, the adolescent knows what is necessary for the situation, but refuses to do it, because he or she is in emotion mind. Linehan (1993) provides many great metaphors for this, and you can even ask the adolescents to give examples of times when they were willful (refusing to do chores even though they knew they would be grounded), and conversely, willing (helping one of their parents out with yard work, even though they were angry about a disagreement earlier). Often, when a client is experiencing willfulness, by using mindfulness, he or she can become aware of it, and use the wise mind to be willing, in the moment. You can also help adolescents identify different mindfulness activities they can use when they are feeling willful—for example, taking a moment to be present and aware of their body, to 'find' their wise mind, before making a decision in the moment.

Cope Ahead for Discharge

This skill includes having adolescents actually envision a situation in which they will experience the urge to engage in a life-threatening behavior, and then envision themselves using distress tolerance skills to resist that urge (see Handout 4.9). This is a skill that adolescents can learn and practice individually, or during group. If working individually, they could role-play the situation with a staff member (for example, an argument with a sibling), and therefore better prepare themselves for actually using skills when they are experiencing emotion dysregulation (Linehan, 2015).

SAMPLE GROUP SESSION FORMAT

We have included a sample group session format here (see Table 7.2), though the skills you teach, and the order and frequency by which you teach them, will vary based on the average length of stay of your program. In standard DBT, completion of skills training is defined by completing all of the skills modules twice; therefore, ideally, you should try to replicate this in your setting (Swenson et al., 2007). However,

Table 7.2 Sample Skills Training Format for Inpatient DBT

Day of the Week	Skills, Activities, and Handouts
Monday	Distress Tolerance: Self Soothe, Willingness Multifamily Skills Group: Behaviorism
Tuesday	Distress Tolerance: Mindfulness of Thoughts
Wednesday	Emotion Regulation: COPE ahead Multifamily Skills Group: Validation
Thursday	Distress Tolerance: Pros and Cons
Friday	Multifamily Skills Group: Behaviorism
Saturday	Distress Tolerance: Self Soothe, Willingness
Sunday	Emotion Regulation: COPE ahead

with a short length of stay, this may be difficult to achieve. Your goal will be to choose the skills you think will be the most helpful for your clients, and present them in a way that regardless of when they are admitted or discharged, they will receive the majority of the skills.

Though we focus solely on skills groups in our sample format, there are a lot of other groups that can be provided throughout the day on an inpatient unit. Goals groups are common (clients identify their goals for the day; see Handout 7.2) and these can be geared towards DBT skills use. Other groups can be focused on problem-solving and consultation for skills use, or even just focus on mindfulness (Swenson et al., 2007). Generally, you will want to teach skills at least several times a week—and with a short time frame, you may want to offer them daily. Our format is set up for a week average stay (common in our experience for acute settings), with skills groups taught daily for 50 minutes, and multifamily skills groups taught three times per week for 90 minutes. Mindfulness is not included in the skills taught, because in this format it should be taught upon admission and utilized several times per day after that.

OUTCOME EVALUATION

Though the assessments we have highlighted in Chapter 5 and Chapter 13 are likely suitable for use in an inpatient setting, we will also highlight a few other options here. Again, as with all of the adaptations in this book, you will want to choose an assessment that fits the overall treatment goals of your clients.

Daily Diary Cards

Though diary cards on an outpatient basis are based on daily skills use, and cover the course of a week, diary cards for acute inpatient stays cover one day, and can be completed hourly. This can be helpful for you to assess whether the client is experiencing a decrease in thoughts and urges to engage in life-threatening behaviors, and whether they are increasing their skills use throughout the day. See Handout 1.5 for a sample diary card for inpatient settings.

Crisis Stabilization Scale (CriSS)

The CriSS (Balkin, 2013) was developed to specifically measure adolescent stabilization in acute care settings. It includes 25 items, and takes about ten minutes to complete. The CriSS has two subscales—Coping, which assesses how the adolescent is using coping skills, and Follow-up, which assesses the level of the client's commitment to follow-up treatment after discharge. Although this assessment does not directly measure DBT coping skills, it can help you evaluate the effectiveness of your program by administering it to your clients upon admission, and then again upon discharge. It can also help you collaborate with your client on his or her treatment plan, and make decisions regarding commitment strategies—for example, if a client scores low on the Follow-up subscale, you may wish to focus on committing the client to engaging in outpatient treatment after discharge.

CHALLENGES AND SOLUTIONS

Funding

Inpatient care is costly, and if your client does not have adequate insurance coverage for treatment, you may have limited ability to treat him or her, if at all. Insurance will cover inpatient care when medical necessity is established—usually this means the clients have to be at risk of harming themselves or others, or actively experiencing psychotic symptoms. In my personal experience, some insurance companies may be more lenient in approving inpatient care for adolescents (e.g., covering a client who has suicidal thoughts but not intent). However, even if your client does receive approval for inpatient treatment, they may only approve two to three days at a time, which can also limit your ability to provide adequate services. Your goal will be to provide evidence of the benefits of full approval for treatment in your program. This may include providing the insurance company with outcome data regarding the program's effectiveness in reducing the frequency of inpatient hospitalizations (thus, saving the insurance company money).

Persistent Therapy-Interfering Behaviors

You will likely encounter some adolescents who persistently engage in therapy-interfering behaviors, despite repeated attempts at engaging the client in behavior chain analyses, and/or working not to reinforce these behaviors, and/or even punishing those behaviors by removing privileges. Your most important asset when this happens is your consultation team. By sitting down and analyzing the client's repeated behaviors, and problem-solving together, you will be able to come up with a solution. However, the key is to not "give up," and if one tactic does not work, simply try another.

For example, during my intensive DBT training, one team brought up a client who consistently disrupted group, either by making sarcastic comments about the content, and/or her peers, or by disrupting group members nearby by whispering to them. Repeated attempts to redirect and recommit the client were unsuccessful, as was removing the client from group (this was actually reinforcing—the client did not want to be there) and removing privileges. All of the teams in the intensive training (approximately ten) engaged in problem-solving to help out this team, and it took a while, but we were finally able to identify something that would reinforce her for behaving during group (not going for participation at this point, just not disrupting)—a Starbucks specialty coffee. The team decided to offer her the opportunity to behave appropriately during group, and if she did so, one of her parents would bring her a coffee. The moral of this story is, don't give up! There is a solution out there; it may just take time and several DBT clinicians to find it.

SUMMARY AND CONCLUSIONS

Implementing a DBT program on an inpatient unit can be challenging; however, the behavioral approach to analyzing life-threatening behaviors may be invaluable for preventing re-admission and increasing the clients' ability to use coping skills. Depending on your setting, some of your main challenges may be a short time frame to teach skills, and ensuring that all of the staff have had adequate training, and are working diligently to provide a DBT milieu that reinforces skillful behavior. Nevertheless, once these aspects have been addressed, your program may not only increase adolescents' quality of life, but that of their families, friends, and the community around them.

REFERENCES

Balkin, R. S. (2013). Validation of the goal attainment scale of stabilization. *Measurement and Evaluation in Counseling and Development*, 46, 261–269. doi:10.1177/0748175613497040

Katz, L. Y., Cox, B. J., Gunasekara, S., & Miller, A. L. (2004). Feasibility of dialectical behavior therapy for suicidal adolescent inpatients. *Journal of The American Academy of Child & Adolescent Psychiatry*, 43(3), 276–282. doi:10.1097/00004583-200403000-00008

Kleindienst, N., Limberger, M. F., Schmahl, C., Steil, R., Ebner-Priemer, U. W., & Bohus, M. (2008). Do improvements after inpatient dialectical behavioral therapy persist in the long term?: A naturalistic follow-up in patients with borderline personality disorder. *Journal of Nervous And Mental Disease*, 196(11), 847–851. doi:10.1097/NMD.0b013e31818b481d

Linehan, M. M. (1993). *Cognitive-behavioral treatment of borderline personality disorder*. New York, NY: Guilford Press.

Linehan, M. M. (2015). *DBT® skills training manual* (2nd ed.). New York, NY: Guilford Press.

McDonell, M. G., Tarantino, J., Dubose, A. P., Matestic, P., Steinmetz, K., Galbreath, H., & McClellan, J. M. (2010). A pilot evaluation of dialectical behavioural therapy in adolescent long-term inpatient care. *Child and Adolescent Mental Health*, 15(4), 193–196. doi:10.1111/j.1475-3588.2010.00569.x

Miller, A. L., Rathus, J. H., & Linehan, M. M. (2007). *Dialectical behavior therapy with suicidal adolescents*. New York, NY: Guilford Press.

Swenson, C. R., Sanderson, C., Dulit, R. A., & Linehan, M. M. (2001). The application of dialectical behavior therapy for patients with borderline personality disorder on inpatient units. *Psychiatric Quarterly*, 72(4), 307–324. doi:10.1023/A:1010337231127

Swenson, C. R., Witterholt, S., & Bohus, M. (2007). Dialectical behavior therapy on inpatient units. In L. A. Dimeff & K. Koerner (Eds.), *Dialectical behavior therapy in clinical practice: Applications across disorders and settings* (pp. 69–111). New York, NY: Guilford Press.

Working Within School Sites

Richard J. Ricard, Mary Alice Fernandez,
Wannigar Ratanavivan, Shanice N. Armstrong,
Mehmet A. Karaman, and Eunice Lerma

In this chapter we will give best practice recommendations for implementing a Dialectical Behavioral Therapy (DBT)-informed skills intervention in middle and high school settings. Given that adolescents spend 30–40% of their day in school environments, it is not surprising that many of the behavioral problems associated with adolescence emerge during the school day. While the American school system continues to focus primarily on the traditional academic preparation of students in core subject areas, teachers and administrators are becoming increasingly aware of the value of school-based mental health intervention services—estimates indicate that between 14 and 20% of children and adolescents will experience emotional or behavioral distress during adolescence (O'Connell, Boat, & Warner, 2009). In addition, adolescents are especially vulnerable to family and social pressure related to rapid maturational changes during puberty, and increasing societal expectations as they transition to adulthood (Arnett, 1999). Therefore, it is imperative we provide adolescents with as much access to mental health resources as possible.

Clinicians can use school-based interventions to address behavioral problems before they escalate and require a more intensive intervention (Mazza, Dexter-Mazza, Miller, Rathus, & Murphy, 2016; Quinn, 2009). Further, the school day provides opportunities for students to practice adaptive coping in the context in which stressors arise—for example, when they experience conflict with peers, or receive a poor grade on an assignment (Cook, Burns, Browning-Wright, & Gresham, 2010). In addition, many of the barriers clinicians face in traditional settings, including parent availability and transportation, are minimized or eliminated in school-based intervention services (Mazza et al., 2016). DBT skills can be easily adapted for classroom or group guidance lessons to increase positive coping skills and healthy youth development (Alvarado & Ricard, 2013; Mazza et al., 2016).

CONSIDERATIONS BEFORE IMPLEMENTING SCHOOL-BASED DBT SKILLS GROUP

Administrative and Staff Commitment

Your primary task before going forward with a DBT program in a school will be attaining commitment and "buy-in" from campus administration. This may be difficult, and you will need to be deliberate in your efforts to work with administrative, teaching, and counseling staff. It will be most helpful if you can emphasize the benefits of the program—including the possibility of decreased behavioral problems and increased academic success. This can be done via a needs assessment you have conducted on site, or with examples of outcome research from other DBT programs in schools. Finally, orient staff and administrators to the goals and process of skills training, the skills deficit model of emotional and behavioral dysregulation, and any anticipated challenges in program implementation with school personnel (Linehan, 2015).

Availability of Resources and Space

You will need to consider where your groups will take place—the room you choose should provide for appropriate space to share information and prevent distraction from other school activities. Standard classroom space is appropriate for implementation of guidance-based approaches, and smaller group room spaces may be helpful for smaller and perhaps more intensive therapeutic group work. Finally, ascertain that you will have appropriate storage space to ethically maintain files and case notes.

Recruitment, Consent, and Assent

Once you have received permission to implement a DBT program, you will need to decide what your treatment targets will be, and this decision should be based on the needs of the school. For example, it may be most important to focus on students with behavioral problems, or those who struggle with specific mental health symptoms. It is also likely that students who struggle with stress management and basic coping skills may benefit from these groups. Regardless, you will also need to consider student characteristics such as gender and age. Try to make groups homogeneous, while also being as inclusive as possible (Miller, Rathus, & Linehan, 2007).

After you have chosen your treatment targets, you will need to consider how you will recruit students to your program. There are a few options for this—students may be referred to services by teachers and other school professionals, or you may wish to identify students via a school-wide screening for mental health and/or behavioral problems (Ricard, Lerma, & Heard, 2013). You can also send home information to parents regarding the group and have them self-refer if they are interested. There are pros and cons to all three of these strategies, and instead it may be helpful to use a combination of these tactics to reach as many participants as possible.

Finally, once possible group participants have been identified, you or another staff member can invite the adolescents' parents in for a meeting so you can explain the program and answer any questions they may have. Though it is mandatory to attain the parent's consent, in DBT it is also necessary to attain assent of the adolescent, as commitment to treatment is one of the largest predictors of success in a DBT program (Rathus & Miller, 2015).

Open vs. Closed Groups

Open groups allow members to enroll at any time while closed groups admit members only at the beginning of the group process. There are benefits to both of these options—in closed groups, members are more likely to develop enhanced cohesion and familiarity with each other; however open groups provide opportunities for participants to experience change and generalize new skills (Linehan, 2015). If the students you will be working with have a history of low or sporadic attendance, open groups may be a better option (Ricard et al., 2013).

Training

DBT is a flexible and manualized approach, and as result, it allows for school-based professionals (e.g., teachers, counselors, teaching assistants) to be trained and become members of a DBT consultation team. This is especially useful if you wish to implement DBT to help adolescents develop basic coping and emotion regulation skills in a guidance class format. However, if the students you are working with struggle with severe mental health symptoms, or have significant behavioral problems, you may be better suited to have a licensed individual with more extensive clinical training implement the group sessions. The most important characteristic of a group facilitator is willingness to practice and use the skills before teaching them, as well as the ability to appropriately self-disclose personal experiences with skills (Mazza et al., 2016).

ADAPTATIONS TO DBT FOR SCHOOLS

A stand-alone DBT skills training group may be the most adaptable element for use on school campuses. In fact, several researchers have successfully implemented DBT skills groups with promising preliminary results (Blackford & Love, 2011; Linehan, 2015; Mazza et al., 2016; Ricard et al., 2013). Two examples illustrative of key adaptations of standard DBT to school settings are provided below, though we will focus mainly on the program we developed, *Teen Talk*.

Skills Training for Emotional Problem-Solving for Adolescents (DBT STEPS-A)

Mazza and colleagues have written the most comprehensive and contemporary approach to a school campus-based DBT infused approach referred to as *Skills Training for Emotional Problem-Solving for Adolescents* (DBT STEPS-A; Mazza et al., 2016). The approach is built upon standard principles of DBT (Linehan, 2015) as well as modifications by Rathus and Miller (2015) for adolescents. The program is applicable to a variety of adolescent student populations ranging from those without any behavioral distress to more challenging students. In addition, it is designed to teach adolescents skills for managing difficult emotions, improving relationships, and enhancing decision-making abilities for solving problems and challenges they encounter in daily living (Mazza et al., 2016).

Teen Talk

A second example of campus-based DBT intervention is the *Teen Talk* program; a program my colleagues (first author) and I have been implementing for the past seven years. *Teen Talk* is an eight-session DBT infused skills program we created at a Disciplinary Alternative Education Program (DAEP) for students who have been removed from their home campus because of disruptive behavioral problems (Ricard et al., 2013). DAEP campuses are required to establish intervention plans that support student success for reintegration into their home school campuses. Campuses must document a student's response to intervention (RTI). The *Teen Talk* program was designed to support the campus's RTI plan for addressing the emotional reactivity and impulsivity that commonly underlies the acute and chronic problematic behaviors of youth on DAEP campuses.

The *Teen Talk* program is organized around small group sessions of 45–50 minutes twice each week. The sessions are led by counseling interns who work adjunctively with the school counselors. Our team also provides additional support to school counselors by receiving individual referrals and providing assistance with school-wide guidance activities. We also conduct school-wide suicide screenings, and are available for crisis intervention and individual sessions with students experiencing distress during their school day. The individual work provides students with the opportunity to process content, and reinforces the use of skills learned during group.

Due to the short time frame of the intervention (four weeks), skills are provided in closed groups that are as homogeneous as possible. Some students exhibit behaviors that are inappropriate for a group setting; those students are seen individually and taught skills using variations of the group skills activities. Our adaptation also involves processing and personal problem-solving during group that is usually reserved for individual sessions in standard DBT. We believe that students need time to process difficult situations in their lives, and so we reserve time for discussion of these issues in the group sessions. However, we work closely with group facilitators to ensure that group sessions are primarily devoted to introducing and practicing skills. Our leaders have developed skill in redirecting group members who attempt to monopolize sessions with personal disclosures and what often might be considered bragging about exploits.

Though *Teen Talk* is characterized as a stand-alone DBT-based skills training group, the program includes adaptations of the standard DBT modes, including a consultation team, individual case management, individual counseling sessions as needed, and limited phone coaching (mostly parent informational contacts mediated by a school counselor). Skills coaching may be critical for adolescent clients so they can seek support and generalize skills throughout the week, and we encourage parent meetings and counselor consultation whenever possible.

Table 8.1 Teen Talk: Treatment Team Members and Roles

Treatment Team Member	Roles
School Counselor	Primary case manager for students Refers students to Teen Talk Services Orients new consultation team members to the site Provides a minimum of one-hour weekly individual site supervision for our clinical team Liaises with teachers and administration Helps facilitate data collection from teachers on DPR and parent posttests Arranges contact with parents when necessary
Group Skills Facilitators	Lead skills groups or individual sessions with students Engage parents and students in orientation to the program Conduct suicide screenings Assist with data collection to support program evaluation *Note: natural change agents (i.e., teachers, school personnel) can also be impactful consultation team members and skills group instructors*
Supervising Faculty	Coordinate the clinical intervention at the school site Provide weekly consultation and supervision

CONSULTATION TEAM MEMBERS AND ROLES

See Table 8.1 for a list of the *Teen Talk* treatment team members and roles. Our consultation team consists of university student counseling interns (masters and doctoral level counselors in training), school counselors, and university faculty members. Our consultation team meets each week to discuss cases and coordinate group activities. During this time, students receive clinical supervision and opportunities to learn and practice new skills. The students then take turns demonstrating skills and intervention techniques to demonstrate mastery before they teach in a group setting (Linehan, 1993). Our skills group facilitators also meet daily with the school counselor who handles referrals, discusses case specifics, and serves as the program liaison to teachers and campus administration.

TREATMENT TARGETS

School-based treatment targets are focused primarily on: promoting student motivation and engagement in learning, keeping each individual student and staff member safe, and maintaining an environment that is conducive to student learning by reducing individual disruptive, aggressive, and harmful behaviors, and maintaining a positive interpersonal climate by teaching pro-social skills and civil interactions. Table 8.2 gives examples of common problem behaviors in this setting.

Table 8.2 DBT Treatment Targets in the Teen Talk Program

Treatment Targets	Examples
Primary Treatment Targets	
Life-Threatening Behaviors	Thoughts and/or urges to harm self or others Engaging in harm to self or others Bringing a lethal weapon to school Engaging in fights with a lethal weapon (e.g., a knife)
Classroom/Campus-Interfering Behaviors	Arguing with peers, teachers, and administrators Fighting with peers Disrupting, skipping, or sleeping in class Vandalism on campus
Therapy-Interfering Behaviors	Skipping group Acting out behavioral or verbally in group Insulting or invalidating others in group
Quality-of-Life-Interfering Behaviors	Drug and alcohol use Behavioral problems at home Stealing, vandalism, and other criminal behaviors Risky and impulsive behaviors
Increase Behavioral Skills	DBT skills modules and opportunities for skill mastery and generalized homework practice Skills for life planning and value clarification

OVERVIEW OF TEEN TALK SKILLS GROUP SESSION FORMAT

The format of the groups is standardized, so regardless of the group leader, each session consists of the same content. The group leader begins by briefly checking in with each student. Then they review the skills learned in the previous session and any homework they had been assigned. The group leader then introduces the new skills, and the clients are invited to practice the skills. Finally, the homework 'challenge' is assigned, the group is closed, and students are dismissed back to class. Table 8.3 includes an overview of the eight-session program.

PROGRAM EVALUATION FOR DBT IN SCHOOLS

Student progress can be measured in several ways. Though we have included the methods of assessment we use in our program, there are a variety of other ways to measure outcomes, and you will want to consider all of your options based on the students you are working with.

Table 8.3 Overview of the Teen Talk Skills Group Sessions

Overview of Skills-Based Group Sessions by Topics and Skill

Session One: Interpersonal Effectiveness and Validation of Others
Session one involves welcoming and introducing students to the group process. The group members introduce themselves to each other. Students are encouraged to talk about why they were referred to the DAEP, their current perceptions of the school, and how they feel about their home school. Group norms for attendance, participation, respect, and confidentiality are discussed. Ice-breaking exercises that emphasize active listening and interpersonal validation (Linehan, 1993) are introduced with corresponding activities. The session sets the tone for group norms on how we expect to interact with each other.

Session Two: Emotion Regulation: Thoughts, Feelings, and Choosing Behavioral Responses
Session two involves the introduction of mindfulness and contact with the inner world of thoughts, feelings, behaviors, and choices (Linehan, 1993). These concepts are introduced with basic activities. Some groups may explore behavior chains.

Session Three: Mindfulness and Emotional Regulation
Session three involves activities related to understanding, describing, and expressing feelings and emotional experiences. This concept is introduced in exercises that help the students to contact and explore their feelings and bodily sensations. The activities are coupled with periods of silence and breathing practice. In a second activity students reflect on the concept of *Minding Your Own Business* and are led in reflection of personal business as in an internal state (thinking, feeling, and emotional experience) in contrast to public behavior. An initial discussion focused on recognition of private thoughts and feelings as personal. Moments of silent reflection and mindful breathing are taught as an approach to "mind" or connecting with our internal selves.

Session Four: Distress Tolerance
Session four focuses on understanding adaptive coping strategies and responses to difficult emotional situations. Distress tolerance skills involve learning how to cope adaptively and survive difficult emotional feelings. As a follow-up to the previous session, discussion focuses on functioning in the context of potentially overwhelming feelings (Linehan, 1993). *Try to Bother Me* is an experiential practice in which one person in a group sits in the middle of a circle of group members and rehearses mindful breathing techniques while the group members try to bother them (i.e., make them laugh, move, or react). Students are encouraged to remember that they can make the choice to remain still and peaceful even in the midst of the chaos that may surround them.

Session Five: Interpersonal Effectiveness Skills
Session five involves teaching effective communication and relating skills. Many students experience conflictual relationships with their families, peers, and school officials (Mitchell, Booker, & Strain, 2011). Students are asked to describe the quality of social interactions with others (family, friends, teachers, counselors) in the past week using the Social Interaction Questionnaire (SIQ; Ricard, 2009).

(Continued)

Table 8.3 (Continued)

Overview of Skills-Based Group Sessions by Topics and Skill

Session Six: Interpersonal Effectiveness (DEAR MAN)
Session six involves a continuation of teaching communication and relating skills initiated in session five. The session introduces the DBT activity of DEAR MAN to structure the discussion. The activity is introduced using a humorous pun by asking the students to draw a "Deer Man" (i.e., a man with deer features like antlers). After students share their depictions, the traditional DEAR MAN acronym activity is introduced and facilitated through rounds of role-play. Through role-play scenarios students practice DEAR MAN communication "to get what you want." The students role-play peer-to-peer, parent-child, and student-teacher interactions.

Session Seven: Distress Tolerance Skills
Students are taught skills for acting the opposite of how they feel. Methods of self-soothing and distracting themselves are adopted from the standard DBT Skills group protocol.

Session Eight: Goal Setting/Committed Action and Smart Goals
The closing session involves a discussion of goal setting and reflecting upon the group experience. *I am SMART* is an activity that utilizes the acronym to describe specific, measurable, attainable, realistic, and time-limited (SMART) goals. Students are coached to describe at least one short-term goal (in the next two to three weeks) and one long-term goal. Students take turns discussing each other's goals and querying each other on the dimensions of SMART. Finally, students are encouraged to commit to specific actions for pursuing goals now. In all cases, students are encouraged to reflect upon their time at the DAEP and return to their home campuses. Encouragement comes in the specific form of asking "How can things go differently at your home school?" And "What are you willing to do to make things go differently?"

Session Nine: Transition and Closing (Optional)
Away You Go involves a leader-prepared individualized narrative letter to each student addressing the process they participated in and the progress they made as a group member. The leader endeavors to provide honest strength-based feedback in the context of encouragement and praise for efforts realized during the group process. The general form of the letter is provided below:
Dear (name),
Throughout these few weeks I have seen your willingness to achieve your goals. You have learned many skills that will help you with many difficult situations. It is up to you to use these skills when needed. I am so proud of your work in our group. Good luck in the coming years.
Counselor Signature

Source: Ricard et al., 2013.

The Social Interaction Questionnaire (SIQ)

The SIQ is an instrument developed by Ricard (2009) to monitor each student's self-assessed quality of interaction with important others (i.e., parents, teachers, friends). *Teen Talk* group facilitators often use this to stimulate discussion as part of the interpersonal effectiveness module.

Daily Progress Report (DPR)

The DPR is a checklist, similar to a daily diary card, designed to assess student behavior and engagement during each class period. Teachers complete the form for each classroom period. Student DPRs are used to assess student compliance with DAEP procedures and policies as well as specific classroom departments. Students are rated (1=credit or 0=no credit) on each of four indicators of classroom behavior (arrives to class on time; participates in class as required; complies with dress code; uses appropriate classroom behavior). Students are rewarded for earning credits by receiving bonus days and recognition, which may result in early release back to their home campuses. Students carry their DPR with them throughout the day, so they can be mindful of their behaviors and use skills as needed. Group sessions can include a review of DPRs, and group facilitators can help the student problem solve to identify skills they could have used in certain situations, and plan for skills use in the future.

Youth Outcome Questionnaire (Y-OQ)

The Y-OQ (Burlingame et al., 2002) is administered to students and parents as the student arrives for orientation to the program. The questionnaire is then re-administered to all participants as a post-assessment on their last day of attendance. The survey takes about five minutes to complete. Participants respond to 30 questions indicating the frequency of situations, behaviors, and moods they experienced in the past week related to six measures of behavioral distress (aggression, somatic disorders, conflict, depression, interpersonal relations, hyperactivity, and impulsivity).

CHALLENGES AND SOLUTIONS

Commitment to treatment is a core concept in DBT; however schools are often fast paced and changing environments, and as result it may be difficult to commit administrators, counselors, and students to the program. School professionals (administrators, teachers, and counselors) are stretched by current responsibilities, and the addition of another program may require extra work. Therefore, it may be challenging for them to maintain commitment to the program long-term. It can also be frustrating for teachers when group facilitators regularly request for students to be dismissed (to counseling) during their class period. In these situations, it will be important for you to keep school personnel informed about how skills group attendance supports the overall educational mission for these students.

As you are probably aware, teenagers often get bored and may lose interest in group sessions over time. To combat this, we work to introduce new and creative activities in sessions. For example, instead of just describing a typical conflict with parents, we may ask the students to role-play as a way to help them think about alternative behavioral solutions. We also use behavioral reinforcement—the adolescents often receive very little individualized attention throughout their day, and as result they appreciate engaging in a positive interaction with an adult during the school day.

We also use the DBT commitment strategies (see Chapter 2) frequently and liberally. For example, during orientation we use *foot in the door* by encouraging students to give our sessions a try and if they don't like them, they don't have to participate. We also use the *freedom to choose* and *absence of alternatives* by emphasizing the fact the students have the choice to take part in the groups rather than the mandate to participate as a response to their behavior. *Teen Talk* intervention is offered to students as an opportunity to learn new ways to manage their emotions if they want to be successful in school.

CONCLUSIONS AND SUMMARY

School-based DBT is focused on helping students identify adaptive solutions to living. It can be used as an adjunct to traditional prevention and guidance activities for all students, as well as with at-risk student populations as a specialized intervention. In the context of the groups, adolescents have supportive access to personal and interpersonal resources, and they can then learn to manage their personal difficulties (Alvarado & Ricard, 2013; Ricard et al., 2013).

A number of researchers have provided best-practice recommendations for evidence-based treatments on middle and high school campuses. Although none of these recommendations are specific to DBT, many of them emphasize the typical structural considerations, practical solutions, and lessons learned from implementation on a school campus (Ruffolo & Fisher, 2009; Fixsen, Naoom, Blase, Friedman, & Wallace, 2005). These investigations have informed the implementation and best recommendation practices discussed in this chapter. Personnel training, sustainability, and evaluation are key components to successful implementation of a DBT program in a school setting. By working to maintain all of these components, you will be able to provide a needed service to students, and increase their chances of academic, personal, and vocational success.

REFERENCES

Alvarado, M. & Ricard, R. J. (2013). Developmental assets and ethnic identity as predictors of thriving in Hispanic adolescents. *Hispanic Journal of Behavioral Sciences*, 35, 510–523. doi:10.1177/0739986313499006

Arnett, J. J. (1999). Adolescent storm and stress, reconsidered. *American Psychologist*, 54, 317–326. doi:10.1037/0003–066x.54.5.317

Blackford, J. & Love, R. (2011). Dialectical behavior therapy group skills training in a community mental health setting: A pilot study. *International Journal of Group Psychotherapy*, 61, 645–657. doi:10.1521/ijgp.2011.61.4.645

Burlingame, G. M., Dunn, T., Hill, M., Cox, M., Wells, M. G., Lambert, M., & Reisinger, C. W. (2002). *Youth outcome questionnaire (YOQ—30.2)*. Stevenson, MD: American Professional Credentialing Services, LLC.

Cook, C. R., Burns, M., Browning-Wright, D., & Gresham, F. M. (2010) *Transforming school psychology in the RTI era: A guide for administrators and school psychologists*. Palm Beach Gardens, FL: LRP.

Fixsen, D. L., Naoom, S. F., Blase, K. A., Friedman, R. M., & Wallace, F. (2005). *Implementation research: A synthesis of the literature* (Research Report No. 231). Tampa, FL: University of South Florida, Louis de la Parte Florida Mental Health Institute, The National Implementation Research Network.

Linehan, M. M. (1993). *Skills training manual for treating borderline personality disorder*. New York, NY: Guilford Press.

Linehan, M. M. (2015). *DBT® skills training manual* (2nd ed.). New York, NY: Guilford Press.

Mazza, J. M., Dexter-Mazza, E. T., Miller, A. L., Rathus, J. H., & Murphy, H. E. (2016). *DBT skills in schools: Skills training for emotional problem solving for adolescents (DBT STEPS-A)*. New York, NY: Guilford Press.

Miller, A. L., Rathus, J. H., & Linehan, M. M. (2007). *Dialectical behavior therapy with suicidal adolescents*. New York, NY: Guilford Press. Retrieved from https://manowar.tamucc.edu/login?url=http://search.ebscohost.com/login.aspx?direct=true&db=psyh&AN=2006-23301-000&site=ehost-live&scope=site

Mitchell, A. D., Booker, K. W., & Strain, J. D. (2011). Measuring readiness to respond to intervention in students attending disciplinary alternative schools. *Journal of Psychoeducational Assessment*, *29*, 547–558. doi:10.1177/0734282911406522

O'Connell, M. E., Boat, T., & Warner, K. E. (2009). *Preventing mental, emotional, and behavioral disorders among young people: Progress and possibilities* [Adobe PDF version]. Retrieved from www.nap.edu/download/12480

Quinn, C. R. (2009). Efficacy of dialectical behaviour therapy for adolescents. *Australian Journal of Psychology*, *61*, 156–166. doi:10.1080/00049530802315084

Rathus, J. H. & Miller, A. L. (2015). *DBT® skills manual for adolescents*. New York, NY: Guilford Press.

Ricard, R. J. (2009). *Social Interaction Questionnaire (SIQ): Measuring social and emotional climate*. Unpublished instrument.

Ricard, R. J., Lerma, E., & Heard, C. C. C. (2013). Piloting a dialectical behavioral therapy (DBT) infused skills group in a disciplinary alternative education program (DAEP). *The Journal for Specialists in Group Work*, *38*, 285–306. doi:10.1080/01933922.2013.834402

Ruffolo, M. & Fischer, D. (2009). Using an evidence-based CBT group intervention model for adolescents with depressive symptoms: Lessons learned from a school-based adaptation. *Child & Family Social Work*, *14*, 189–197. doi:10.1111/j.1365

Substance Abuse and Mental Health Services Administration. (2014). *Results from the 2013 national survey on drug use and health: Mental health findings* (NSDUH Series H-49, HHS Publication No. (SMA) 14–4887). Rockville, MD: Substance Abuse and Mental Health Services Administration, (p. 2).

Eating Disorders
K. Michelle Hunnicutt Hollenbaugh

In this chapter, we will discuss adaptations to DBT specifically related to eating disorders (abbreviated DBT-ED). Millions of adolescents in the U.S. are diagnosed with an eating disorder every year (Swanson, Crow, Le Grange, Swendsen, and Merikangas, 2011). Eating disorders have extreme physical consequences, including low blood pressure, emaciation, cardiac problems, and, in severe cases, death (American Psychiatric Association, 2013). These disorders are also especially dangerous for adolescents, as they are highly correlated with other mental health diagnoses and increased suicidal thoughts and attempts (Swanson et al., 2011). In light of these findings, we are charged with helping adolescents overcome disordered eating with the best approach possible. DBT is well suited for treating eating disorders, because eating disordered behaviors are often directly related to emotion dysregulation.

CONSIDERATIONS BEFORE IMPLEMENTING DBT

The research on DBT-ED is preliminary, and the bulk of this research is on adults who struggle with bulimia and binge eating disorder (BED). Though a lot of the research on DBT-ED for adolescents has taken place in outpatient settings, it has also been implemented in intensive outpatient and day treatment settings. Based on the current literature, there are three different ways to implement DBT-ED for adolescents: DBT-ED in addition to a current evidence-based treatment, full DBT for stage one clients with added aspects for disordered eating, and DBT-ED for stage three clients (Safer, Telch, & Chen, 2009; Federici, Wisniewski, & Ben-Porath, 2012; Bhatnagar & Wisniewski, 2015).

Dialectical Behavior Therapy in Addition to Current Treatment

The majority of research on DBT-ED is focused on implementing DBT in addition to traditional structured treatments for eating disorders that already have an evidence base. Researchers posit that using DBT as a supplement to traditional formats could be more effective in helping clients increase coping skills and decrease emotion dysregulation (Bhatnagar & Wisniewski, 2015). Further, the current evidence-based treatments available are not effective for all adolescents—some clients are considered treatment resistant, and the implementation of DBT in addition to traditional treatment modes may increase positive outcomes for those clients (Wisniewski, Safer, & Chen, 2007).

Adding DBT to a current treatment for eating disorders probably sounds like a lot (and it is), so this is why it is usually only offered in this format for adolescents who are exhibiting severe symptoms, and are not experiencing positive treatment outcomes. If you decided to do this, you will need to delineate treatment targets based on the client's immediate needs (Bhatnagar & Wisniewski, 2015). In most adaptations where DBT is implemented in addition to current treatment, all treatment modes (e.g., skills group, individual and family sessions, consultation group, intersession skills coaching) are implemented. However, this can be time consuming and expensive, and can include up to two individual and/or family sessions and a family skills group session weekly. Therefore, it may be more prudent to only implement some modes of treatment, or combine modes to address treatment targets. These adaptations will vary depending on the setting and resources available; however special attention should be placed on maintaining the fidelity of the treatment as much as possible.

One example is the combination of DBT and Family-Based Treatment (FBT; Lock & Le Grange, 2012). Researchers state that these two modalities complement each other via nonjudgmental stances to treatment, and active but nondirective therapeutic approaches. In this model, adolescents attended individual sessions, family sessions, and multifamily skills groups every week. Adolescents were referred to the FBT-DBT program (as opposed to the FBT-only program) when they were actively engaging in life-threatening behaviors, were not showing progress in FBT only, were engaging in significant and severe therapy-interfering behaviors, or had comorbid diagnoses that also needed to be addressed (Bhatnagar & Wisniewski, 2015).

Full DBT With Added Aspects to Address Eating Disorder Symptoms

There are a few publications that highlight adaptations for clients who struggle with disordered eating and meet criteria for stage one in DBT. Treatment in these implementations adheres to the standard DBT model, and includes adaptations for eating disorder symptoms. For example, skills instruction may be tailored to discuss managing disordered eating, or you can include a full module that addresses nutrition and eating behaviors (Federici, Wisniewski, & Ben-Porath, 2012). Other alterations may include having the clients weigh themselves during individual sessions, and changes in the rules around phone coaching (this will be discussed in detail later in this chapter; Chen, Matthews, Allen, Kuo, & Linehan, 2008).

Dialectical Behavior Therapy for Stage Three Clients

The adaptation of DBT-ED has the most published literature. As you'll remember from Chapter 1, stage three clients do not engage in life-threatening behaviors, either because they have already been through stages one and two in a DBT program, or they did not engage in these behaviors in the first place. Clients in this stage have insight into the fact that their eating disorder behaviors are interfering with their quality of life, and therefore they are motivated to engage in DBT treatment to specifically address these behaviors. Since life-threatening behaviors are not a concern

EATING DISORDERS

with these clients, treatment targets typically start with therapy-interfering behaviors. Researchers have also included an extra module on nutrition and eating behaviors in this adaptation (Safer, Telch, & Chen, 2009).

THE BIOSOCIAL THEORY AND EMOTION DYSREGULATION IN EATING DISORDERS

In addition to the traditional biosocial theory of emotion dysregulation that highlights a biological predisposition for emotional vulnerability (see Chapter 1), Wisniewski and Kelly (2003) posited that individuals struggling with eating disorders also struggle with a nutritional vulnerability. These clients are biologically predisposed to have difficulty recognizing when they are hungry and when they are full, which can lead to eating disordered behaviors. Similarly, the invalidating environment can include messages about body image that individuals receive from peers, family, media, and

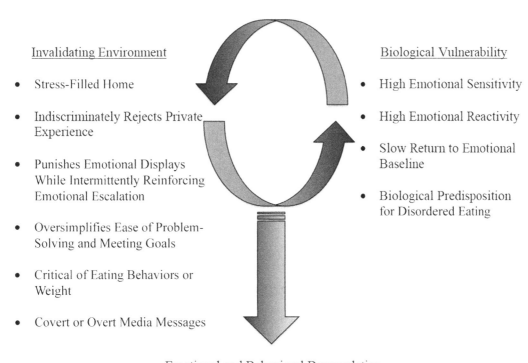

Figure 9.1 Biosocial Theory as Applied to Eating Disorders

culture (Wisniewski et al., 2007). These messages can be overt—for example, an adolescent being bullied for being overweight, or an adolescent's parents criticizing her eating behaviors. However, these messages can also be covert—for example, when an adolescent is frequently exposed to messages in the media about body images (see Figure 9.1 for a biosocial theory applied to eating disorders).

ADDITIONAL TREATMENT TEAM MEMBERS

Medical Doctor

As we mentioned, eating disorders can have extremely harmful physical consequences. As a result, you will want to seriously consider having a physician, nurse practitioner, or physician assistant as a member of the consultation team. At the very least, the client should have a medical professional that he or she sees regularly and that you can have contact with as an ancillary team member. Medical professionals can monitor the client's health, and also report on any behaviors the client may be engaging in that might be considered life threatening. They can also provide support and reinforcement for the client to use new skills instead of problem behaviors related to his or her eating disorder.

Nutritionist

In addition to a medical professional, you will also want to consider having a nutritionist as a member of your treatment team. The nutritionist can provide individual sessions to help the client develop healthy eating patterns, and/or lead skills groups on nutrition to educate clients on the basic functions of food and the body. If you don't have a nutritionist as part of your program, you can still work with a nutritionist as an ancillary team member. The nutritionist can be informed of the client's treatment plan, and then work with the client based on those treatment targets to develop an individualized eating plan.

ADAPTATIONS TO TREATMENT TARGETS FOR EATING DISORDERS

See Chapter 1 for a review of hierarchical treatment targets in DBT. Table 9.1 depicts examples of treatment targets for clients struggling with eating disorders. Life-threatening behaviors may vary based on the adolescent, the severity and frequency of the behaviors, and the physical health of the adolescent. Regardless, usually eating disordered behaviors are not deemed life threatening unless a medical doctor reports an imminent threat to the adolescent's health (Wisniewski et al., 2007).

Secondary Treatment Targets

Wisniewski and Ben-Porath (2015) highlighted several dialectical dilemmas that emerge specifically while working with clients struggling with eating disorders. These

Table 9.1 Treatment Targets in DBT for Eating Disorders

Treatment Targets	Examples
Primary Treatment Targets	
Life-Threatening Behaviors	Urges, thoughts, or behaviors that harm self or others Eating disorder behaviors that have been deemed life threatening by a medical doctor
Therapy-Interfering Behaviors	Not completing homework Arriving late to session Lying about eating disordered behaviors, or omitting information about these behaviors Refusing to weigh in Refusing to maintain agreed-upon weight **Parents:** Not providing transportation to treatment Not attending treatment Not engaging in or attempting to practice skills
Quality-of-Life-Interfering Behaviors	Engaging in binging, purging, or restricting behaviors Engaging in excessive exercise Urges to binge, purge, or restrict Engaging in Apparently Irrelevant Behaviors (AIBs) Accessing pro-eating disorder online media **Parents:** Engaging in AIBs that can lead to the adolescent engaging in disordered eating behaviors (e.g., keeping certain foods in the house)
Increasing Behavioral Skills	Mindfulness (mindful eating) Emotion Regulation Interpersonal Effectiveness Distress Tolerance (Urge Surfing, Adaptive Denial) Walking the Middle Path Burning Bridges and Building New Ones Alternate Rebellion Dialectical Abstinence
Secondary Treatment Targets	
Eating Disorder Specific Dialectical Dilemmas	
Structured Eating Plans vs. No Eating Plan at All	The adolescent vacillates between over-controlling eating, to not being mindful of eating at all

(*Continued*)

Table 9.1 (Continued)

Treatment Targets	Examples
No Activity vs. Over-Activity	Not being physically active at all one day, excessively exercising the next
Apparent Compliance vs. Active Defiance	The client claims to be engaging in skills use but is not vs. actively refusing to engage in aspects of treatment (for example, weighing in or keeping a food diary)

dialectical dilemmas can be considered secondary treatment targets, and are therefore only addressed after the primary treatment targets have been satisfactorily resolved.

Structured Eating Plans vs. No Eating Plan at All

This dialectical dilemma refers to the extreme vacillation that clients with bulimia and binge eating disorder engage in between a rigid over-structuring of their eating plan and/or significant restriction of calorie intake and having absolutely no structure to their eating at all, which includes binging. By highlighting this dichotomy, clients and clinicians can work collaboratively to find the dialectic (perhaps with the help of a nutritionist), and follow the path to mindful eating.

No Activity vs. Over-Activity

Another dialectical dilemma that is common for clients struggling with eating disorders is either engaging in over-activity (extreme and/or frequent exercise activities) vs. not engaging in any activity at all. Adolescents may waver between both, or simply be on one side of this dilemma persistently. Identifying this dilemma, and generating examples for when this can happen, is helpful, including problem-solving regarding how to consistently balance between both.

Apparent Compliance vs. Active Defiance

This is an interesting dilemma, and may be especially true for adolescents struggling with eating disorders. Apparent compliance refers to when the client is engaging in all requested activities in order to appear engaged in treatment, but is not actually experiencing meaningful changes. For example, the client may claim to be engaging in agreed-upon behaviors, but, upon investigation, it is found that the client is not actually doing so (e.g., a client reports active completion of food logs but repeatedly fails to produce them in session). Active defiance is exactly as it sounds—when a client refuses to engage in treatment-related behaviors. When this happens, the clinician should go back to utilizing dialectical and commitment strategies to recommit the client to treatment.

SPECIFIC SKILLS AND ADAPTATIONS RELATED TO EATING DISORDERS

There are a few skills that researchers have developed or adapted specifically for clients struggling with eating disorders. Some of these skills were originally adapted for treating substance dependence with DBT; however Safer et al. (2009) have adapted them for BED and bulimia as well.

Dialectical Abstinence

This strategy relates specifically to binge eating for stage three clients (see Handout 9.1). Dialectical abstinence is the idea that the client will commit to abstaining from binge eating permanently. This commitment is usually made during the pretreatment phase, and is considered essential for the client to continue in treatment. However, the dialectic involved is that the client must also commit to reducing binge eating when it does occur by using skills to either stopping the binge eating, or not engage in binge eating again. The premise of this is that when the client has been abstaining from an eating disorder behavior and then experiences a 'slip' so to speak, he or she may be feeling discouraged and as result give up and fall back into the pattern of disordered eating. This synthesis of two seeming conflicting ideas will allow flexibility for the client to completely abstain when he or she is not engaged in binge eating, while also working to reduce binge eating when such an episode does occur (Wisniewski et al., 2007). The idea of committing to completely abstaining from binge eating is often extremely difficult for some clients to consider. However, the counselor can use the commitment strategies reviewed in Chapter 2 (e.g., weighing the pros and cons, foot in the door/door in the face) to engage the client in this commitment and use metaphors to help clients understand the concept. Wisniewski et al. (2007) provide the example of a football player—though at the beginning of each play, the quarterback's goal is to score a touchdown, in the event he does not score a touchdown, he doesn't give up. Instead, he still tries to gain as many yards as possible, while still keeping the goal of scoring a touchdown during the next play.

Burning Bridges

Though we discuss this skill in the context of substance use in Chapter 11, it is conceptualized a little bit differently for eating disorders. In DBT-ED, *burning your bridges* is included in the distress tolerance module—the client is invited to engage in radical acceptance regarding the idea that he or she will "burn the bridge" to binging and purging behaviors, and no longer use them as a way to manage emotions (see Handout 9.2). You can then help the client identify other skills they can use to replace the old problem behaviors. You can be creative with this skill; for example, you could include imagery exercises in which the client envisions actually burning or destroying the bridge to those behaviors (Safer et al., 2009).

Urge Surfing

With this skill, clients are encouraged to be aware of the urge to binge and purge, but not to act on it (see Handout 9.3). They are taught to be aware of the urge, experience it as an ebb and flow (like surfing a wave), and in that awareness remind themselves that the urge will pass. By engaging in this activity without acting on the urge, clients are better able to regulate their emotions and engage in more adaptive coping behaviors, which is an important concept to reinforce (Safer et al., 2009). Again, creativity may be helpful to engage adolescents, either through a mindfulness activity where you lead them through imagery of surfing through urges (while playing sounds of the ocean in the background), or having them draw pictures of the ocean and what surfing the urge would look like to them.

Mindful Eating

Mindful eating is a common skill in many treatment approaches for eating disorders. Mindful eating is an exercise in which clients are encouraged to be acutely aware of every bite they are taking, and to slowly savor the flavors, smells, and textures of their foods. By engaging in this practice regularly, clients will be better able to use their mindfulness skills to be aware of their eating behaviors, and avoid dialectical dilemmas such as over-structured eating vs. no structure to eating at all. Clients can engage in mindful eating exercises during group settings with other clients or alone. Mindfulness may be more difficult for adolescents to master; therefore you may want to spend more time practicing mindful eating in session, and use a variety of different food items to help them learn to use all of their senses (and be aware of any emotional reactions they may be having) while eating. See Handout 9.4 for a worksheet on this topic.

Alternate Rebellion

Adolescents may engage in eating disorder behaviors as a method of rebelling against authority figures—for example, parents, teachers, or even the clinician. The adolescent may feel that she has little control—but eating behaviors are one thing she can control. The goal of the alternate rebellion skill is to help clients validate their urge to rebel, but do so in a manner that is not harmful and does not include engaging in eating disordered behaviors (see Handout 9.5). You may need to be creative to come up with some ideas, but some ideas can include listening to loud or offensive music, (temporarily) changing his or her physical appearance, or even writing down swear words on a piece of paper (and then tearing it up and throwing it away).

Phone Coaching Rules

One mode of DBT treatment that researchers have adapted is the intersession skills coaching (Safer et al., 2009; Wisniewski & Ben-Porath, 2005). Traditionally, in adult

DBT, if a client engages in a problem behavior, the rule is that they may not contact the clinician for 24 hours after they have engaged in that behavior (Miller et al., [2007] actually discourage against this rule for adolescents—you will need to make your own decisions on this based on the needs of your clients). However, clinicians found that 24 hours was too long for clients who struggle with disordered eating, and within that time frame, he or she would have several opportunities to continue to binge or purge. As result, researchers suggest that this rule be altered in DBT-ED. Some programs specify a number of hours the client must wait before calling, while others state the client must wait until the next meal or snack. Regardless, this time frame can be changed based on the needs of the adolescent, as the goal of phone coaching is to support the client in using new skills to manage emotions. These boundaries can be discussed during the pretreatment sessions, and then revisited for alterations as needed.

SAMPLE GROUP SESSION FORMAT

The sample group session format presented in Table 9.2 includes all five traditional DBT modules (Miller et al., 2007) in a six-week format, with the mindfulness module that includes eating disorder specific skills and psychoeducation on eating disorders and nutrition (Safer et al., 2009). Sessions can last between one and a half and two hours, with the first half focused on review and homework, and the second half focused on new skills. Mindfulness practice should be conducted at least once per session (see *Mindfulness Exercises* in Handout 4.2 for a list of sample mindfulness exercises). Though the skills adapted for eating disorders are mainly taught in the mindfulness and distress tolerance modules, you may wish to incorporate them into each of the modules, especially if you have a lot of new participants starting at the beginning of a new module.

Table 9.2 Sample Skills Training Schedule for DBT-ED

Module/Session	Skills, Activities, and Handouts
Mindfulness: Module 1	
Session 1	Orientation to DBT and Skills Training Group Rules Biosocial Theory of Eating Disorders Dialectical Abstinence
Session 2	Reasonable, Emotion, and Wise Mind Basics of Nutrition Eating Disorders and Their Consequences

(*Continued*)

Table 9.2 (Continued)

Module/Session	Skills, Activities, and Handouts
Session 3	Mindfulness Practice—What Is Mindfulness? Mindfulness What Skills (Observe, Describe, Participate)
Session 4	Mindfulness How Skills (One-Mindfully Effectively, Nonjudgmentally)
Session 5	Mindful Eating
Session 6	Apparently Irrelevant Behaviors Alternate Rebellion

Distress Tolerance: Module 2

Session 1	Review of Group Rules and DBT Skills Training, the Biosocial Theory, and Eating Disorders as needed Introduction to Distress Tolerance and Eating Disorders
Session 2	Urge Surfing Adaptive Denial Burning Bridges
Session 3	Distract With Wise Mind ACCEPTS, Self Soothe With the Six Senses
Session 4	IMPROVE the Moment
Session 5	Pros and Cons, TIPP
Session 6	Acceptance Skills, Willingness, and Willfulness

Walking the Middle Path: Module 3

Session 1	Review of Group Rules and DBT Skills Training, the Biosocial Theory, and Eating Disorders as needed Introduction to the Walking the Middle Path Module
Session 2	Dialectics
Session 3	Dialectical Dilemmas
Session 4	Validation
Session 5	Behaviorism
Session 6	Problem-Solving and Behavior Chain Analysis

Emotion Regulation: Module 4

Session 1	Review of Group Rules and DBT Skills Training, the Biosocial Theory, and Eating Disorders as needed Introduction to Emotion Regulation for eating disorders
Session 2	ABC—Accumulating positive experiences, Build mastery, Cope ahead (Apparently Irrelevant Behaviors)
Session 3	PLEASE—treat Physical illness, balance Eating, Avoid drugs, balance Sleep, get Exercise

Module/Session	Skills, Activities, and Handouts
Session 4	Mindfulness of Current Emotions
Session 5	Check the Facts
Session 6	Opposite Action
Interpersonal Effectiveness: Module 5	
Session 1	Review of Group Rules and DBT Skills Training, the Biosocial Theory, and Eating Disorders as needed Introduction to Interpersonal Effectiveness
Session 2	GIVE—Gentle, Interested, Validate, Easy manner
Session 3	DEAR MAN—Describe, Express, Assert, Reinforce, be Mindful, Appear confident, Negotiate
Session 4	FAST—be Fair, no Apologies, Stick to values, be Truthful
Session 5	Factors to consider when asking for something or saying no
Session 6	THINK—Think, Have empathy, Interpretations, Notice, Kindness

OUTCOME EVALUATION

In addition to the measures mentioned in previous chapters for emotion dysregulation, if you are implementing DBT-ED it is important to assess for eating behaviors as well. Though we include a few examples here, there may be other methods by which you can measure your outcomes—focus on what the goal of your program is, and then choose accordingly.

Diary Cards

Remember, diary cards can be an important indicator of progress in treatment, and can be tailored to the specific problem behaviors you have targeted. Diary cards are used in a simplistic fashion—simply keep track of how many times a client engaged in a behavior on a week-by-week basis. This should give you a good idea if the frequency of occurrences is going down (or up); in addition to letting you know if the frequency of skills use is increasing. Handout 1.3 is a sample diary card for eating disorders, and Handout 9.6 is a sample Food Log that can also help you track progress.

Body Mass Index (BMI)

Depending on the behaviors the adolescent is struggling with, BMI may be an important indicator of treatment progress. If the adolescent is struggling with anorexia, an increase in BMI may be an indication of weight gain, and positive treatment progress. Though the goal for clients who struggle with binge eating disorder and/or bulimia may not necessarily be to lose weight, weight loss can also be an indicator of treatment success. There is controversy surrounding the use of specific BMI scores as benchmarks, due to the differences in body types and bone structure. Therefore, you should not aim for a specific BMI as part of goal setting for the client, but instead just use the BMI as one indicator of progress in treatment (Safer et al., 2009).

Child Eating Disorders Examination and Questionnaire

The Child Eating Disorders Examination (ChEDE; Bryant-Waugh, Cooper, Taylor, & Lask, 1996) was developed based on the adult version, the Eating Disorder Examination (EDE; Cooper & Fairburn, 1987). The ChEDE is a standardized, semi-structured interview that the clinician administers by asking the adolescent questions and recording the responses. It can be used for children and adolescents ages 8–18 and includes four subscales based on cognitive and behavioral symptoms of eating disorders: restraint, eating concern, weight concern, and shape concern (Van Durme, Craeynest, Braet, & Goossens, 2015). You also have the option of administering this assessment as a self-report questionnaire—the Child Eating Disorder Examination Questionnaire is based on the ChEDE (ChEDE-Q; Decaluwé & Braet, 1999) and includes similar questions regarding eating disorder symptoms over the last four weeks. Regardless of which method you use, you should be able to get a solid grasp on your client's eating behavior. By administering this assessment several times over the course of treatment, you will be able to adequately measure treatment progress.

CHALLENGES AND SOLUTIONS

One of the biggest challenges you may face is committing the client to treatment. We say it in every chapter, but it is true! As always, your commitment strategies will be invaluable to you during the pretreatment phase, and when you need to recommit the client throughout treatment. Implementing DBT in addition to another treatment for eating disorders can be expensive and intensive. You can combat this by combining modes of treatment where possible, and only referring clients to this treatment who have not been successful in other treatment approaches. As we've also said repeatedly, DBT is extremely flexible—so you can pick and choose the aspects you wish to implement into your current treatment, and leave the rest. Just be sure that you are being intentional in what you're doing, and why you're doing it.

SUMMARY AND CONCLUSIONS

DBT-ED is structured to treat the underlying emotion dysregulation related to eating disorders (Safer et al., 2009). In addition, the behavioral aspects of DBT will help you work with adolescents and their parents to be sure you are not reinforcing problem behaviors, and instead reinforcing new, coping behaviors. Unfortunately, there is little research on using DBT with adolescents and eating disorders. Though the research that is available is promising, evidence-based approaches should be considered before implementing DBT in place of another approach.

REFERENCES

American Psychiatric Association (APA). (2013). *Diagnostic and statistical manual of mental disorders* (5th ed.). Arlington, VA: American Psychiatric Publishing.

Bhatnagar, K. & Wisniewski, L. (2015). Integrating dialectical behavior therapy with family therapy for adolescents with affect dysregulation. In K.L. Loeb, D. Le Grange, & J. Lock (Eds.), *Family therapy for adolescent eating and weight disorders: New applications* (pp. 305–327). New York, NY: Routledge/Taylor & Francis Group.

Bryant-Waugh, R. J., Cooper, P. J., Taylor, C. L., & Lask, B. D. (1996). The use of the eating disorder examination with children: A pilot study. *International Journal of Eating Disorders*, *19*, 391–397.

Chen, E. Y., Matthews, L., Allen, C., Kuo, J. R., & Linehan, M. M. (2008). Dialectical behavior therapy for clients with binge-eating disorder or bulimia nervosa and borderline personality disorder. *International Journal of Eating Disorders*, *41*(6), 505–512. doi:10.1002/eat.20522

Cooper, Z. & Fairburn, C. (1987). The eating disorder examination: A semi-structured interview for the assessment of the specific psychopathology of eating disorders. *International Journal of Eating Disorders*, *6*(1), 1–8. https://doi.org/10.1002/1098-108X(198701)6:1<1::AID-EAT2260060102>3.0.CO;2-9

Decaluwé, V. & Braet, C. (1999). *Child eating disorder examination—questionnaire* [Dutch translation]. Unpublished manuscript, Belgium: Ghent University.

Federici, A., Wisniewski, L., & Ben-Porath, D. (2012). Description of an intensive dialectical behavior therapy program for multidiagnostic clients with eating disorders. *Journal of Counseling & Development*, *90*(3), 330–338. doi:10.1002/j.1556-6676.2012.00041.x

Lock, J. & Le Grange, D. (2012). *Treatment manual for anorexia nervosa: A family-based approach* (2nd ed.). New York, NY: Guilford Press.

Miller, A. L., Rathus, J. H., & Linehan, M. M. (2007). *Dialectical behavior therapy with suicidal adolescents*. New York, NY: Guilford Press. Retrieved from https://manowar.tamucc.edu/login?url=http://search.ebscohost.com/login.aspx?direct=true&db=psyh&AN=2006-23301-000&site=ehost-live&scope=site

Safer, D. L., Telch, C. F., & Chen, E. Y. (2009). *Dialectical behavior therapy for binge eating and bulimia*. New York, NY: Guilford Press.

Swanson, S. A., Crow, S. J., Le Grange, D., Swendsen, J., & Merikangas, K. R. (2011). Prevalence and correlates of eating disorders in adolescents. Results from the national comorbidity survey replication adolescent supplement. *Archives of General Psychiatry*, *68*(7), 714–723. https://doi.org/10.1001/archgenpsychiatry.2011.22

Van Durme, K., Craeynest, E., Braet, C., & Goossens, L. (2015). The detection of eating disorder symptoms in adolescence: A comparison between the children's eating disorder examination and the children's eating disorder examination questionnaire. *Behaviour Change*, *32*(3), 190–201. doi:10.1017/bec.2015.10

Wisniewski, L. & Ben-Porath, D. D. (2005). Telephone skill-coaching with eating-disordered clients: Clinical guidelines using a DBT framework. *European Eating Disorders Review*, *13*(5), 344–350. doi:10.1002/erv.657

Wisniewski, L. & Ben-Porath, D. D. (2015). Dialectical behavior therapy and eating disorders: The use of contingency management procedures to manage dialectical dilemmas. *American Journal of Psychotherapy*, *69*(2), 129–140.

Wisniewski, L. & Kelly, E. (2003). The application of dialectical behavior therapy to the treatment of eating disorders. *Cognitive and Behavioral Practice*, *10*(2), 131–138. doi:10.1016/S1077-7229(03)80021-4

Wisniewski, L., Safer, D., & Chen, E. (2007). Dialectical behavior therapy and eating disorders. In L. A. Dimeff, K. Koerner, L. A. Dimeff, K. Koerner (Eds.), *Dialectical behavior therapy in clinical practice: Applications across disorders and settings* (pp. 174–221). New York, NY: Guilford Press.

Conduct Disorder, Probation, and Juvenile Detention Settings

K. Michelle Hunnicutt Hollenbaugh and Jacob M. Klein

In this chapter we discuss the use of DBT with adolescents who have been diagnosed with conduct disorder, and/or are involved with the legal system in some manner. This includes adolescents referred on an outpatient basis due to behavior problems, as well as adolescents in residential juvenile detention settings. There are several reasons you may find DBT helpful when working with this population. Many adolescents who have legal difficulties struggle with mental illness and emotion dysregulation. However, their symptoms present differently than other adolescents, and they struggle primarily with the ability to regulate anger (Cavanaugh, Solomon, & Gelles, 2011). One study found that over half of incarcerated adolescents have a history of significant traumatic experiences, prior mental health treatment, and a substance use disorder diagnosis (Stewart & Trupin, 2000). Though it is rarely implemented, research shows that mental health treatment can increase rehabilitation for offenders, and as a result, reduce rates of recidivism (McCann, Ivanoff, Schmidt, & Beach, 2007). When adolescents do not receive proper treatment for their mental health problems, and instead experience incarceration or punitive consequences, they may actually experience an increase in symptoms (Quinn & Shera, 2009).

Many aspects of DBT overlap with evidenced-based treatments for conduct disorder in adolescents, including multisystemic therapy (MST; Henggeler, Schoenwald, Borduin, Rowland, & Cunningham, 2009). For example, MST also includes intersession contact with the clinician, involvement and skills training of parents, and the introduction of behavioral and cognitive-behavioral skills. Including other aspects of DBT—for example, dialectics and validation—may increase treatment outcomes with this population.

The behavioral approach to problem-solving and change in DBT fits well with reinforcing and extinguishing behaviors related to these disorders. Conversely, as you have likely noticed, validation is a major facet of DBT, and using validation in the context of change can increase positive treatment outcomes. Unfortunately, many evidence-based approaches for behavioral problems in adolescents focus very little on validating the client, and therefore DBT may be a very helpful option for clients who do not respond to traditional treatment approaches (Cavanaugh et al., 2011). Further, when working with this population, counselor (and other team member) burnout can be high. DBT specifically targets staff engagement through the consultation team, which can decrease frequency of burnout (McCann et al., 2007; Waltz, 2003). Finally, offenders who receive DBT treatment as part of their rehabilitation may also continue with DBT treatment after this time is over and while transitioning from residential to outpatient treatment, which will further increase positive outcomes and reduce the likelihood of recidivism (Vitacco & Van Rybroek, 2006).

CONSIDERATIONS BEFORE IMPLEMENTING DBT

There are several things to consider before you implement DBT with this population. As we've said with other adaptations in this book, research on DBT with this population is preliminary, and other evidence-based treatments may be preferable. A second consideration is administration and staff buy-in, especially in residential settings. Staff generalization in skills training is paramount to the success of DBT in a detention or residential setting. All staff should be well trained in DBT skills as well as skills coaching strategies. This can be done through regular trainings, implementation of DBT skill use during team meetings, and modeling of skill use by leaders and directors (McCann et al., 2007). Regardless of the setting, administration will also need to have a full understanding of the treatment and be committed to making changes related to implementation. Lack of support from administration can lead to lack of funding and/or inconsistency in treatment implementation, which can ultimately lead to treatment failure (see Chapter 2).

Parental Involvement and Commitment to Treatment

Even if the adolescent is mandated to treatment (either by his or her parents or legally), it is important that he or she commit to DBT voluntarily (Galietta & Rosenfeld, 2012). Therefore, clients should be given a choice to engage in the DBT program, or some other treatment option. It may take a significant amount of time before the client is willing to fully engage in the treatment; however it is paramount that he or she makes that choice. Remember, even if you cannot attain full commitment, partial commitment may be enough for the adolescent to start the program until you can use strategies to commit them fully (refer back to the commitment strategies in Chapter 2).

One of the primary predictors of treatment success with this population is parental involvement—perhaps more so than other diagnoses covered in this book, since symptoms of these disorders are usually directly related to adolescents' interactions with their parents as authority figures. The majority (if not all) of the evidence-based treatments for conduct disorders either include parents in treatment, or focus solely on the parents and parenting strategies, therefore committing the parents to treatment may be just as important as committing the adolescent. Though it may not always be possible to include the parents (for example, in a juvenile detention setting), by teaching both parents and adolescents DBT skills, they can work together to extinguish target behaviors and increase positive coping skills.

Validation and Nonjudgmental Stance

It is imperative that you approach treatment dialectically when working with adolescents who have committed criminal acts or have problems with conduct. From a dialectical viewpoint, both the clinician and the adolescent are aware that the adolescent must take responsibility for his or her actions *and* the clinician is also accepting and validating of the adolescent's perspective, including previous experiences that led up to problem behaviors. Clinicians also take a nonjudgmental stance towards the adolescent's behaviors, and separate the behaviors from being "good" or "bad" but instead view them objectively as a problem that needs to be solved (Waltz, 2003). One of the underlying tenants in DBT is that the clinician should not "validate the invalid," and this can be especially difficult when working with adolescent offenders. By avoiding validation of the behavior or the offense, it can then be difficult to find anything to validate. The key is remembering that you can always validate the underlying emotions (anger, hurt, etc.) while simultaneously not validating the criminal or harmful problem behavior. For example, you can say "I can understand how you felt angry and disrespected when your teacher told you to stop talking in class, *and* yelling and knocking over your desk is not an effective way to manage your emotions and relationships, or get your needs met" (Waltz, 2003).

THE BIOSOCIAL THEORY OF CONDUCT DISORDER AND CRIMINAL BEHAVIORS

The biosocial theory of emotion dysregulation (see Chapter 1) can be adapted to address symptoms of conduct disorders, and more specifically, criminal behaviors (see Figure 10.1). There is a wide range of severity for behavior disorders, and the emotion dysregulation these adolescents experience may be due to a biological sensitivity to emotions. However, McCann et al. (2007) also postulated that individuals who exhibit criminal behaviors may actually be experiencing an *insensitivity* to emotions. The adolescent may not even realize he or she is experiencing strong emotions until they are at an extreme level, and this may then lead to aggressive, harmful, and criminal behaviors.

In addition to this possible insensitivity to emotions, researchers have hypothesized that for individuals who struggle with criminal behaviors and conduct disorder, the invalidating environment may consist of *disturbed caring*, an environment in which antisocial behaviors are modeled. Though this is not always the case, in these situations the adolescent may view and/or experience physical abuse, inconsistent discipline, and low supervision (McCann et al., 2007).

Regardless, as we discussed previously, your goal will be to take a nonjudgmental stance when working with parents and adolescents. Remember that the invalidating environment can be transactional, and that invalidation of the adolescent may be directly related to his or her behavioral problems and his or her parents struggling to find ways to manage these behaviors successfully.

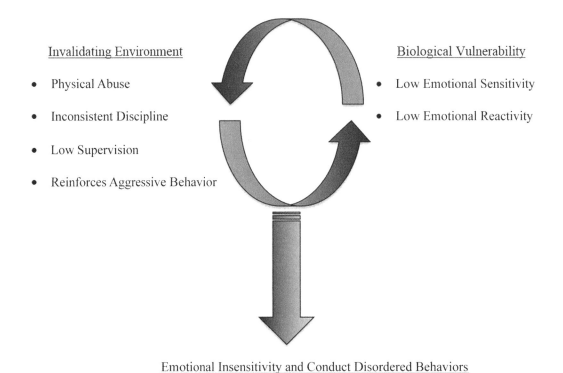

Figure 10.1 Biosocial Theory as Applied to Conduct Disorder/Criminal Behavior

TREATMENT TARGETS WITH ADOLESCENTS WITH BEHAVIORAL PROBLEMS

Though the treatment hierarchy remains the same when working with adolescents with behavioral problems, adaptations may be necessary to fit residential settings. For example, instead of focusing on decreasing therapy-interfering behaviors, the treatment targets may include decreasing unit-destroying behaviors. As shown in Table 10.1, these behaviors include any activity the adolescent engages in that interferes with therapeutic functioning on a residential unit (McCann et al., 2007; Trupin, Steward, Beach, & Boesky, 2002). Depending on the severity of the adolescent's mental health symptoms, you may wish to alter or add different treatment targets—for example, pretreatment goals may include stabilization on medication for management of severe mental health symptoms (Vitacco & Van Rybroek, 2006). Nonetheless, treatment targets should be linked back to criminal behavior and the consequences of all those behaviors (Quinn & Shera, 2009).

Life-threatening and quality-of-life-interfering behaviors are adapted to include any behaviors that are threatening and harmful to others, in addition to the adolescent. Secondary targets may include decreasing criminal identification and increasing citizenship (McCann et al., 2007). Remember, treatment targets focus on the problem behavior, but can also include thoughts, urges, and emotions related to those behaviors, and therefore, all of these aspects should be monitored (Fruzzetti &

Table 10.1 DBT Treatment Targets and Hierarchy With Conduct Disorders and in Juvenile Detention Settings

Treatment Targets	Examples
Primary Treatment Targets	
Life-Threatening Behaviors	Harm to self or others Urges, plans, threats, or thoughts to harm self or others
Unit-Destroying Behaviors	Fighting with other adolescents Arguing/fighting with staff Destroying unit property Causing disruption in group
Therapy-Interfering Behaviors	Not reporting quality-of-life- or life-threatening behaviors to the counselor Not completing diary card or homework Arriving late to session Not attending session Angry or irritable mood Argumentative or defiant behavior
	Parents: Not providing transportation to treatment Not attending treatment Not engaging in or attempting to practice skills
	Clinician: Being judgmental and/or punitive
Quality-of-Life-Interfering Behaviors	Substance use (see also: Chapter 8) Stealing Antisocial behaviors Risky sex Vandalism Lying Fighting Academic issues
Increasing Behavioral Skills	Mindfulness Interpersonal Effectiveness Emotion Regulation (Anger Management) Distress Tolerance Walking the Middle Path
Secondary Treatment Targets	
Decrease Criminal Identification	Learn validation and empathy
Increase Citizenship	Pro-social skills
Dialectical Dilemma—Excessive Leniency vs. Authoritarian Control	Parents allowing the adolescent to not return home several nights of the week without any consequences, then suddenly grounding the adolescent for six months.

Levensky, 2000). Finally, when possible, it is important to include treatment targets related to the parents, as they may be unintentionally reinforcing problem behaviors.

ADDITIONAL TREATMENT TEAM MEMBERS AND ROLES

School Counselor

School counselors can be especially helpful ancillary team members when your client is having behavioral problems at school. Your goal will be to educate the counselor on the client's treatment targets and the DBT approach. The counselor can then work with teachers to ascertain that problem behaviors are not being reinforced, and that the use of new coping skills is reinforced. The counselor can also serve as a skills coach throughout the school day when necessary. The adolescent would then be reinforced for seeking out coaching from the counselor before he or she engages in disruptive and problematic behaviors at school. Ideally, teachers would be aware of this and allow the student to leave class to seek out coaching when needed. Just as with intersession phone coaching, abuse of the opportunity for skills coaching (e.g., requesting to meet with the school counselor to avoid taking a test) should not be reinforced (the counselor would immediately send the student back to class) and the counselor should inform the individual therapist, who will spend a significant amount of time in the next session engaging the adolescent in a problem-solving behavior chain (see Chapter 2) regarding this therapy-interfering behavior.

Probation Officers/Residential Staff

As we've said in other chapters, anyone involved in the adolescent's rehabilitation should be at least minimally aware of the basics of DBT. If not, they may unintentionally reinforce problem behaviors. This is easier said than done—many individuals who work with the legal system, including staff on residential units and probation officers have become accustomed to approaching adolescents with a punitive and authoritarian approach. In addition, they may experience a dialectical dilemma between keeping themselves safe (using restraints, etc.) and coaching the client to engage in skills use and distress tolerance to manage the situation (McCann et al., 2007). The DBT consultation team can provide problem-solving and support as needed to help other professionals maintain a commitment to the DBT approach.

ADAPTATIONS TO DBT FOR BEHAVIORAL PROBLEMS AND LEGAL SETTINGS

There are several adaptations for DBT implementation for adolescents with behavioral problems and in juvenile correctional settings. These include added modules, changes in length based on the setting, and use of various treatment modes. Though adaptations for outpatient and residential settings might be different, there are also many overlaps, and you may be working with the same adolescent in both settings. Therefore, we will discuss them together, and where there are differences we will note them.

Mindfulness

Relational Mindfulness

We also discussed this skill in the chapter on DBT with families, as it specifically focuses on being mindful of others (see Handout 5.2). By being aware of others, the adolescent can increase empathy and decrease behaviors that are harmful to others (McCann et al., 2007). You can encourage your client to use relationship mindfulness by having him or her think of one specific person and observe and describe them nonjudgmentally (at first, it's best if this is someone they either feel neutral or positive about). After the adolescent has had some practice, he or she can be mindful of someone they have conflict with—for example, a parent, teacher, or probation officer. By nonjudgmentally describing the individual, they will hopefully be able to see the other's perspective more clearly, which will increase their ability to be empathetic toward that individual.

Do What Works

This skill is included in Rathus and Miller's (2015) skills manual and fits perfectly for adolescents who struggle with managing anger and impulsivity towards authority figures and parents (see Handout 10.1). The steps to this skill are 1) Focus on your goals, and 2) Do what needs to be done to achieve your goals, including: not letting your emotions control your behaviors, playing by the rules, and acting as skillfully as you can. A metaphor that works really well with this skill is playing in a football or basketball game. Players have to play by the rules, or get penalized and/or be removed from the game. Though in the moment, getting in a fight with a player on the opposite team may seem worth it, the bigger picture is winning the game. "Doing what works" in this scenario is using distress tolerance skills to avoid a fight, and instead focus on playing the game. It may help to show a short video clip of a famous basketball or football player walking away from a possible conflict, and then discuss what the process may have been like for that player, and what they notice about his or her body language in the video (Rathus & Miller, 2015).

Emotion Regulation

Anger outbursts will likely be common quality-of-life- and therapy-interfering target behaviors when you are working with this population. Anger, irritability, and related behaviors are diagnostic criteria for conduct disorder, and these behaviors can lead to innumerable other problems when the client is unable to manage this emotion effectively. All of the different facets of anger, including triggers, false beliefs, and specific behavioral consequences can be addressed via diary cards and skills.

Though it is imperative to help adolescents understand and explore anger, it is also important not to overlook the other emotions as well. Anger is a secondary emotion, and the adolescent may experience many emotions at one time, which increases likelihood of maladaptive behaviors in an effort to regulate them (Galietta & Rosenfeld, 2012; Fruzzetti & Levensky, 2000). This module can be altered to help adolescents understand the primary emotions that underlie anger, which are usually sadness and hurt. You can also focus on how to communicate emotions effectively to others, and the link between their thoughts and their emotions.

Acts of Kindness

The goal of this skill is to help adolescents develop empathy and be aware of how their behaviors affect others (see Handout 10.2; McCann, Ball, & Ivanoff, 2000). Clients are taught that an act of kindness is done willingly, without expectation of anything in return. They can use the list of kind things on the handout for ideas (for example, giving a compliment, unexpectedly helping out with a chore around the house, or helping a teacher with something at school), and they are encouraged to use this skill often. The goal of this skill is to help the adolescent experience positive emotions, which will reinforce him or her for engaging in acts of kindness.

Act Opposite to Anger and Apathy

This skill can help adolescents identify the emotion they are currently experiencing, and then act opposite to that emotion in order to manage it effectively without engaging in a harmful behavior (see Handout 4.8). Though you will obviously want to help adolescents use this skill when they are experiencing anger, McCann, Ball, and Ivanoff (2000) also adapted this skill to help juvenile offenders act opposite to apathy and detachment. Some examples include engaging in random acts of kindness (see above), participating fully in group and individual sessions (even when he or she does not want to), listening mindfully and validating others, and engaging in interactive activities with family and friends.

Cope Ahead to Manage Anger

This skill can be useful in helping the adolescent plan for situations in which he may become angry and be at risk for engaging in harmful and/or problem behaviors (Linehan, 2015; see Handout 4.9). This can include interactions with parents, teachers, and peers. The client can then problem solve and decide how to handle it using positive coping skills (for example, the STOP distress tolerance skill). Your client will then imagine what the situation will be like, and envision using the identified skills. By doing this, your clients will be able to effectively "cope ahead" instead of engaging in destructive or harmful behaviors. This can also go hand in hand with the behavior chain for problem-solving (see Handout 1.6)—the client can complete the behavior chain, and then use the imagery to imagine himself or herself using the newly identified skills (Linehan, 2015).

Distress Tolerance

STOP

This skill is an acronym, for Stop, Take a step back, Observe, and Proceed mindfully (Linehan, 2015). This can be a fun and helpful skill to practice in group sessions with clients. For example, having the clients imagine a situation in the past (that is likely to happen again) in which they engaged in a harmful or aggressive behavior. The clients can be invited to act out their body language and "set up" the scene, so to speak, up to the point where they actually engaged in the problem behavior. Then, they can role-play how they will use the STOP skill in the future, and keep themselves from engaging in the problem behavior.

Intersession Skills Coaching

Skills coaching between sessions for adolescents who struggle with behavioral problems will look different based on your setting. For example, similar to an inpatient unit, coaching in a juvenile detention center may be conducted by unit staff on an as-needed basis (McCann et al., 2007). In an outpatient setting, it may be difficult to engage clients who struggle with criminal behaviors, and therefore it may be more helpful for you to actually schedule times that the client will call for skills coaching. Some clinicians who work with offenders have actually removed the 24-hour rule (the client cannot call the clinician until 24 hours after the problem behavior occurred). You may also wish to consider removing this rule, because clients who have behavioral problems are unlikely to be reinforced by contact with the clinician (especially if they have been mandated to treatment), and this removes the necessity of this rule (Galietta & Rosenfeld, 2012).

SAMPLE GROUP SESSION FORMAT

The sample group session format included in Table 10.2 presents all five traditional DBT modules (Rathus & Miller, 2015) in a six-week format, with each module including the new and adapted skills related specifically to criminal and harmful behaviors (McCann et al., 2007). Session length may vary—for residential settings, groups may last an hour, and outpatient groups may last an hour and a half. Usually the traditional format will work best, with the first half focused on review and homework, and

Table 10.2 Sample Skills Training Schedule for DBT for Conduct/Behavioral Problems

Module/Session	Skills, Activities, and Handouts
Mindfulness: Module 1	
Session 1	Orientation to DBT and Skills Training Group Rules Biosocial Theory of Conduct Disorder Psychoeducation on Conduct Disorder and Emotion Dysregulation
Session 2	Reasonable, Emotion, and Wise Mind Mindfulness Practice—What Is Mindfulness?
Session 3	Mindfulness What Skills (Observe, Describe, Participate)
Session 4	Mindfulness How Skills One-Mindfully Nonjudgmentally
Session 5	Mindfulness How Skills Effectively (Do What Works)
Session 6	Relational Mindfulness
Distress Tolerance: Module 2	
Session 1	Review of Group Rules and DBT Skills Training, the Biosocial Theory, and Conduct Disorder as needed Introduction to Distress Tolerance
Session 2	STOP Skill
Session 3	Distract With Wise Mind ACCEPTS, Self Soothe With the Six Senses
Session 4	IMPROVE the Moment
Session 5	Pros and Cons, TIPP
Session 6	Acceptance Skills, Willingness, and Willfulness
Walking the Middle Path: Module 3	
Session 1	Review of Group Rules and DBT Skills Training, the Biosocial Theory, and Conduct Disorders as needed Introduction to the Walking the Middle Path Module
Session 2	Dialectics
Session 3	Dialectical Dilemmas
Session 4	Validation
Session 5	Behaviorism
Session 6	Problem-Solving and Behavior Chain Analysis
Emotion Regulation: Module 4	
Session 1	Review of Group Rules and DBT Skills Training, the Biosocial Theory, and Conduct Disorders as needed Introduction to Emotion Regulation for conduct/anger

Module/Session	Skills, Activities, and Handouts
Session 2	ABC—Accumulating positive experiences, Build mastery, COPE ahead to manage anger
Session 3	PLEASE—treat Physical illness, balance Eating, Avoid drugs, balance Sleep, get Exercise
Session 4	Mindfulness of Current Emotions
Session 5	Check the Facts Acts of Kindness
Session 6	Act Opposite to Anger and Apathy
Interpersonal Effectiveness: Module 5	
Session 1	Review of Group Rules and DBT Skills Training, the Biosocial Theory, and Conduct Disorder as needed Introduction to Interpersonal Effectiveness
Session 2	GIVE—Gentle, Interested, Validate, Easy manner
Session 3	DEAR MAN—Describe, Express, Assert, Reinforce, be Mindful, Appear confident, Negotiate
Session 4	FAST—be Fair, no Apologies, Stick to values, be Truthful
Session 5	Factors to consider when asking for something or saying no
Session 6	THINK—Think, Have empathy, Interpretations, Notice, Kindness

the second half focused on new skills. Mindfulness practice should be conducted at least once per session (see Handout 4.2). To review some of the standard skills listed here, refer back to Chapter 5.

OUTCOME EVALUATION

Alongside the traditional methods of measuring treatment progress in DBT, you will want to incorporate a method of measuring the specific treatment targets related to working with juvenile offenders and adolescents with behavior problems. You can do this fairly easily with a combination of informal and formal assessment methods.

Diary Cards

See Handout 1.4 for a diary card that includes behaviors that are common treatment targets for this population. This can include number of re-offenses, disciplinary actions, and aggressive or destructive behaviors. As the diary card is self-report, the client may be reluctant to complete it, or to be honest in completing it. You can approach this using the door-in-the-face commitment strategy (see Chapter 2)—start by asking the client to complete the full card, and if you are met with resistance, ask the client to complete a very small portion instead. As the client (hopefully) has made the voluntary choice to engage in DBT treatment, you can also remind him or her of that when discussing the importance of honesty in completing diary cards. If you do become aware that the client has not been honest regarding problem behaviors that have occurred throughout the week, this can be treated as a therapy-interfering behavior, and addressed in individual sessions via behavior chain analysis.

Child Behavior Checklist

The Child Behavior Checklist (U.S. Department of Justice, National Institutes of Justice, Office of Justice Data Resources Program, 2002) assessment is really popular, and can be used for children and adolescents. It includes several measures, a report form for parents and teachers, and a youth self-report form. It includes statements regarding the client's behavior, and then the respondent can rate the frequency she or he engages in certain behaviors based on a Likert scale. The school age version includes 120 questions, and can also be helpful in diagnosis.

State-Trait Anger Expression Inventory-2

The State-Trait Anger Expression Inventory-2 (STAXI-2; Spielberger, 1999) assessment is considered appropriate for adolescents age 16 and older, and this may be a limitation depending on the age range of the adolescents you are working with. This short assessment (5–10 minutes) includes 57 items and six scales—State Anger, Trait Anger, Anger Expression-In, Anger Expression-Out, Anger Control-In, and Anger Control-Out (Lievaart, Franken, & Hovens, 2016). Though you may not find all of these scales helpful in your outcome evaluation, you can choose one or two of these scales instead, which can reduce the amount of time the adolescent will need to take to complete the assessment, and give you an accurate picture of the specific variable you wish to analyze.

CHALLENGES AND SOLUTIONS

Commitment to Treatment

Adolescents who have behavioral problems are often difficult to engage in treatment. As we've mentioned, this is likely due to the fact they have been required to attend treatment, and therefore, commitment to treatment may take longer with this population. DBT commitment strategies can be used to help engage the client. For example, the adolescent may be willing to commit to a shorter term of treatment, or towards positive goals that are perhaps not directly related to criminal offenses (foot in the door). You may also want to highlight the freedom to choose, and the absence of alternatives: "It's your choice—you can stay in the current program, that you have already told me you find to be 'worthless,' or you could try out this new program, and we can work together towards goals we both agree will improve your life and get your probation officer and your parents off of your back" (Miller, Rathus, & Linehan, 2007). The adolescent may need to be committed and recommitted to treatment often. Similarly, parents may need to engage in the commitment process several times. This is especially important during transition periods and after the client has been released from residential care, as parent commitment may help the client use skills, and reduce the likelihood of re-offense.

Finally, for adolescents involved in the legal system, you may be asked to release records, or appear in court to describe treatment progress. This can pose ethical issues that you will need to be upfront with your client about at the beginning of treatment, and be clear about who will have access to the records, and what you will and will not share with others. Not only will this facilitate the development of the therapeutic alliance, but you will be modeling honestly and genuineness to the client.

CONCLUSIONS

Though the majority of published literature on DBT with juvenile offenders and adolescents with conduct disorder is conceptual, preliminary results are promising (Nelson-Gray et al., 2006). Using aspects and adaptations of DBT may be helpful for your practice. Be sure to weigh the pros and cons of the different aspects of treatment, and consider supplementing current treatment with a DBT approach. The major tenants of DBT, including a nonjudgmental approach, and working towards change in the context of validation, may be invaluable for adolescents who have become accustomed to a punitive and authoritarian approach.

REFERENCES

Cavanaugh, M. M., Solomon, P. L., & Gelles, R. J. (2011). The Dialectical Psychoeducational Workshop (DPEW) for males at risk for intimate partner violence: A pilot randomized controlled trial. *Journal of Experimental Criminology*, *7*(3), 275–291. doi:10.1007/s11292-011-9126-8

Fruzzetti, A. E. & Levensky, E. R. (2000). Dialectical behavior therapy for domestic violence: Rationale and procedures. *Cognitive and Behavioral Practice*, *7*(4), 435–447. doi:10.1016/S1077–7229(00)80055–3

Galietta, M. & Rosenfeld, B. (2012). Adapting dialectical behavior therapy (DBT) for the treatment of psychopathy. *The International Journal of Forensic Mental Health*, *11*(4), 325–335. doi:10.1080/14999013.2012.746762

Henggeler, S. W., Schoenwald, S. K., Borduin, C. M., Rowland, M. D., & Cunningham, P. B. (2009). *Multisystemic therapy for antisocial behavior in children and adolescents* (2nd ed.). New York, NY: Guilford Press.

Lievaart, M., Franken, I. A., & Hovens, J. E. (2016). Anger assessment in clinical and nonclinical populations: Further validation of the State-Trait Anger Expression Inventory-2. *Journal of Clinical Psychology, 72*(3), 263–278. doi:10.1002/jclp.22253

Linehan, M. M. (2015). *DBT® skills training manual* (2nd ed.). New York, NY: Guilford Press.

McCann, R. A., Ball, E. M., & Ivanoff, A. (2000). DBT with an inpatient forensic population: The CMHIP forensic model. *Cognitive and Behavioral Practice, 7*(4), 447–456. doi:10.1016/S1077-7229(00)80056-5

McCann, R. A., Ivanoff, A., Schmidt, H., & Beach, B. (2007). Implementing dialectical behavior therapy in residential forensic settings with adults and juveniles. In L. A. Dimeff & K. Koerner (Eds.), *Dialectical behavior therapy in clinical practice: Applications across disorders and settings* (pp. 112–144). New York, NY: Guilford Press.

Miller, A. L., Rathus, J. H., & Linehan, M. M. (2007). *Dialectical behavior therapy with suicidal adolescents*. New York, NY: Guilford Press.

Nelson-Gray, R. O., Keane, S. P., Hurst, R. M., Mitchell, J. T., Warburton, J. B., Chok, J. T., & Cobb, A. R. (2006). A modified DBT skills training program for oppositional defiant adolescents: Promising preliminary findings. *Behaviour Research and Therapy, 44*(12), 1811–1820. doi:10.1016/j.brat.2006.01.004

Quinn, A. & Shera, W. (2009). Evidence-based practice in group work with incarcerated youth. *International Journal of Law And Psychiatry, 32*(5), 288–293. doi:10.1016/j.ijlp.2009.06.002

Rathus, J. H. & Miller, A. L. (2015). *DBT® skills manual for adolescents*. New York, NY: Guilford Press.

Spielberger, C. D. (1999). *State-Trait Anger Expression Inventory-2*. Lutz, FL: Psychological Assessment Resources.

Stewart, D. G. & Trupin, E. W. (2000, March). *Identifying serious mental and emotional disturbance with the MAYSI*. In A. Kavanaugh & D. Peuschold (chairs), *The Massachusetts Youth Screening Inventory*. Symposium presented at meeting of the American Psychology-Law Society, New Orleans.

Trupin, E. W., Stewart, D. G., Beach, B., & Boesky, L. (2002). Effectiveness of dialectical behaviour therapy program for incarcerated female juvenile offenders. *Child and Adolescent Mental Health, 7*(3), 121–127. doi:10.1111/1475-3588.00022

U.S. Department of Justice, National Institutes of Justice, Office of Justice Data Resources Program (2002). *Project on Human Development in Chicago Neighborhoods (PHDCN) child behavior checklist, wave 3, 2000–2002* (Instrument for ICPSR 13679). Retrieved from www.icpsr.umich.edu/files/PHDCN/wave-3-instruments/13679-cbcl.pdf

Vitacco, M. J. & Van Rybroek, G. J. (2006). Treating insanity acquittees with personality disorders: Implementing dialectical behavior therapy in a forensic hospital. *Journal of Forensic Psychology Practice, 6*(2), 1–16. doi:10.1300/J158v06n02_01

Waltz, J. (2003). Dialectical behavior therapy in the treatment of abusive behavior. *Journal of Aggression, Maltreatment & Trauma, 7*(1–2), 75–103. doi:10.1300/J146v07n01_05

11

Substance Use Disorders

K. Michelle Hunnicutt Hollenbaugh

In this chapter, we will review adaptations of DBT for adolescents who struggle with substance use disorders (SUDs). Adolescent alcohol and drug use is common, and research shows that up to 90% of adolescents who struggle with alcohol and drugs struggle with symptoms of emotion dysregulation as well (Chan, Dennis, & Funk, 2008). In fact, research shows that many adolescents use substances as a way to cope with difficult emotions (Bukstein & Horner, 2010). Adolescents who use substances are more likely to engage in impulsive behaviors and experience more extreme mental health symptoms than adolescents who do not use substances, and DBT can help adolescents replace substance use with more effective coping mechanisms (McMain, Sayrs, Dimeff, & Linehan, 2007). Although the results are preliminary, there is a large body of research on using DBT to address substance use, and DBT has been found to increase treatment compliance and help clients maintain sobriety longer than other clients who received standard treatment for alcohol and drug dependency (e.g., 12-step programs and support groups; Linehan et al., 1999).

CONSIDERATIONS BEFORE IMPLEMENTING DBT

There are several evidence-based treatments for adolescents who struggle with substance use (for example, multi-dimensional family therapy), and researchers have adapted DBT to supplement those treatments (Dietz & Dunn, 2014; Rathus & Miller, 2015). DBT can be especially useful for adolescents who struggle with an SUD and emotion dysregulation, or whose substance use seems directly related to emotion dysregulation. DBT may also be an excellent option for adolescents who have not experienced positive outcomes in other treatment approaches (McMain et al., 2007). As with the other diagnoses we discuss in this book, you will need to consider the available treatment modalities and the needs of your clients before adapting or adopting DBT in your practice.

ADAPTATIONS FROM STANDARD DBT FOR SUBSTANCE USE DISORDERS

Researchers have adapted many of the traditional DBT skills to address SUDs (McMain et al., 2007). They have also included a few new skills that you will notice are similar to those used in other treatments for substance use. Harvey and Rathbone (2013) suggested an emphasis on distress tolerance skills, as adolescents who engage in substance use might struggle most with impulsivity and the inability to regulate intense emotions in the moment. Some of the adapted skills we discuss below are distress tolerance skills, to be used in the moment to fight the urge to use, which can be considered a crisis situation by DBT standards. Therefore, not only are these adapted skills important, but you will likely want to spend extra time emphasizing all of the distress tolerance skills and communicate how helpful they can be in maintaining sobriety.

Clear Mind, Clean Mind, and Addict Mind

In DBT for substance use, there are three additional states of mind—*clear mind*, *clean mind*, and *addict mind* (McMain et al., 2007). See Figure 11.1 for a depiction of these three states of mind, and Handout 11.1. Addict mind represents the state of mind the adolescents are in when they are actively using substances—their thoughts and behaviors are consumed by their substance use. Conversely, the clean mind is the state of mind clients are in immediately after they have stopped using the substance. Though they are sober, they are also in a sort of "honeymoon" phase that often occurs immediately upon becoming sober—their thoughts and behaviors are so consumed with their elation at achieving sobriety, that they may not be aware of the challenges they will face when working to maintain sobriety. However, the clear mind is the dialectic of the addict and the clean mind. When clients are in clear mind, they are aware of any potential pitfalls that they may face in maintaining sobriety, and use newly attained skills to manage their emotions effectively. Similar to the states of mind in standard DBT (emotion mind, reasonable mind, and wise mind; see Chapter 1), adolescents can attain clear mind by using mindfulness skills.

Dialectical Abstinence

This concept is also included in the adaption of DBT for eating disorders (see Chapter 9). The idea is for adolescents to make an intentional commitment to not use

---

ADDICT MIND → CLEAN MIND → CLEAR MIND

Addict Mind: singularly focused on using. Thoughts and behaviors are all geared towards using or preparing to use. Impulsive.

Clean Mind: not using but not well. Naïve to potential dangerous situations, prone to high risks, and open to falling back into using behaviors. Believes self to be safe and invincible to future problems.

Clear Mind: both clean and aware of the potential for relapse. Safeguards the self from potential people, places, and things that might trigger old behaviors. Sets up a support system to help with cravings.

Figure 11.1 Clear Mind, Clean Mind, Addict Mind

substances ever again. However, they simultaneously also commit to reducing substance use when it does happen (see Handout 9.1). Obviously, the dialectic here is committing to not using at all, *and* committing to reducing use when it happens. This is an important commitment—adolescents who have identified substance use as a problem behavior must make a commitment to themselves and to others that they will no longer engage in this behavior. However, often when adolescents experience a "slip" and use a substance after committing to sobriety, they experience guilt and shame, and corresponding negative thoughts. They may then completely give in to their urges to use and fully relapse. By committing to a reduction of use if/when this does happen, the adolescent can plan ahead to use effective coping skills in the moment, and hopefully will then continue to make progress towards treatment goals. Usually a sports metaphor is good for helping adolescents understand this concept—McMain et al. (2007) use the example of when a runner sets out to run a race. The runner is absolutely committed to winning that race; however, in the event it becomes clear that she is not going to win, she commits to doing the best that she can, and perhaps getting second or third place, as opposed to completely giving up and dropping out of the race.

Urge Surfing

This skill is common in other interventions for SUDs. When the adolescent experiences an urge to use, he or she is encouraged to experience the desire to use, and be aware of it, but then use skills until that urge has passed—they can use mindfulness skills to envision themselves "riding" the urge like a surfer riding a wave (see Handout 9.3). This then will give the adolescent the time to use distress tolerance skills to control thoughts and emotions until the urge has passed, and remove him or herself from the situation, if needed. For example, adolescents can remind themselves that they have the choice of using later, if they wish, which can help them feel more in control while not giving in to the urge (McMain et al., 2007).

Apparently Irrelevant Behaviors

This is not necessarily a technique, but more like the coping ahead emotion regulation skill in standard DBT. Basically, the client works to identify apparently irrelevant behaviors (AIBs) that can ultimately lead to substance use (see Handout 11.2). For example, an AIB could be giving an old friend (who uses, and is likely to offer him or her the opportunity to use as well) a ride home, or, simply not getting enough sleep (which leads to the client feeling distressed and therefore more likely to use). The hallmark of an AIB is that it is a behavior that at the time seems unimportant, but it can (and frequently does) actually lead to relapse. AIBs are often identified through completing a behavior chain after the client has used a substance, but they also can be identified via diary cards, and by noticing emotional patterns and related activities throughout the week. For example, if the client is reviewing the diary card and notices she always experiences an urge to use on Wednesdays, she may realize that every Wednesday she goes to the music store she spent time in a lot when she was high. Though this behavior did not seem like something that would be harmful, the adolescent can then problem solve to identify an alternative activity on that day (McMain et al., 2007).

Alternate Rebellion

This technique is also taught to clients who struggle with eating disorders. Adolescents naturally engage in rebellion against authority, and this skill focuses on the idea that substance use can be a form of rebellion (see Handout 9.5). When you teach adolescents this technique, you are teaching them to rebel in an alternative, less harmful way. Again focusing on the dialectic—you can validate the desire to rebel, while problem-solving for change in reducing substance use. Some examples of alternate rebellion activities may include changing hair color, or dressing in outlandish clothing. The activity may vary based on what specifically the adolescent wishes to rebel against, but regardless the goal is to help the client feel satisfied in rebelling while also not being harmful to him or herself or others (McMain et al., 2007).

Burning Bridges and Building New Ones

Similar to urge surfing, this technique is common in many SUD treatment approaches. The name of the skill is actually a metaphor for intentionally ending relationships with people who facilitated the adolescent's substance use. You can work collaboratively with your client to "burn" bridges to the past—for example, deleting his or her dealer's phone number, and telling the dealer not to call. Then, you can work together to help your client "build" new bridges to the future—for example, making new, sober friends and creating new activities and hobbies. By simultaneously engaging in both of these exercises, he or she can increase the chances of maintaining sobriety (McMain et al., 2007). You can have fun being creative with this idea—engage your clients in a mindfulness exercise where they envision themselves actually burning these bridges, or have them draw a picture of what the metaphor means to them. In a safe, supervised, and controlled atmosphere, they could even find things that represent their old lifestyle and actually burn them as a symbolic gesture of closing off any routes to their old lifestyle (see Handouts 9.2 and 11.3).

Adaptive Denial

Adaptive denial is a skill that involves helping the adolescent change his or her thoughts about substance use (see Handout 11.4). The clients work to convince themselves that they do not really want to use substances, and instead, reframe thoughts to convince themselves that they actually wish to engage in some other activity (thus, denial). This is another strategy to help your clients get through the moment when they experience an urge to use. You will want to help your client decide on the alternative activity beforehand, and it should be something the adolescent enjoys doing, so he or she will be positively reinforced. This could include playing sports, spending time with sober friends, going to the movies, or playing a video game (McMain et al., 2007).

ADDITIONAL TREATMENT TEAM MEMBERS AND ROLES

In addition to the traditional treatment team members, there may be a few additional ancillary treatment team members for adolescents with SUDs. Your clients may (or may not) find a 12-step program helpful, and therefore they may have a sponsor that they seek out for guidance and assistance in maintaining sobriety. Ideally, this sponsor will be aware of your client's contingency plans, and the premise of DBT, so when your client does turn to him or her for guidance, the sponsor can respond and guide your client in a manner aligned with DBT principles. Though many adolescents who struggle with SUDs do not have any legal problems, a large amount find themselves in treatment as a direct consequence of their legal troubles. As a result, another common treatment team member is a probation officer, who is assigned to your client to monitor him or her, ensure compliance with probation requirements, and possibly administer drug tests. By seeking a release of information for your client's probation officer, you can communicate with this individual to make sure your goals are aligned, and then the probation officer can contact you if any issues arise, so you can work together to find the best outcome for the client.

ADDITIONAL TREATMENT MODES

12-Step Support Groups

As aforementioned, support groups similar to or including Alcoholics Anonymous and Narcotics Anonymous may be helpful for your clients. Though the majority of these groups are for adults, many cities have a group or two geared towards adolescents. Though 12-step programs are not for everyone, for many they can be an extremely helpful venue of support to maintain sobriety.

Parenting/Family Skills Groups

Some researchers have suggested separate parent and family skills groups when working with adolescents who struggle with SUDs (Harvey & Rathbone, 2013). They also encourage parents to have their own skills coach. This can help validate parents as well as help them develop skills and ideas to reinforce positive behaviors. Further, they discussed the fact that although some parents do decide to use drug testing to manage and measure drug use, they have found it far more effective to focus on reinforcing the adolescent for sobriety and positive behaviors, than focus on drug testing and punishments. See Handout 4.14 for information on this topic.

Treatment Targets

See Table 11.1 for examples of hierarchical treatment targets when treating SUDs. In most substance use treatments, the goal is for the client to attain abstinence. However, with adolescents this expectation may simply be unreasonable. Instead, you may need to focus on harm reduction, and reduction of substance use, while simultaneously working to commit your client to completely abstain from drug use. When your client refuses to work on reducing or ceasing drug use, you instead can focus on quality-of-life- and therapy-interfering behaviors that the adolescent will agree to work on, and then try to connect those behaviors to drug use as appropriate (Harvey & Rathbone, 2013).

Table 11.1 Adapted Treatment Targets for Treating Clients With SUDs

Treatment Targets	Examples
Primary Treatment Targets	
Life-Threatening Behaviors	Urges, thoughts, or behaviors that harm self or others Substance use that has been deemed life threatening by a medical doctor
Therapy-Interfering Behaviors	Not completing homework Arriving late to session Attending session under the influence of substances, or not attending session because of substance use **Parents:** Not providing transportation to treatment Not attending treatment Not engaging in or attempting to practice skills
Quality-of-Life-Interfering Behaviors	Substance use Urges to use substances Behaviors surrounding substance use Symptoms of withdrawal associated with abstinence
Increasing Behavioral Skills	Mindfulness Emotion Regulation Interpersonal Effectiveness Distress Tolerance (Urge Surfing, Adaptive Denial) Walking the Middle Path Burning Bridges and Building New Ones Alternate Rebellion Dialectical Abstinence
Secondary Treatment Targets	
Common Parent/Child Dialectical Dilemmas	
Excessive leniency vs. authoritarian control	Parents ignoring outright substance use behaviors, then suddenly grounding the adolescent for 6 months.

Treatment Targets	Examples
Normalizing pathological behaviors vs. pathologizing normative behaviors	Vacillating between treating frequent and serious substance use as normal, and treating other typical adolescent developmental behaviors as pathological (e.g., staying out past curfew).
Forcing autonomy vs. fostering dependence	Expecting the adolescent to cease substance use with little to no guidance vs. taking over and making all decisions for the adolescent.

SAMPLE GROUP SESSION FORMAT

There are many different ways to implement skills groups, and you will want to adapt your delivery based on the needs of your clients. The sample group session format in Table 11.2 presents all five traditional DBT modules (Rathus & Miller, 2015) in a six-week format, with the mindfulness module that includes the substance use specific skills and psychoeducation on substance use. These skills can be taught to adolescents and parents/family members in a multifamily group format, or to a group of only adolescents. Each session should last about one and a half to two hours, with the first half focused on review and homework, and the second half focused on new skills. Mindfulness practice should be conducted at least once per session (see Handout 4.2). Though the skills adapted for SUDs are mainly taught in the mindfulness and distress tolerance modules, you may wish to incorporate them into each of the modules, especially if you have a lot of new participants starting at the beginning of a new module.

OUTCOME EVALUATION

One of the most important things you will consider is how to evaluate the success of your program. Though we provide a few suggestions here, remember to focus specifically on the goals of your program, and then identify methods of assessment that align accordingly.

Urine Screens

Urine screens are a very common method of evaluation in substance use treatments, and Rizvi, Monroe-DeVita, and Dimeff (2007) suggest using random urine screens to evaluate the success of your program. Though this may not be helpful for all substances, it may be worth considering, if it is a reasonable option for your site. However, remember Harvey and Rathbone (2013) encourage the use of positive reinforcement of sobriety, and believe that can be more effective than focusing on urine screens, so you should also keep this in mind.

Table 11.2 Sample Skills Module Format

Module/Session	Skills, Activities, and Handouts
Mindfulness: Module 1	
Session 1	Orientation to DBT and Skills Training Group Rules Biosocial Theory of Emotion Dysregulation Education on Substance Use and Adolescent Brain Development Dialectical Abstinence
Session 2	Reasonable, Emotion, and Wise Mind Addict, Clean, and Clear Mind
Session 3	Mindfulness Practice—What Is Mindfulness? Mindfulness What Skills (Observe, Describe, Participate)
Session 4	Mindfulness How Skills (One-Mindfully Effectively, Nonjudgmentally)
Session 5	Burning Bridges and Building New Ones
Session 6	Apparently Irrelevant Behaviors Alternate Rebellion
Distress Tolerance: Module 2	
Session 1	Review of Group Rules and DBT Skills Training, the Biosocial Theory, and Substance Use and Adolescent Development as needed Introduction to Distress Tolerance and Substance Use
Session 2	Urge Surfing Adaptive Denial
Session 3	Distract With Wise Mind ACCEPTS, Self Soothe With the Six Senses
Session 4	IMPROVE the Moment
Session 5	Pros and Cons, TIPP
Session 6	Acceptance Skills, Willingness, and Willfulness
Walking the Middle Path: Module 3	
Session 1	Review of Group Rules and DBT Skills Training, the Biosocial Theory, and Substance Use and Adolescent Development as needed Introduction to the Walking the Middle Path Module
Session 2	Dialectics
Session 3	Dialectical Dilemmas (as related to substance use)
Session 4	Validation
Session 5	Behaviorism
Session 6	Problem-Solving and Behavior Chain Analysis

Module/Session	Skills, Activities, and Handouts
Emotion Regulation: Module 4	
Session 1	Review of Group Rules and DBT Skills Training, the Biosocial Theory, and Substance Use and Adolescent Development as needed Introduction to Emotion Regulation for SUDs
Session 2	ABC—Accumulating positive experiences, Build mastery, Cope ahead (Apparently Irrelevant Behaviors)
Session 3	PLEASE—treat Physical illness, balance Eating, Avoid drugs, balance Sleep, get Exercise
Session 4	Mindfulness of Current Emotions
Session 5	Check the Facts
Session 6	Opposite Action
Interpersonal Effectiveness: Module 5	
Session 1	Review of Group Rules and DBT Skills Training, the Biosocial Theory, and Substance Use and Adolescent Development as needed Introduction to Interpersonal Effectiveness
Session 2	GIVE—Gentle, Interested, Validate, Easy manner
Session 3	DEAR MAN—Describe, Express, Assert, Reinforce, be Mindful, Appear confident, Negotiate
Session 4	FAST—be Fair, no Apologies, Stick to values, be Truthful
Session 5	Factors to consider when asking for something or saying no
Session 6	THINK—Think, Have empathy, Interpretations, Notice, Kindness

Diary Cards

See Handout 1.3 for a diary card that is tailored for adolescents who struggle with substance use. As with all DBT interventions, the diary card is an extremely important tool for keeping track of problem behaviors, and skills use. By aggregating this data, you will be able to get a clear picture of how successful your program is at meeting treatment targets.

Adolescent Substance Abuse Subtle Screening Inventory—Adolescent

The Substance Abuse Subtle Screening Inventory—Adolescent (ASSI-A2; Lazowski, Miller, Boye, & Miller, 1998) was designed to screen for the presence of a substance use disorder in adolescents. It has several subscales, includes questions that can identify whether the adolescent is responding in a defensive manner, and also has questions that do not seem directly related to substance use to help identify when your client may not be being completely truthful. Though there is a cost to administer this test, it may be worth it to have a formalized psychometric assessment to use to assess the presence of substance use.

CHALLENGES AND SOLUTIONS

We have emphasized commitment strategies several times in other chapters, and I know you are probably tired of hearing about it (see Chapter 2 to review DBT commitment strategies). However, they really can be paramount when specifically targeting substance use with adolescents. This is mainly because the majority of adolescents do not believe their substance use is a problem, and therefore have no desire to stop using. You can use commitment strategies, in addition to motivational interviewing and assessment of the stages of change, to help the client gain insight into the problems substance use may be causing them (Dietz & Dunn, 2014).

Relapse is common for individuals who struggle with SUDs. By focusing on dialectical abstinence and distress tolerance skills, your client will learn to work through urges to use to decrease and then eliminate relapse. However, relapse can be disheartening for you and your client, especially after a sustained period of sobriety. When this happens, you will need to work together to remember that relapse is part of the process, and that the client cannot "fail" DBT treatment. In addition, by using your dialectical strategies (see Chapter 2) you can help the client "make lemonade out of lemons" and use the relapse as an opportunity to increase his or her ability to use skills.

KEY POINTS TO CONSIDER/CONCLUSIONS

As we mentioned in the beginning, though DBT for SUDs is a promising approach, there still is not a lot of research on it. As result, you'll want to be intentional about how you implement it—either in addition to another, evidence-based approach, or when other approaches have been unsuccessful. DBT is flexible enough that you can adapt it in many ways, and this may include just implementing specific skills that you think will work best for your clients. Regardless, you will need to focus on your commitment strategies to help your client see how his or her substance use is keeping him or her from living a life worth living.

REFERENCES

Bukstein, O. G. & Horner, M. S. (2010). Management of the adolescent with substance use disorders and comorbid psychopathology. *Child and Adolescent Psychiatric Clinics of North America*, *19*(3), 609–623. doi:10.1016/j.chc.2010.03.011

Chan, Y., Dennis, M. L., & Funk, R. R. (2008). Prevalence and comorbidity of major internalizing and externalizing problems among adolescents and adults presenting to substance abuse treatment. *Journal of Substance Abuse Treatment*, *34*(1), 14–24. doi:10.1016/j.jsat.2006.12.031

Dietz, A. R. & Dunn, M. E. (2014). The use of motivational interviewing in conjunction with adapted dialectical behavior therapy to treat synthetic cannabis use disorder. *Clinical Case Studies*, *13*(6), 455–471. doi:10.1177/1534650114521496

Harvey, P. & Rathbone, B. H. (2013). *Dialectical behavior therapy for at-risk adolescents: A practitioner's guide to treating challenging behavior problems*. Oakland, CA: New Harbinger Publications.

Lazowski, L. E., Miller, F. G., Boye, M. W., & Miller, G. A. (1998). Efficacy of the Substance Abuse Subtle Screening Inventory-3 (SASSI-3) in identifying substance dependence disorders in clinical settings. *Journal of Personality Assessment*, *71*(1), 114–128. doi:10.1207/s15327752jpa7101_8

Linehan, M. M., Schmidt, H. I., Dimeff, L. A., Craft, J. C., Kanter, J., & Comtois, K. A. (1999). Dialectical behavior therapy for patients with borderline personality disorder and drug-dependence. *The American Journal on Addictions*, *8*(4), 279–292. doi:10.1080/105504999305686

McMain, S., Sayrs, J. R., Dimeff, L. A., & Linehan, M. M. (2007). Dialectical behavior therapy for individuals with borderline personality disorder and substance dependence. In L. A. Dimeff & K. Koerner (Eds.), *Dialectical behavior therapy in clinical practice: Applications across disorders and settings* (pp. 145–173). New York, NY: Guilford Press.

Rathus, J. H. & Miller, A. L. (2015). *DBT® skills manual for adolescents*. New York, NY: Guilford Press.

Rizvi, S. L., Monroe-DeVita, M., & Dimeff, L. A. (2007). Evaluating your dialectical behavior therapy program. In L. A. Dimeff & K. Koerner (Eds.), *Dialectical behavior therapy in clinical practice: Applications across disorders and settings* (pp. 326–350). New York, NY: Guilford Press.

12

Other Diagnoses for Consideration
K. Michelle Hunnicutt Hollenbaugh

In this chapter we are going to touch on a few other diagnoses that have some existing research with DBT. These diagnoses include bipolar disorder, major depressive disorder, and anxiety disorders, including post-traumatic stress disorder (PTSD). The current research on using DBT with these diagnoses is preliminary, but promising. Research has shown that DBT treatment can help clients decrease symptoms of anxiety and depression, and increase their use of positive coping skills (Neacsiu, Eberle, Kramer, Wiesmann, & Linhean, 2014; Cook & Gorraiz, 2016). Another pilot study demonstrated that DBT adapted for adolescents with bipolar disorder significantly increased positive outcomes in comparison to treatment as usual (Goldstein et al., 2015). Finally, several studies support the use of DBT with clients struggling with anxiety disorders, including PTSD (Harned & Linehan, 2008; Bohus et al., 2013). Though we will not go as in depth on each of these diagnoses as we have on topics in other chapters, we will share possible applications of DBT for these disorders, and how you might use these adaptations in your practice.

CONSIDERATIONS BEFORE IMPLEMENTING DBT

As in previous chapters in the text, DBT is often utilized as an adjunct to other evidence-based treatments, or is implemented when the client has not responded well to other treatments. Due to the vast array of symptoms clients might present due to these disorders, it will be important to tailor skills for the individual client. Though we will only discuss a few adaptations of DBT for these disorders, remember that DBT is a flexible treatment, and all aspects of the treatment can be adapted to intentionally address treatment targets related to emotion dysregulation.

ADAPTATIONS FOR ANXIETY

Treatment targets for anxiety should be behaviors that the client can control—for example, panic attacks might not be a treatment target, but things the client can control that lead up to the panic attack may be—for example, worry thoughts or catastrophizing. See Table 12.1 for a list of examples of treatment targets related to symptoms of anxiety. When choosing skills to use with clients who struggle with

Table 12.1 DBT Treatment Targets and Hierarchy for Anxiety Disorders

Treatment Targets	Examples
Primary Treatment Targets	
Life-Threatening Behaviors	Harm to self or others Urges, plans, threats, or thoughts to harm self or others
Therapy-Interfering Behaviors	Not completing diary card or homework Arriving late to session Not attending session Being willful
	Parents: Not providing transportation to treatment Not attending treatment Not engaging in or attempting to practice skills
Quality-of-Life-Interfering Behaviors	Worry thoughts Experiential avoidance Catastrophizing Judgmental thoughts
Increasing Behavioral Skills	Mindfulness/Relaxation Interpersonal Effectiveness Emotion Regulation Distress Tolerance Walking the Middle Path

anxiety, be aware of skills that may trigger panic attacks or even flashbacks for clients who struggle with PTSD (e.g., mindfulness exercises).

Mindfulness of Worry Thoughts

By utilizing the "what" and "how" skills in DBT mindfulness, clients can be aware of their anxiety in the moment—this includes awareness of their thoughts and beliefs, as well as any physical sensations that might communicate to them they are beginning to experience anxiety (Gratz, Tull, & Wagner, 2005). For many clients, worry thoughts are automatic, and they are not aware they are having them. By using mindfulness, your clients can be present in the moment, and then be aware of when they are experiencing worry thoughts. This can be helpful not only in analyzing those thoughts ("Do I really have something to worry about right now?") but also noticing the other sensations they are experiencing when they are having those thoughts—including emotional reactions and physical sensations.

Cope Ahead for Panic Attacks

We have mentioned this skill in previous chapters, as it is flexible and easy to adapt for target behaviors. By teaching your clients how to cope ahead for panic attacks, they can identify situations in which they foresee experiencing anxiety, identify specific skills they will use in that situation to manage that anxiety, and then use imagery to picture themselves using skills in the situation (see Handout 4.9). You will want to be sure the client has a foundation in skills use and managing worry thoughts before having him or her practice this skill. Mindfulness exercises before, during, and after this exercise may be necessary, as imagining the situation can be anxiety inducing in itself.

Acting Opposite of Anxiety

This skill can be a helpful way for your clients to face anxiety-inducing situations; however the client needs to be able to objectively think about the cause of the anxiety, and decide whether it is warranted or not (see Handout 4.8). Linehan (2015) discusses acting opposite of fear, and the same behaviors can be applicable for anxiety. To act opposite to anxiety, the client will face the situation he or she has anxiety about, instead of avoiding. He or she can do this while using other distress tolerance and mindfulness skills, including check the facts, and observe, describe, and participate skills.

Mindfulness of Others for Interpersonal Effectiveness

Adolescents who struggle with anxiety in social situations may become so focused on themselves and their anxiety that they have difficulty with relationships—they may have trouble making friends or standing up for themselves. By focusing on others, they can actually decrease their personal anxiety, and act more effectively in the moment (see Handout 5.2). I once worked with an adolescent who would become so anxious in social situations that when he started talking, he wouldn't know when to stop. As result, he often either said things he didn't mean to say, or his peers would stop listening to him. By working on being mindful of others, instead of focusing on his anxiety in the moment, he focused on the person he was talking to, and how they were responding to him. We focused on facial expressions and body language. As result, he was able to manage his anxiety, speak less, and listen more.

Walking the Middle Path—Validation of Self

Adolescents who struggle with anxiety may think negative thoughts about themselves related to their anxiety—they may be judging themselves, or believe (correctly or incorrectly) that others are judging them. By working with your clients to help them validate themselves, they can decrease judgmental thoughts and increase their ability to cope with anxiety (see Handouts 4.12 and 4.13). They can do this by identifying the negative thoughts they have about themselves, or believe others are having about them. Then they can challenge them with validating statements. If your clients have difficulty with this, remind them of the validating statements they make towards other group members, or their friends. They can then practice transferring those validating statements to themselves.

Adaptations Related to PTSD

Though we have not developed any handouts related to this adaptation, we believe it is important to note that there has been research conducted related to treating PTSD in the context of DBT. This adaptation integrates exposure-based treatments, and is called DBT-Prolonged Exposure (DBT-PE; Becker & Zayfert, 2001; Harned & Linehan, 2008; Bohus et al., 2013; Welch, Osborne, & Pryzgoda, 2010). There are three levels of PTSD-PE. Level 1 includes teaching psychoeducational skills from DBT to increase the client's coping skills during exposure therapy. Level 2 includes skills and DBT-based strategies—for example, validation and dialectical strategies used by the clinician to increase commitment. Level 3 is the full implementation of DBT, with the inclusion of exposure-based treatment when life-threatening and therapy-interfering treatment targets have been achieved (Welch et al., 2010). All three of these adaptations are based on assessment of the specific needs of the client, including frequency and severity of symptoms. For example, level 1 clients may be able to use emotion regulation and distress tolerance to be aware of and cope with emotions during exposure activities. In level 2, clinicians might incorporate treatment targets and commitment strategies for clients who are engaging in therapy-interfering behaviors, or have more severe symptoms that must be addressed. Level 3 would likely be reserved for clients who engage in life-threatening behaviors and experience severe emotion dysregulation.

PTSD is considered a stage two treatment target in DBT, and therefore you will want to be sure you have addressed any life-threatening and therapy-interfering behaviors before moving on to address symptoms of PTSD. There are several adaptations to standard DBT in DBT-PE, including increased commitment to treatment, regular assessment of life-threatening behaviors, and the introduction of exposure activities at a slower pace, with a higher level of involvement by the therapist (Harned & Linehan, 2008). Remember research on DBT with PTSD is preliminary, and therefore another evidence-based treatment may be a better fit for your population, for example, Trauma-Focused Cognitive-Behavioral Therapy (Cohen, Mannarino, Berliner, & Deblinger, 2000). You can also consider using aspects of DBT in conjunction with another approach.

ADAPTATIONS FOR DEPRESSION

Symptoms of depression are highly correlated with suicidal and self-harm behaviors. Unfortunately, there is very little published literature on specifically working with adolescents struggling with depression. This may be due to the fact that there are several evidence-based treatments for childhood depression already in place (Chorpita et al., 2011). However, the majority of these treatments are based in CBT, an approach that is also included throughout the DBT skills modules. In addition, like other adaptations, DBT may be helpful for adolescents who have already tried other types of treatment, and not experienced significant positive treatment outcomes. See Table 12.2 for some examples of DBT treatment targets for adolescents who struggle with depression.

Table 12.2 DBT Treatment Targets and Hierarchy for Depression

Treatment Targets	Examples
Primary Treatment Targets	
Life-Threatening Behaviors	Self-injury Thoughts/urges to self injure Suicide attempts/thoughts/plans/urges Thoughts of hurting others
Therapy-Interfering Behaviors	Not reporting quality-of-life- or life-threatening behaviors to the counselor Not completing diary card or homework Arriving late to session Not attending session
	Parents: Not providing transportation to treatment Not attending treatment Not engaging in or attempting to practice skills
Quality-of-Life-Interfering Behaviors	Sleeping/staying in bed too much Isolating Irritability/anger outbursts Substance use Impulsive behaviors Eating too much or too little Academic problems Behavioral problems
Increasing Behavioral Skills	Mindfulness Interpersonal Effectiveness Emotion Regulation Distress Tolerance Walking the Middle Path

Loving Kindness

Linehan (2015) included the loving kindness mindfulness exercise as a way for the clients to share love with themselves or with others. This exercise can be particularly helpful for adolescents who struggle with depression by having them share loving kindness with themselves. This exercise consists of cognitively sending kind messages to yourself—much like self-validation, only this takes a step further because it is not just validating, but sending love and positivity. Though your clients may find this difficult at first, and may become distracted, you should encourage them to continue to practice until they can engage in this exercise with relative ease.

Acting Opposite to Symptoms of Depression

We have discussed this skill frequently in this book because it is easily adapted, and can be applied to any emotion your client struggles with. For adolescents who struggle with depression, it can also be applied to other symptoms related to major depressive disorder (see Handout 4.8). For example, in addition to acting opposite to depression and sadness by watching funny movies, or engaging in activities that make the client feel happy or competent, he or she can also act opposite to anhedonia by getting involved and participating in activities, to fatigue by being active and getting out of the house to engage in activities, and to guilt by using self-validation (see Handout 4.13). One of the best ways to identify what an opposite action will be for the client is having the adolescent identify what he wants to do—for example, go to bed and stay in bed all day—and then think of the exact opposite of that, which can be extreme, and at times humorous—for example, going out and running a marathon. You can then work together to find an activity that is within reason, and the client is willing to do—like taking a walk. This approach not only helps the client act opposite to depression, but by identifying something extreme and ridiculous, you have used the door-in-the-face commitment strategy, so the client is more likely to be willing to take a walk after comparing it to running a marathon (Linehan, 2015).

ADAPTATIONS FOR BIPOLAR DISORDER

Though DBT is not typically considered for the treatment of Bipolar Disorder (BD), researchers posit that BD is directly related to emotion dysregulation (Goldstein et al., 2015). In addition, the risk of suicide in adolescents struggling with BD is high, with up to 75% endorsing suicidal ideations (Goldstein et al., 2005). Researchers also cite the fact that there is a paucity of research and implementation of BD treatments specifically for adolescents, and treatment approaches and goals in DBT align well to address emotion dysregulation, suicidality, treatment compliance, and interpersonal deficits (Miklowitz & Goldstein, 2010). Some researchers have adapted DBT for BD by teaching skills in individual family sessions, and by extending the length of treatment to one year to allow for generalization of skills over the course of mood cycles (Goldstein, Axelson, Birmaher, & Brent, 2007). They also shortened the length of the group sessions to one hour, citing experiences with adolescents with BD having difficulty concentrating for longer periods of time. See Table 12.3 for examples of treatment targets for clients who struggle with BD.

Goldstein and colleagues (2007) highlighted the importance of individualizing skills to specific mood states—this is simply due to the fact some skills may be more helpful when the client is feeling depressed as opposed to manic. This important distinction will help clients focus on which skills will work best for them, and which may not be helpful. For example, when the adolescent is feeling depressed, he or she may wish to focus on "acting opposite" to his or her emotion as an emotion regulation skill. However, this may not be appropriate if the client is cycling into an elevated mood, and therefore he or she may choose an *observe* or *describe* mindfulness skill to increase awareness and manage emotions instead.

Table 12.3 DBT Treatment Targets and Hierarchy for Bipolar Disorder

Treatment Targets	Examples
Primary Treatment Targets	
Life-Threatening Behaviors	Self-injury Thoughts/urges to self injure Suicide attempts/thoughts/plans/urges Thoughts of hurting others
Therapy-Interfering Behaviors	Not reporting quality-of-life- or life-threatening behaviors to the counselor Not completing diary card or homework Arriving late to session Not attending session Angry or irritable mood Argumentative or defiant behavior Not taking medication as prescribed (or not taking it at all) **Parents:** Not providing transportation to treatment Not attending treatment Not engaging in or attempting to practice skills
Quality-of-Life-Interfering Behaviors	Substance use (see also: Chapter 11) Stealing Risky sex Academic issues
Increasing Behavioral Skills	Mindfulness Interpersonal Effectiveness Emotion Regulation Distress Tolerance Walking the Middle Path

Mindfulness States of Mind—Manic Mind and Depressed Mind

Skills trainers not only discussed the reasonable mind, wise mind, and emotion mind, but they focused on the different types of emotion mind the adolescent might experience as related to BD—for example, mania and depression (Miklowitz & Goldstein, 2010). While reviewing each state of mind, adolescents can discuss their thoughts and emotions during different mood cycles—for example, negative and suicidal thoughts in depressed mind, and grandiose and racing thoughts in manic mind. They can also identify any warning signs to when one of these moods may occur, and discuss the mindfulness activities they can use during these mood states to manage emotions and act skillfully to keep from engaging in problem behaviors.

Mindfulness of Emotions

In alignment with the manic and depressed states of mind, the mindfulness of current emotions skill can be adapted specifically for adolescents who struggle with BD. This skill can be used in the moment to help adolescents notice all aspects of their emotional state—including physical sensations, thoughts related to their emotions, and also how other people are receiving them. For example, if the adolescent uses this skill and is aware of being happy, he or she may not recognize any other warning signs in his or her thoughts or sensations. However, being aware of how other people are reacting to him or her can help tell the adolescent if he or she is, in fact, cycling into a manic episode (for example, if peers seem overwhelmed or confused during conversations, or shocked by behaviors). Being mindful of all these things in the moment can help the adolescent be aware of where he or she is with regard to mood cycling, and then choose skills as needed to manage emotions and seek support.

Radical Acceptance

Radical acceptance may also be a helpful skill to tailor specifically for adolescents with BD (see Handout 4.10). Not only would this include practicing acceptance of the fact they are struggling with increased challenges related to their diagnosis, but also with regard to medication compliance. Adolescents (and adults) are often resistant to psychotropic medication to manage BD, due to the side effects that often come along with mood stabilizers. As result, it is essential to focus on the importance of medication compliance, and this can be done by helping adolescents radically accept medication as an aspect of BD. They can acknowledge that accepting it does not mean they approve of it, like it, or that they do not have the option to work to change it (for example, by working with their psychiatrist to find a medication that is tolerable).

OUTCOME EVALUATION

Though many assessments mentioned in previous sections can be applicable for working with these diagnoses, you may also wish to consider assessments specific to the treatment targets and symptoms you wish to reduce. A few of those options are listed here.

Youth Outcome Questionnaire 2.10 and SR 2.0

The Youth Outcome Questionnaire (Y-OQ) 2.10 and SR 2.0 (Wells, Burlingame, Lambert, Hoag, & Hope, 1996) are both flexible instruments that can be used together—the Y-OQ 2.10 is completed by the parent, and the Y-OQ SR (self-report) is completed by the adolescent. These instruments have six scales—intrapersonal distress, somatic, interpersonal relationships, social problems, behavioral dysfunction, and a critical items scale. Both have 64 Likert-scaled questions. The Y-OQ is popular and clinicians use it frequently to measure outcomes in outpatient settings, so this may be a good choice if you wish to measure a few different symptoms.

The Beck Depression Inventory and the Beck Anxiety Inventory

The Beck Depression Inventory (BDI; Beck, Steer, & Brown, 1996) and Beck Anxiety Inventory (BAI; Beck & Steer, 1993) are both popular instruments because they are short, fairly inexpensive, easy to administer, and very straightforward. There is a lot of research behind these instruments so they may also be a solid choice for you if you are looking to measure either depression or anxiety (or both). These instruments are short enough that you could administer them frequently to track progress—perhaps monthly or weekly depending on the severity of your client's symptoms and the intensity of your treatment.

CHALLENGES AND SOLUTIONS

Adolescents who struggle with these disorders will present with a variety of different challenges, and this will depend on your setting and the population you choose to work with. In general, we recommend that you spend a lot of time assessing the severity of the client's symptoms before deciding how to implement DBT and which skills might be most useful for that client. For example, clients with very severe depression may have a difficult time with the acting opposite skill in the beginning, while other clients with less severe symptoms may find it extremely helpful. Therefore, you will likely need to tailor the skills you teach to each individual client, which may be time consuming, but will increase positive treatment outcomes.

KEY POINTS TO CONSIDER/CONCLUSIONS

DBT can be a great tool for you to use when working with adolescents struggling with these disorders, but likely should be implemented in conjunction with other evidence-based treatments. As with the other adaptations of DBT, family involvement can be extremely helpful, and possibly necessary, depending on the severity of the client's disorder. This may be especially true for clients who struggle with bipolar disorder, as parents may need help identifying problem behaviors and helping the client use skills to manage extreme emotions during depressive and manic episodes. Regardless, a dialectical approach of validation and change can help these adolescents effectively regulate their emotions.

REFERENCES

Beck, A. T. & Steer, R. A. (1993). *Beck anxiety inventory manual*. San Antonio, TX: Psychological Corporation.

Beck, A. T., Steer, R. A., & Brown, G. K. (1996). *Manual for the Beck depression inventory-II*. San Antonio, TX: Psychological Corporation.

Becker, C. B. & Zayfert, C. (2001). Integrating DBT-based techniques and concepts to facilitate exposure treatment for PTSD. *Cognitive and Behavioral Practice*, 8(2), 107–122. doi:10.1016/S1077-7229(01)80017-1

Bohus, M., Dyer, A. S., Priebe, K., Krüger, A., Kleindienst, N., Schmahl, C., . . . Steil, R. (2013). Dialectical behaviour therapy for post-traumatic stress disorder after childhood sexual abuse in patients with and without borderline personality disorder: A randomised controlled trial. *Psychotherapy and Psychosomatics*, 82(4), 221–233. doi:10.1159/000348451

Chorpita, B. F., Daleiden, E. L., Ebesutani, C., Young, J., Becker, K. D., Nakamura, B. J., . . . Starace, N. (2011). Evidence-based treatments for children and adolescents: An updated review of indicators of efficacy and effectiveness. *Clinical Psychology: Science and Practice*, 18(2), 154–172. doi:10.1111/j.1468-2850.2011.01247.x

Cohen, J. A., Mannarino, A. P., Berliner, L., & Deblinger, E. (2000). Trauma-focused cognitive behavioral therapy for children and adolescents: An empirical update. *Journal of Interpersonal Violence*, 15(11), 1202–1223. doi:10.1177/088626000015011007

Cook, N. E. & Gorraiz, M. (2016). Dialectical behavior therapy for nonsuicidal self-injury and depression among adolescents: Preliminary meta-analytic evidence. *Child and Adolescent Mental Health*, 21(2), 81–89. doi:10.1111/camh.12112

Goldstein, T. R., Axelson, D. A., Birmaher, B., & Brent, D. A. (2007). Dialectical behavior therapy for adolescents with bipolar disorder: A 1-year open trial. *Journal of the American Academy of Child & Adolescent Psychiatry*, 46(7), 820–830. doi:10.1097/chi.0b013e31805c1613

Goldstein, T. R., Birmaher, B., Axelson, D., Ryan, N. D., Strober, M. A., Gill, M. K., . . . Keller, M. (2005). History of suicide attempts in pediatric bipolar disorder: Factors associated with increased risk. *Bipolar Disorders*, 7(6), 525–535. doi:10.1111/j.1399-5618.2005.00263.x

Goldstein, T. R., Fersch-Podrat, R. K., Rivera, M., Axelson, D. A., Merranko, J., Yu, H., & . . . Birmaher, B. (2015). Dialectical behavior therapy for adolescents with bipolar disorder: Results from a pilot randomized trial. *Journal of Child and Adolescent Psychopharmacology*, 25(2), 140–149. doi:10.1089/cap.2013.0145

Gratz, K. L., Tull, M. T., & Wagner, A. W. (2005). Applying DBT mindfulness skills to the treatment of clients with anxiety disorders. In S. M. Orsillo & L. O. Roemer (Eds.), *Acceptance and mindfulness-based approaches to anxiety: Conceptualization and treatment* (pp. 147–161). New York, NY: Springer Science + Business Media. doi:10.1007/0-387-25989-9_6

Harned, M. S. & Linehan, M. M. (2008). Integrating dialectical behavior therapy and prolonged exposure to treat co-occurring borderline personality disorder and PTSD: Two case studies. *Cognitive and Behavioral Practice*, 15(3), 263–276. doi:10.1016/j.cbpra.2007.08.006

Linehan, M. M. (2015). *DBT® skills training manual* (2nd ed.). New York, NY: Guilford Press.

Miklowitz, D. J. & Goldstein, T. R. (2010). Family-based approaches to treating bipolar disorder in adolescence: Family-focused therapy and dialectical behavior therapy. In D. J. Miklowitz & D. Cicchetti (Eds.), *Understanding bipolar disorder: A developmental psychopathology perspective* (pp. 466–493). New York, NY: Guilford Press.

Neacsiu, A. D., Eberle, J. W., Kramer, R., Wiesmann, T., & Linehan, M. M. (2014). Dialectical behavior therapy skills for transdiagnostic emotion dysregulation: A pilot randomized controlled trial. *Behaviour Research and Therapy*, 5940–5951. doi:10.1016/j.brat.2014.05.005

Welch, S. S., Osborne, T. L., & Pryzgoda, J. (2010). Augmenting exposure-based treatment for anxiety disorders with principles and skills from dialectical behavior therapy. In D. Sookman & R. L. Leahy (Eds.), *Treatment resistant anxiety disorders: Resolving impasses to symptom remission* (pp. 161–197). New York, NY: Routledge/Taylor & Francis Group.

Wells, M. G., Burlingame, G. M., Lambert, M. J., Hoag, M. H., Hope, C. A. (1996). Conceptualization and measurement of patient change during psychotherapy: Development of the Outcome Questionnaire and Youth Outcome Questionnaire. *Psychotherapy: Theory, Research, Practice, and Training*, *33*, 275–283.

Comorbid Diagnoses and Life-Threatening Behaviors

K. Michelle Hunnicutt Hollenbaugh

Although comorbid diagnoses and life-threatening behaviors may not seem related, they are both related to a higher level of symptom severity in adolescents, and therefore can both be related to higher risk for chronic mental health problems, and poor treatment outcomes. Our goal in this chapter is to highlight some specific ways to address these severe symptoms via DBT. We will discuss skills coaching in more detail, as well as conducting behavior chain analyses for problem behaviors. We will also discuss treatment planning for adolescents who have more than one diagnosis.

LIFE-THREATENING BEHAVIORS

Life-threatening behaviors are the primary treatment target in DBT. Though life-threatening behaviors can vary based on the diagnosis, the most common include self-harm and suicidal behaviors, thoughts, and urges, and so these are the symptoms we will focus on in this chapter (Miller, Rathus, & Linehan, 2007). Studies have shown that up to half of adolescents in the U.S. may have engaged in non-suicidal self-injury at some point in their lives (Lloyd-Richardson, Perrine, Dierker, & Kelley, 2007; Yates, Tracy, & Luthar, 2008). In addition, suicide has been found to be the number three leading cause of death among adolescents, and up to 8% of adolescents report a previous suicide attempt (Centers for Disease Control and Prevention, National Center for Injury Prevention and Control, 2007) while up to 30% of adolescents diagnosed with depression endorsed having thoughts of suicide within the past year (Avenevoli, Swendsen, He, Burstein, & Merikangas, 2015). Suicide and self-injury are considered two different problem behaviors, because an adolescent engaging in self-injury often is not attempting suicide, and instead trying to manage intense, dysregulated emotions. However, they are highly correlated—adolescents who engage in self-injury are at higher risk for suicide, and up to 60% of individuals who engage in self-injury also have thoughts of suicide (Klonsky, Victor, & Saffer, 2014; Whitlock et al., 2013).

Every facet of DBT is designed to address suicide and self-harm behaviors, which makes it an ideal treatment approach for adolescents who struggle with these symptoms. Specifically, behavior chains help the client problem solve and stop reinforcement of life-threatening behaviors. Intersession skills coaching reinforces the client for using positive coping skills. CBT skills taught during the psychoeducational group sessions help clients distract from intense emotions, and engage in more effective coping strategies. Finally, the clinician utilizes a dialectical approach to commit the client to treatment (Linehan, 1993).

Assessment of Self-Harm and Suicidal Behaviors

There are a few formal assessments that can be helpful to monitor and manage adolescent self-harm and suicide-related behaviors. Though you will definitely want to have the client complete a detailed assessment regarding life-threatening behaviors upon admission, you may also decide to administer them at regular intervals throughout treatment, so that you can track treatment progress.

Diary Cards

We highlight the diary card as an assessment tool in every chapter, and there's a reason for it—the diary card is by far the easiest way for you to track problem behaviors in DBT. We discuss it more in detail in Chapter 4 (see Handouts 1.2–1.5). By having the adolescent complete the diary card weekly, you can keep track of how many self-harm behaviors and/or suicidal thoughts he or she engages in and experiences in each week (and address them via completing a behavior chain analysis, which we discuss later in this chapter). You can then keep track over time, to evaluate whether the frequency of these behaviors and thoughts are decreasing.

Beck Scale of Suicide Ideation

The Beck Scale of Suicide Ideation (BSS; Beck & Steer, 1991) is a short and efficient self-report instrument, with 21 questions that are specifically related to suicidal thoughts and behaviors over the past week. Though this assessment can be easy for you to use and administer frequently, it does not include questions on self-harm behaviors that are unrelated to suicide, and therefore you may need to use another method of evaluation in conjunction with this assessment to gain adequate information on both types of behaviors (for example, the diary card).

Suicide Attempt Self-Injury Interview

The Suicide Attempt Self-Injury Interview (SASII; Linehan, Comtois, Brown, Heard, & Wagner, 2006) is an assessment that covers both suicidal thoughts/attempts and self-harm behaviors. This assessment is in the format of a formal interview, is extremely thorough, and goes through each attempt/self-harm episode in detail on six scales—suicide intent, interpersonal influence, emotion relief, suicide communication, lethality, and rescue likelihood. However, the downfall of this is that it may be time consuming, and therefore may not be suitable for some settings.

Treatment Planning With Life-Threatening Behaviors

As we've mentioned, life-threatening behaviors are always the first treatment target addressed in DBT treatment. However, you may have difficulty identifying whether a behavior is actually considered life threatening. Usually, any thoughts, behaviors, or urges that are not directly related to harming themselves or harming others are considered quality-of-life- or therapy-interfering behaviors (Linehan, 1993). However, depending on what the behavior is, you may decide that it is actually life threatening, and therefore you need to address that behavior first (for example, a pregnant teen who is drinking heavily). This is a decision you can make in collaboration with the adolescent and his or her parents, and you can also seek guidance from your DBT consultation team.

Another challenge you may face is that the adolescent may be unwilling to identify a life-threatening behavior as a treatment goal. However, it is paramount that the adolescent be in agreement regarding which treatment targets you will work towards, otherwise, success will be unlikely. You can use your commitment strategies (Chapter 2), and shaping, to work with the client to attain at least partial commitment. This can include shorter time frames—for example, a commitment not to self-harm until the next counseling session. It can also include agreeing on treatment targets related to the life-threatening behavior—for example, if they are more likely to engage in self-harm when drinking, alcohol use might be an acceptable alternative treatment target. You can then continue to use commitment strategies, and help the adolescent build skills use, until he or she is willing to fully commit to working on the life-threatening behavior.

Behavior Chain Analysis for Life-Threatening Behaviors

We briefly discussed the behavior chain analysis (BCA) in Chapter 2, and we will cover it in more detail here as an essential facet of DBT for addressing life-threatening behaviors. Once you and the client have mutually agreed-upon problem behaviors, and the client is tracking these behaviors regularly via the diary card, then when the problem behavior does occur, the next step is to help the adolescent complete the BCA. At first, this may be an extremely difficult task. Adolescents (and adults) who are not familiar with going through the process of all of the thoughts, feelings, and behaviors that led to a problem behavior may have difficulty identifying all of these factors and how they are related. You will need to walk the client through each step, and help him or her identify these things. See Figure 13.1 for an example of a completed diary card regarding an adolescent's self-harm behaviors, and Handout 1.6 for our version of the BCA. The first step is always identifying and writing down the problem behavior, and the consequences of that behavior. After that, I usually encourage the client to identify any vulnerabilities to the problem behavior—basically, what was going on in the client's life that already made him or her more susceptible to engaging in this behavior? This can be a variety of things, including lack of sleep, stress at school, or some other stressor that the adolescent is having difficulty dealing with

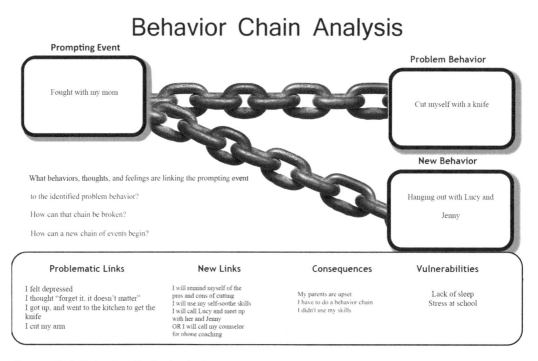

Figure 13.1 Behavior Chain Analysis
Source: Adapted by permission from Linehan, M.M. (2015) *DBT Skills Handouts and Worksheets*. New York: Guilford Press.

emotionally (e.g., a fight with a friend). Then, we try to identify the prompting event. Sometimes, this is easily identifiable—an argument with a parent, or a break-up with a boyfriend or girlfriend. Other times, it may not be a clear, isolated event—and you may have to back up and walk the client step by step through the day. Once you have identified it (a thought, e.g., "I think I'm worthless") then you can walk through all of the other tiny steps to the behavior (e.g., I felt depressed, I got up and went to the kitchen to get a knife). Then, you help the adolescent create the new chain of events by starting with the behavior the client is going to engage in instead. The important distinction here is that the alternative chain should lead to something the client will do, not just the lack of the problem behavior. This can include taking a walk, or spending time with friends. Finally, the adolescent builds the steps to this new behavior, which can include engaging in distress tolerance skills and contacting the clinician for phone coaching (Linehan, 1993).

Phone Coaching for Life-Threatening Behaviors

We briefly discuss phone coaching in Chapter 2; however, we will discuss here it in more detail. The DBT approach to handling life-threatening behaviors may feel dissonant to your clinical training—we are often taught that if clients are a risk to themselves or others, that we must immediately intervene to get them help, and this often means inpatient hospitalization. However, in DBT the goal is to avoid hospitalization if possible, as this can inadvertently reinforce the client's life-threatening behavior. As a result, phone coaching guidelines are structured around helping clients advocate for themselves, and reinforcing them for using skills to cope in crisis situations, instead of engaging in life-threatening behaviors. As we mentioned in Chapter 2, clients must call the clinician before engaging in the life-threatening behavior—and are strongly reinforced for doing so. In DBT for adults, clients are required to wait 24 hours after engaging in a life-threatening behavior to contact the clinician; however, Miller, Rathus, & Linehan (2007) advise against this for adolescents. Therefore, if the adolescent calls after engaging in a life-threatening behavior, the clinician will need to assess for safety, and then terminate the call as quickly as possible. If the client is hospitalized, she or he can have no contact with the clinician during hospitalization, unless it is deemed necessary to help the client towards successful skills use and discharge (this decision can be made with the assistance of the consultation team).

The idea of intersession phone contact with clients may be anxiety inducing, especially with clients who struggle with pervasive emotion dysregulation. Linehan (1993) noted that the majority of skills coaching calls last ten minutes or less, and are focused solely on helping the client identify skills he or she can use in the moment. Be mindful of your personal boundaries—for example, not taking calls after a certain time of night, as this will help prevent burnout (Ben-Porath, 2004). You will also want to set up clear guidelines for phone coaching in the beginning of treatment—not only should clients call before engaging in any life-threatening behaviors, but they should also be sure to call before their intensity of their emotions gets too high, and they are unable to problem solve in the moment via phone coaching (Ben-Porath, 2004). In fact, some clinicians require the client try at least two skills before contacting the clinician for coaching (Ben-Porath and Koons, 2005).

Regardless of the structure and limits surrounding phone coaching, it is still a large responsibility for the clinician. Your job will be to help the client problem solve in an efficient and supportive manner. At times this may be challenging, as the client may digress into a discussion of the history of the current problem, or other topics unrelated to problem-solving. When this happens, you will need to redirect the client back to the current situation and skills use. If the client continues to be willful and not engage in problem-solving behavior, then you will need to terminate the call. Throughout these interactions, be mindful of voice tone and supportive responses. When the phone call is appropriate, provide supportive responses. Conversely, if the call is inappropriate, be "business like" and keep supportive responses to a minimum (Ben-Porath, 2004).

In the event that the client does call you inappropriately (e.g., outside the guidelines you delineated at the beginning of treatment), you then need to engage the client in a behavior chain analysis regarding this call during the next scheduled session. This serves two purposes—it will help you and the client problem solve so the behavior doesn't happen again, and it can also help extinguish this behavior.

Clients often do not wish to engage in behavior chains, and would rather be discussing other things, and are therefore less likely to call you inappropriately again. If inappropriate phone calls continue, you can decide to have the client take a phone call "vacation"—this is to protect you from burnout as well as help the client reflect on his or her behaviors before having the opportunity to call you again (Linehan, 1993).

So, after all of this, you may still end up with a client on the phone who either refuses to contract for safety, or has engaged in a self-harm behavior. First, you will want to assess the client's immediate safety. For self-harm, you will need to assess if his or her injuries are life threatening. For suicidal thoughts, you will want to assess if the client has a plan, means, or intent—if the client has two of these three factors, then you will need to go focus more on ensuring the safety of the client as opposed to skills coaching (Ben-Porath & Koons, 2005). If the client needs medical attention, or needs to be hospitalized, then you will go through the steps to ensure his or her safety; however again, you will need to minimize supportive responses and end the call as soon as possible.

COMORBID DIAGNOSES

As you may imagine, when an adolescent is struggling with more than one psychiatric disorder, the severity of his or her symptoms will increase. Up to 64% of adolescents who have been diagnosed with major depressive disorder have also been diagnosed with another psychiatric disorder. In one study, researchers found that as many as 40% of participants met criteria for at least three disorders (Small et al., 2008). The most common comorbid diagnoses include anxiety and behavioral disorders, as well as ADHD and substance use disorders (Avenevoli et al., 2015). Adolescents with comorbid disorders are also less likely to experience positive treatment outcomes, and spend more time in treatment than adolescents struggling with one disorder (Andrews, Slade, & Issakidis, 2002).

DBT is a flexible treatment, and as result, it can be an extremely helpful approach if you are working with a client who struggles with more than one diagnosis. By utilizing the DBT format of the hierarchical treatment targets, you will be able to organize treatment goals, while emphasizing skills that will be the most helpful for the client's unique symptomology.

Assessment of Comorbid Diagnoses

In addition to diary cards, and the assessments we have listed in the outpatient chapter for general program evaluation, you may also find the assessments outlined in Chapter 12 helpful, as they target a variety of diagnoses. We have also included a few other assessments you may find helpful not only assessing for the severity of the client's symptoms, but for evaluating the effectiveness of your program.

Kiddie-Sads-Present and Lifetime Version

The Kiddie-Sads-Present and Lifetime Version (K-SADS-PL; Kaufman, Birmaher, Brent, & Rao, 1997) is a semi-structured interview, designed to assess for a variety of mental health disorders. It is thorough, incorporates responses from parents and children, and includes several steps, including supplemental diagnostic questionnaires for specific diagnoses. It is also free for clinical use, and could be easily included in the initial interview. However, due to the detail involved in completing this interview, it can be time consuming, and the current available version has yet to be updated for the changes in the DSM-5 (American Psychiatric Association, 2013).

Brief Symptom Inventory (BSI)

The Brief Symptom Inventory (BSI; Derogatis & Melisaratos, 1983) is a shortened version of the SCL-R-90 (Derogatis & Fitzpatrick, 2004) and can be used with adolescents age 13 and older. It includes 53 self-report questions, and has a fairly short administration time of 8–10 minutes. It includes nine different symptom scales, as well as three overall scales based on total symptoms and severity. This scale is flexible enough for frequent use to assess treatment progress, and it encompasses a large variety of symptoms and diagnoses.

Treatment Planning With Comorbid Diagnoses

Treatment planning for a client who has several diagnoses may seem overwhelming at first. However, the hierarchical structure of DBT treatment targets facilitates the clinician's ability to easily identify the most important symptoms to focus on, regardless of the diagnosis.

Life-Threatening Behaviors

Remember that decreasing life-threatening behaviors is considered the most crucial treatment target in DBT. When an adolescent is struggling with multiple disorders, it can be difficult to discern whether a behavior should be considered life threatening. For example, driving fast is not considered a life-threatening behavior, unless the adolescent is intentionally engaging in this behavior with the intent to harm him or herself, or it is extreme to the point of acute danger (Miller et al., 2007). Or, as we mentioned in Chapter 9, eating disordered behaviors are considered quality-of-life interfering, unless a medical doctor deems them life threatening. To assess whether a behavior should be considered life threatening, gather as much detail as you can during the initial interview, and discuss the behavior with the adolescent as well as parents and other family members. If you are still unable to discern whether a behavior should be considered life threatening, consult with your DBT team, as other clinicians can analyze the behavior objectively, help you identify any aspects you have missed, or provide insight based on their experiences (Miller et al., 2007).

Therapy-Interfering Behaviors

Behaviors that interfere with the actual therapeutic process are likely similar for an adolescent with several diagnoses as they are for those with just one. However, an adolescent with comorbid diagnoses may exhibit more of these behaviors than other adolescents. For example, an adolescent who has been diagnosed with ADHD in addition to depression may not only struggle with the behaviors related to symptoms of depression (e.g., missed appointments due to low energy) but behaviors related to ADHD (inability to concentrate during session or group, disrupting others in group, etc.). Therapy-interfering behaviors may also be more severe, due to a higher level of emotion dysregulation. For example, the adolescent may have more difficulty overcoming typical barriers to treatment (e.g., using skills to overcome anxiety and attend group) due to the complexity and severity of his or her emotions. Similarly, therapy-interfering behaviors that the clinician or family members engage in may also be more severe. Comorbid diagnoses often increase symptom severity, which increases the likelihood of clinician burnout, and the likelihood of extreme behaviors by family members that can impede treatment (e.g., extreme disciplinary measures that limit the client's ability to use skills effectively).

Quality-of-Life-Interfering Behaviors

Again, these are likely the same regardless of the number of diagnoses; however, the risk of these behaviors being more frequent and more severe is higher with adolescents who experience extreme and complex emotions. These behaviors may cover a broader array of life situations and types of behaviors, and it may seem too difficult or overwhelming to attempt to address all of them. We recommend working in conjunction with the adolescent and his or her parents to find a few that are either the most extreme, or the most concerning for all parties involved. Once the adolescent believes he or she is successfully managing those specific behaviors, the therapist and adolescent can work together to identify other important quality-of-life-interfering behaviors to target.

Increasing Behavioral Skills

One of the basic assumptions in DBT is that new skills must be learned and utilized in all contexts (Linehan, 1993). Therefore, it may be helpful for you to spend more time when discussing each skill, to be sure that you address all of the client's symptoms. For example, when reviewing diary cards, you could work with the client to identify when he or she used a specific skill to manage a certain situation and behavior. By using a dialectical approach that emphasizes flexibility, validation, and change, you can help clients optimize their use of skills for home, school, and work.

SUMMARY AND CONCLUSIONS

In this chapter, we have discussed how to approach treatment planning for adolescents who struggle with severe symptoms, either via multiple diagnoses or life-threatening behaviors. One of the things I have always loved about DBT is that it provides me with the tools to work with clients who struggle with a multitude of severe and life-threatening symptoms. I find it empowering to not shy away from working with clients who struggle with extreme pervasive emotion dysregulation, and I hope DBT can help you feel empowered to do the same.

REFERENCES

American Psychiatric Association (APA) (2013). *Diagnostic and statistical manual of mental disorders* (5th ed.). Arlington, VA: American Psychiatric Publishing.

Andrews, G., Slade, T., & Issakidis, C. (2002). Deconstructing current comorbidity: Data from the Australian national survey of mental health and well-being. *The British Journal of Psychiatry*, *181*(4), 306–314. doi:10.1192/bjp.181.4.306

Avenevoli, S., Swendsen, J., He, J., Burstein, M., & Merikangas, K. R. (2015). Major depression in the national comorbidity survey—adolescent supplement: Prevalence, correlates, and treatment. *Journal of the American Academy of Child & Adolescent Psychiatry*, *54*(1), 37–44. doi:10.1016/j.jaac.2014.10.010

Beck, A. T. & Steer, R. A. (1991). *Beck Scale for suicide ideation manual*. San Antonio, TX: Psychological Corporation.

Ben-Porath, D. D. (2004). Intercession telephone contact with individuals diagnosed with borderline personality disorder: Lessons from dialectical behavior therapy. *Cognitive and Behavioral Practice*, *11*(2), 222–230. doi:10.1016/S1077-7229(04)80033-6

Ben-Porath, D. D. & Koons, C. R. (2005). Telephone coaching in dialectical behavior therapy: A decision-tree model for managing inter-session contact with clients. *Cognitive and Behavioral Practice*, *12*(4), 448–460. doi:10.1016/S1077-7229(05)80072-0

Centers for Disease Control and Prevention, National Center for Injury Prevention and Control. (2007). *Web-Based Injury Statistics Query and Reporting System* (WISQARS). Retrieved from www.cdc.gov/ncipc/wisqars

Derogatis, L. R. & Fitzpatrick, M. (2004). The SCL-90-R, the Brief Symptom Inventory (BSI), and the BSI-18. In M. E. Maruish (Ed.), *The use of psychological testing for treatment planning and outcomes assessment: Instruments for adults* (Vol. 3, 3rd ed., pp. 1–41). Mahwah, NJ: Lawrence Erlbaum Associates Publishers.

Derogatis, L. R. & Melisaratos, N. (1983). The brief symptom inventory: An introductory report. *Psychological Medicine*, *13*(3), 595–605. doi:10.1017/S0033291700048017

Kaufman, J., Birmaher, B., Brent, D., & Rao, U. (1997). Schedule for affective disorders and schizophrenia for school-age children-present and lifetime version (K-SADS-PL): Initial reliability and validity data. *Journal of the American Academy of Child & Adolescent Psychiatry*, *36*(7), 980–988. doi:10.1097/00004583-199707000-00021

Klonsky, E. D., Victor, S. E., & Saffer, B. Y. (2014). Nonsuicidal self-injury: What we know, and what we need to know. *The Canadian Journal of Psychiatry/La Revue Canadienne De Psychiatrie*, *59*(11), 565–568.

Linehan, M. M. (1993). *Cognitive-behavioral treatment of borderline personality disorder*. New York, NY: Guilford Press.

Linehan, M. M., Comtois, K. A., Brown, M. Z., Heard, H. L., & Wagner, A. (2006). Suicide Attempt Self-Injury Interview (SASII): Development, reliability, and validity of a scale to assess suicide attempts and intentional self-injury. *Psychological Assessment*, *18*(3), 303–312.

Lloyd-Richardson, E. E., Perrine, N., Dierker, L., & Kelley, M. L. (2007). Characteristics and functions of non-suicidal self-injury in a community sample of adolescents. *Psychological Medicine*, *8*, 1183–1192.

Miller, A. L., Rathus, J. H., & Linehan, M. M. (2007). *Dialectical behavior therapy with suicidal adolescents*. New York, NY: Guilford Press.

Small, D. M., Simons, A. D., Yovanoff, P., Silva, S. G., Lewis, C. C., Murakami, J. L., & March, J. (2008). Depressed adolescents and comorbid psychiatric disorders: Are there differences in the presentation of depression? *Journal of Abnormal Child Psychology*, *36*(7), 1015–1028. doi:10.1007/s10802-008-9237-5

Whitlock, J., Muehlenkamp, J., Eckenrode, J., Purington, A., Baral Abrams, G., Barreira, P., & Kress, V. (2013). Non-suicidal self-injury as a gateway to suicide in young adults. *Journal of Adolescent Health*, *52*(4), 486–492. doi:10.1016/j.jadohealth.2012.09.010

Yates, T. M., Tracy, A. J., & Luthar, S. S. (2008). Non-suicidal self-injury among "privileged" youths: Longitudinal and cross-sectional approaches to developmental process. *Journal of Consulting and Clinical Psychology*, *76*(1), 52–62.

Summary and Conclusions
K. Michelle Hunnicutt Hollenbaugh

Our goal in this text was to provide you with usable materials and information to adapt DBT for adolescents with a variety of different symptoms and in a variety of settings. I hope that we have achieved that goal, and that this information can facilitate your implementation of a DBT program that fits the needs of your population and your setting. There were a few recommendations that were consistent throughout the book, and we will review a few of those here, as well as provide some additional thoughts and suggestions we have from personal experience. Finally, we will highlight a variety of resources on DBT you will be able to use in conjunction with this text.

MAJOR POINTS FOR CLINICIANS

Adaptation Considerations

Though DBT is flexible, and can be easily adapted, you also need to be aware of your goals in treatment, and how DBT fits with those goals. For example, just teaching the skills can certainly be helpful for clients, but it will likely not be as effective as implementing all of the modes of treatment, and/or utilizing the therapist strategies involved in the treatment (Linehan, 2015). If you wish to implement DBT to elicit lasting and significant behavior change in your client, the current evidence supports the use of full DBT. For example, I recently received an email from a clinician asking for advice because she was using DBT with her clients and they were having trouble applying the skills to daily life, and continued to engage in problem behaviors. Upon further investigation, I realized she had taught the skills in session, but she had not implemented any of the behavioral problem-solving, or dialectical and commitment strategies that can be key in the success of DBT. Once I explained the other facets of DBT that she had not included, she realized she had not sufficiently educated herself on the treatment, and decided to seek training before going further. I believe this may be a common occurrence, and clinicians may teach a few skills from the manual and then experience disappointment when the results are not what they expected. At any rate, be sure that you are intentional in how you implement DBT, and that you are well prepared before going forward.

Treatment Commitment

We've talked a lot about commitment. At this point, I'm sure you're tired of hearing about it. Regardless, we're going to mention it again. We have emphasized this point repeatedly because Linehan (2015) and Rathus and Miller (2015) stress its importance—but I also believe that as clinicians, we can get caught up in the routine of treatment, and sometimes forget about how important it is that the client makes a conscious decision to take part in the treatment in the first place. For example, during one of my DBT trainings, the trainers began to implement behavior chain analyses for attendees who arrived to the training late. However, there was one major issue with this—they had not asked us for a commitment to be on time, and as result, there was a lot of dissent from the attendees that was then resolved by the group formally committing to arriving on time.

A similar example involves a client I had when I first started implementing DBT several years ago. I described the treatment and the process, and then explained the diary card, gave it to her, and sent her on her way. However, week after week, she returned without completing the diary card. I would insist on her completing the diary card in session, which was upsetting for the client. It was a total disaster—she hadn't committed to the treatment, or made a commitment to complete the diary cards. I had simply implemented it under the assumption that it was something she was willing to do. As a result, this strained our relationship, and I had to start back at the beginning to rebuild therapeutic trust.

Training

You will also need to be mindful of the level of training you will need to administer DBT effectively. If you are only planning on incorporating some of the skills sporadically within your current treatment, you may not need as much training as if you were implementing a full DBT program. Regardless, remember that there is *a lot* involved in DBT; because of the level of complexity, it may take you awhile to get a full handle on all of it. The more you immerse yourself in it, and use it in your daily life, the more familiar you will become with the material, and the more effective you will be with your clients.

Outcome Evaluation

Another aspect we've highlighted in each section is the importance of outcome evaluation. It is extremely important that you utilize a method of assessment to keep track of your clients' individual progress, as well as the effectiveness of your overall program. Not only will this facilitate your ability to serve your clients in the best manner possible, it will also help you gather data that you can use to provide evidence to stakeholders of the effectiveness of your program. This data can also help you attain reimbursement from third-party payers, and receive support from administrators. As we have mentioned throughout the text, there are a lot of different ways to do this, from simply using diary cards and counting frequency of problem behaviors, to formalized assessments with reports from parents, teachers, and adolescents. Nonetheless, be sure to assess all of the different outcome variables you wish to target.

CURRENT AND FUTURE DIRECTIONS IN DBT

Researchers continue to publish new information on the effectiveness of DBT. Though the research is promising, there still is a lack of sufficient quality studies in DBT with adolescents, and researchers continue to work to design and publish more research on the topic. Recently published data has shown evidence of brain change related to emotion regulation for patients who had received DBT treatment (Goodman et al., 2014). Research continues on the dismantlement of DBT to identify if there are some aspects of the treatment that are more effective than others. For example, one recent study showed that a DBT skills group was more effective in reducing emotion dysregulation than an activities-based support group (Neacsiu, Eberle, Kramer, Wiesmann, & Linehan, 2014).

Another area for future research is regarding the fidelity of the treatment in adaptations of DBT (McCay et al., 2016). DBT has been implemented in numerous settings and with a variety of adaptations for adolescents. As a result, we need to give attention to the importance of the conformity of the treatment, and that clients are aware any adaptions from traditional DBT in the treatment they are receiving.

Finally, researchers are continuing to take specific aspects of DBT and expand upon them for use in different approaches—for example, therapy-interfering behaviors (Chapman & Rosenthal, 2016). Researchers are also working to develop and evaluate new formalized assessments to measure aspects of DBT—for example, therapist validation strategies (Carson-Wong & Rizvi, 2016; Stein, Hearon, Beard, Hsu, & Björgvinsson, 2016).

OTHER RESOURCES ON DBT

Books

There are numerous books published on DBT, by a variety of researchers and clinicians. We will only list a few here that we are familiar with and believe will be helpful for you.

Foundational Texts

Linehan, M. M. (1993). *Cognitive-behavioral treatment of borderline personality disorder*. New York, NY: Guilford Press.
Linehan, M. M. (2015). *DBT® skills training handouts and worksheets* (2nd ed.). New York, NY: Guilford Press.

Linehan, M. M. (2015). *DBT® skills training manual* (2nd ed.). New York, NY: Guilford Press.
Miller, A. L., Rathus, J. H., & Linehan, M. M. (2007). *Dialectical behavior therapy with suicidal adolescents*. New York, NY: Guilford Press.
Rathus, J. H. & Miller, A. L. (2015). *DBT® skills manual for adolescents*. New York, NY: Guilford Press.

Texts for Specific Populations and Settings

Dimeff, L. A. & Koerner, K. (2007). *Dialectical behavior therapy in clinical practice: Applications across disorders and settings*. New York, NY: Guilford Press.
Fruzzetti, A. E. (2006). *The high conflict couple: A dialectical behavior therapy guide to finding peace, intimacy, & validation*. Oakland, CA: New Harbinger.
Harvey, P. & Rathbone, B. H. (2015). *Parenting a teen who has intense emotions: DBT skills to help your teen navigate emotional & behavioral challenges*. Oakland, CA: New Harbinger.
Mazza, J. J., Dexter-Mazza, E. T., Miller, A. L., Rathus, J. H., Murphy, H. E., & Linehan, M. M. (2016). *DBT® skills in schools: Skills training for emotional problem solving for adolescents (DBT STEPS-A)*. New York, NY: Guilford Press.
Safer, D. L., Telch, C. F., & Chen, E. Y. (2009). *Dialectical behavior therapy for binge eating and bulimia*. New York, NY: Guilford Press.

Texts to Facilitate Implementation

Swenson, C. R. (2016). *DBT® principles in action: Acceptance, change, and dialectics*. New York, NY: Guilford Press.
Koerner, K. (2012). *Doing dialectical behavior therapy: A practical guide*. New York, NY: Guilford Press.

Websites

There are several websites that provide information on DBT. However, there are a few websites that you should be familiar with, especially if you wish to develop a program or continue training in DBT.

- Behavioral Tech (www.behavioraltech.org) is an organization founded by Marsha Linehan, and is the main DBT website that includes information on DBT, a contact list for intensively trained DBT teams, and information for online and in-person trainings. They also provide case consultation as needed. Though there are definitely other resources for DBT trainings, this provides a wide variety of options, including the intensive ten-day training for teams, which is considered the gold standard for DBT training.
- DBT-Linehan Board of Certification (www.dbt-lbc.org) is the website for information regarding becoming a Linehan Board-Certified DBT clinician. The process to become a Certified DBT clinician includes attaining a specified number of hours of training, sitting for a written test, and then submitting videotapes of counseling sessions to provide verification that you understand the material, and

that you are able to apply it. Though certification is not necessary to provide DBT services, it does increase your credibility in the field, and will enable you to say that you are officially certified. Be wary of other websites that claim to provide DBT certification, as they are not affiliated with Behavioral Tech, and are not considered the official certification.
- www.dbtselfhelp.com is a website that is managed by former or current participants in DBT treatment. Though it is an informal website, it does provide useful resources, including a format to make your own diary cards.

Smart Phone Applications

With the increase in technology use, especially with adolescents, smart phone applications (apps) may be a perfect venue to increase skills use and treatment compliance. There are numerous options, including diary card apps that can be personalized to the client, and formatted into a PDF to print and bring to session. There are also apps that include the different skills and practice exercises. Be sure to verify all of the aspects of any smart phone application before suggesting it to your client.

REFERENCES

Carson-Wong, A. & Rizvi, S. (2016). Reliability and validity of the DBT-VLCS: A measure to code validation strategies in dialectical behavior therapy sessions. *Psychotherapy Research*, *26*(3), 332–341. doi:10.1080/10503307.2014.966347

Chapman, A. L. & Rosenthal, M. Z. (2016). *Managing therapy-interfering behavior: Strategies from dialectical behavior therapy*. Washington, DC: American Psychological Association. doi:10.1037/14752-000

Goodman, M., Carpenter, D., Tang, C. Y., Goldstein, K. E., Avedon, J., Fernandez, N., . . . Hazlett, E. A. (2014). Dialectical behavior therapy alters emotion regulation and amygdala activity in patients with borderline personality disorder. *Journal of Psychiatric Research*, *57*, 108–116. doi:10.1016/j.jpsychires.2014.06.020

Linehan, M. M. (2015). *DBT® skills training manual* (2nd ed.). New York, NY: Guilford Press.

McCay, E., Carter, C., Aiello, A., Quesnel, S., Howes, C., & Johansson, B. (2016). Toward treatment integrity: Developing an approach to measure the treatment integrity of a dialectical behavior therapy intervention with homeless youth in the community. *Archives of Psychiatric Nursing*, *30*(5), 568–574. doi:10.1016/j.apnu.2016.04.001

Neacsiu, A. D., Eberle, J. W., Kramer, R., Wiesmann, T., & Linehan, M. M. (2014). Dialectical behavior therapy skills for transdiagnostic emotion dysregulation: A pilot randomized controlled trial. *Behaviour Research and Therapy*, 5940–5951. doi:10.1016/j.brat.2014.05.005

Rathus, J. H. & Miller, A. L. (2015). *DBT® skills manual for adolescents*. New York, NY: Guilford Press.

Stein, A. T., Hearon, B. A., Beard, C., Hsu, K. J., & Björgvinsson, T. (2016). Properties of the dialectical behavior therapy ways of coping checklist in a diagnostically diverse partial hospital sample. *Journal of Clinical Psychology*, *72*(1), 49–57. doi:10.1002/jclp.22226

Handout 1.1

Biosocial Theory

Invalidating Environment

- Stress-Filled Home
- Indiscriminately Rejects Private Experience
- Punishes Emotional Displays While Intermittently Reinforcing Emotional Escalation
- Oversimplifies Ease of Problem-Solving and Meeting Goals

Biological Vulnerability

- High Emotional Sensitivity
- High Emotional Reactivity
- Slow Return to Emotional Baseline
- Biological Predisposition

Emotional and Behavioral Dysregulation

- Doesn't Know How to Express Emotions Appropriately
- Negative Coping Techniques Such as Substance Abuse, Eating Disorders, and Self-Harm

Source: Adapted with permission from Linehan, M. M. (2015). *DBT® skills training manual* (2nd ed.). New York, NY: Guilford Press.

©2018, *Dialectical Behavior Therapy With Adolescents*, K. Michelle Hunnicutt Hollenbaugh and Michael S. Lewis, Routledge

Handout 1.2

Diary Card

Name: _____ Beginning Date: _____

Date	Self-Harm Urge	Self-Harm Action	Suicidal Ideations 0-5	Phone Consult Y/N	Targets Urge	Action	Urge	Action	Urge	Action	Urge	Action	Happiness 0-5	Care 0-5	Anger 0-5	Fear 0-5	Shame 0-5	Hurt 0-5	Sadness 0-5
M																			
Tu																			
W																			
Th																			
F																			
S																			
Su																			

Suicidal Ideation: 0 – No Thoughts 1 – Some Thoughts 2 – Intense Thoughts 3 – Very Intense 4 – Making a Plan 5 – Ready to Enact a Plan

Source: Adapted with permission from Linehan, M. M. (2015). *DBT® skills training manual* (2nd ed.). New York, NY: Guilford Press.

©2018, *Dialectical Behavior Therapy With Adolescents*, K. Michelle Hunnicutt Hollenbaugh and Michael S. Lewis, Routledge

Handout 1.3

Diary Card 2

Name: _____ Beginning Date: _____

Date	Active Denial		Dialectical Abstinence		Burning Bridges		Building Bridges		Urge Surfing		Cravings	Care	Anger	Fear	Shame	Hurt	Sadness
	Thought	Used	Urge	Action	Urge	Action	Urge	Action	Urge	Action	0-5	0-5	0-5	0-5	0-5	0-5	0-5
M																	
Tu																	
W																	
Th																	
F																	
S																	
Su																	

Columns grouped under **Targets**: Active Denial, Dialectical Abstinence, Burning Bridges, Building Bridges, Urge Surfing.
Columns grouped under **Emotions**: Anger, Fear, Shame, Hurt, Sadness.

Source: Adapted with permission from Linehan, M. M. (2015). *DBT® skills training manual* (2nd ed.). New York, NY: Guilford Press.

©2018, *Dialectical Behavior Therapy With Adolescents*, K. Michelle Hunnicutt Hollenbaugh and Michael S. Lewis, Routledge

Handout 1.4

Diary Card 3

Name: _____ Beginning Date: _____

Date	Targets										Emotions					
	Re-offending		Act of Rebellion		Aggressive Behaviors					Violent	Care	Anger	Fear	Shame	Hurt	Sadness
	Thought	Used	Urge	Action	Urge	Action	Urge	Action	Urge	Action	0-5	0-5	0-5	0-5	0-5	0-5	0-5
M																
Tu																
W																
Th																
F																
S																
Su																

Source: Adapted with permission from Linehan, M. M. (2015). *DBT® skills training manual* (2nd ed.). New York, NY: Guilford Press.

©2018, *Dialectical Behavior Therapy With Adolescents*, K. Michelle Hunnicutt Hollenbaugh and Michael S. Lewis, Routledge

Handout 1.5

Daily Diary Card

Name: _____

Date	Primary Target: Urge	Primary Target: Action	Suicidal Ideations 0-5	Participation Y/N	Skill Usage Thought	Use	Thoughts	Use	Thought	Use	Thought	Use	Happiness 0-5	Care 0-5	Anger 0-5	Fear 0-5	Shame 0-5	Hurt 0-5	Sadness 0-5
9a																			
10a																			
11a																			
12p																			
1p																			
2p																			
3p																			
4p																			
5p																			
6p																			
7p																			
8p																			
9p																			
10p																			
11p																			

Source: Adapted with permission from Linehan, M. M. (2015). *DBT® skills training manual* (2nd ed.). New York, NY: Guilford Press.

©2018, *Dialectical Behavior Therapy With Adolescents*, K. Michelle Hunnicutt Hollenbaugh and Michael S. Lewis, Routledge

Handout 1.6

Behavior Chain Analysis

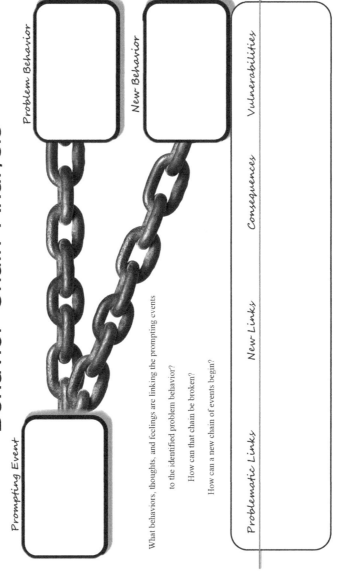

Source: Adapted with permission from Linehan, M. M. (2015). *DBT® skills training manual* (2nd ed.). New York, NY: Guilford Press.

©2018, *Dialectical Behavior Therapy With Adolescents*, K. Michelle Hunnicutt Hollenbaugh and Michael S. Lewis, Routledge

Handout 1.7

Skills Diary Card

Skill	M	Tu	W	Th	F	S	Su
Participation: Be a part of the situation and fully engage in the experience							
Wise Mind: Balance the emotional mind and reasonable mind							
DEAR MAN: Describe, Express, Assert, Reinforce, Mindful, Appear confident, Negotiate							
GIVE: Gentle, Interested, Validation, Easy manner							
FAST: Fair, no Apologies, Stick to values, be Truthful							
PLEASE: address Physical illness, balance Eating, Avoid drugs, balance Sleep, Exercise daily							
Fact Checking: Look for evidence for thoughts rather than making assumptions							
Problem Solving: Identify the goal, brainstorm possible solutions, and enact a plan							
Self-Soothe: Use the five senses mindfully to emotionally regulate							
Validate Yourself: Acknowledge your contributions, thoughts, and feelings							
Validate Another: Acknowledge someone else's contributions, thoughts, and feelings							
Pros and Cons: Weigh out the benefits and costs of a situation before making a choice							
Emotional Identification: Mindfully assess your current emotional state							

Key: 1) Didn't use or think about using skill 2) Thought about the skill but chose not to use it 3) Used the skill but it was ineffective 4) Effectively utilized the skill

Source: Adapted with permission from Linehan, M. M. (2015). *DBT® skills training manual* (2nd ed.). New York, NY: Guilford Press.

©2018, *Dialectical Behavior Therapy With Adolescents*, K. Michelle Hunnicutt Hollenbaugh and Michael S. Lewis, Routledge

Handout 2.1

Commitment Strategies

Review these potential strategies and explore which will help your client commit to treatment

Foot in the Door	Asking the client for a small commitment (one easily achievable), and then request increasingly larger commitments
Door in the Face	Asking the client for a huge commitment (one nearly impossible), then, when the client refuses, request a smaller, more acceptable commitment
Connecting Prior Commitments to the Present	Reminding the client of previous commitments in a reinforcing and affirming way in order to recommit them to a present goal or behavior
Playing the Devil's Advocate	Changing the script on the client and suggesting perhaps they won't be able to succeed or hold to their commitment, in turn prompting them to argue for their ability to succeed and recommit
Evaluating Pros & Cons	Objectively weighing the benefits and difficulties of committing to DBT treatment
Freedom to Choose	Emphasizing that the client has the ability to freely choose to stay in treatment or not, but that their alternatives may not be better
Cheerleading	Praising the client for their successes and reinforcing their ability to maintain their commitment to treatment

Source: Adapted with permission from Linehan, M. M. (2015). *DBT® skills training manual* (2nd ed.). New York, NY: Guilford Press.

©2018, *Dialectical Behavior Therapy With Adolescents*, K. Michelle Hunnicutt Hollenbaugh and Michael S. Lewis, Routledge

Handout 3.1

My Treatment Team

Below is a list of your treatment team members and what roles they will play

Team Member Name

Role	Description	Name
Team Leader	The Team Leader is in charge of your treatment and the treatment team and may have many roles	_____
Skills Trainer	Will lead your psychoeducational groups and homework	_____
Primary Clinician	Will work with you in individual therapy and facilitate family sessions	_____
Case Manager	Coordinates and links you to outside resources as necessary and is your overall advocate	_____
Physician	In charge of your physical health and well-being	_____
Psychiatrist	Facilitates medications and monitors their management	_____
Other	These may include other important people in your life such as teachers, coaches, or extended family members	_____

©2018, *Dialectical Behavior Therapy With Adolescents*, K. Michelle Hunnicutt Hollenbaugh and Michael S. Lewis, Routledge

Handout 3.2

Treatment Team Contacts

Below is a list of your treatment team members, contact information, and why you would contact them

Team Leader: _____ Psychiatrist: _____

Phone Number: _____ Phone Number: _____

Meeting Times: _____ Meeting Times: _____

Contact If: _____ Contact If: _____

Skills Trainer: _____ Additional Member: _____

Phone Number: _____ Phone Number: _____

Meeting Times: _____ Meeting Times: _____

Contact If: _____ Contact If: _____

Primary Clinician: _____ Additional Member: _____

Phone Number: _____ Phone Number: _____

Meeting Times: _____ Meeting Times: _____

Contact If: _____ Contact If: _____

Case Manager: _____ Additional Member: _____

Phone Number: _____ Phone Number: _____

Meeting Times: _____ Meeting Times: _____

Contact If: _____ Contact If: _____

Physician: _____ Additional Member: _____

Phone Number: _____ Phone Number: _____

Meeting Times: _____ Meeting Times: _____

Contact If: _____ Contact If: _____

©2018, *Dialectical Behavior Therapy With Adolescents*, K. Michelle Hunnicutt Hollenbaugh and Michael S. Lewis, Routledge

Handout 3.3

Weekly Medication Management

Name: _____

These are the medications I'm currently taking:

Name	Dosage	Time(s) Taken	Circle Days Taken
_____	_____	_____	M T W Th F S Su
_____	_____	_____	M T W Th F S Su
_____	_____	_____	M T W Th F S Su
_____	_____	_____	M T W Th F S Su
_____	_____	_____	M T W Th F S Su
_____	_____	_____	M T W Th F S Su

Note here any differences you're experiencing with thinking, mood, or side effects that seem related to your medication:

_____

_____

_____

_____

©2018, *Dialectical Behavior Therapy With Adolescents*, K. Michelle Hunnicutt Hollenbaugh and Michael S. Lewis, Routledge

Handout 3.4

Confidentiality

Our treatment team takes great care to respect your information and keep it private within the bounds of our treatment policies, our professional boards of ethics, and the law. What this means is that outside of some specific instances, you can trust our treatment team to hold what you share contained within the treatment team.

There are some exceptions as outlined here:

Parents and Guardians: They have legal rights to your information. However, we will discuss with them only what we believe is necessary to further your treatment to the best of our ability.

━ ▪ ▪ ━ ▪ ▪ ━ ▪ ▪ ━ ▪ ▪ ━ ▪

Risk of Harm: If there is substantial reason to believe that you are imminently at risk to yourself or have plans to harm another person we will break confidentiality in order to keep everyone safe. Additionally, we are bound by law to report any abuse of any children, elderly, or disabled individuals to also keep them safe. The information we will share is limited to specifically the information needed to care for you or others.

━ ▪ ▪ ━ ▪ ▪ ━ ▪ ▪ ━ ▪ ▪ ━ ▪

Treatment Team: The treatment team will share information with one another in order to make your treatment easier for you and us. There may be some information we share formally in your records or shared informally at meetings or in conversation relevant to your treatment.

©2018, *Dialectical Behavior Therapy With Adolescents*, K. Michelle Hunnicutt Hollenbaugh and Michael S. Lewis, Routledge

Handout 3.5

DBT Information Sheet

This information is being provided to you as a provider for this client who is also under our care. This will help you understand a little about the nature of their treatment and outlines some of the specific treatment goals in order to coordinate our efforts to best help. Please contact us if you have questions.

> What is Dialectical Behavioral Therapy?
> DBT is a style of treatment that uses multiple modes (individual therapy, group therapy, phone coaching, skills training) to help clients modify problem behaviors. DBT uses an interprofessional consultation team approach in order to meet the client's physical, mental, and emotional needs. We teach the client skills like mindfulness, emotional regulation, acceptance skills, and distress tolerance in order to decrease problematic or life-threatening behaviors and increase positive coping skills. The goal is to provide a path to a life worth living, build self-worth, and set healthy life goals.

Treatment is built around treatment goals. Below are some of this client's target behaviors that you may be able to help with or which you need to be aware.

Treatment Target: _____

Treatment Target: _____

Treatment Target: _____

Treatment Target: _____

©2018, *Dialectical Behavior Therapy With Adolescents*, K. Michelle Hunnicutt Hollenbaugh and Michael S. Lewis, Routledge

Handout 3.6

Provider Communication Form

Client's Name: _____ Date: _____

Provider Name: _____

Please provide details on the nature of your interaction with this client and any information you think would be helpful for his/her treatment team to know.

Nature of Visit: _____
_____
_____

Affect and Disposition of Client: _____
_____
_____

Client's Response and Behavior: _____
_____
_____

Plan or Follow-up: _____
_____
_____

Concerns or Additional Information: _____
_____
_____

Thank you for your time to provide this feedback. Please send it with the client to return to the treatment team. If you would like to speak with a treatment team member please provide your contact information here: _____

©2018, *Dialectical Behavior Therapy With Adolescents*, K. Michelle Hunnicutt Hollenbaugh and Michael S. Lewis, Routledge

Handout 3.7

Client Report

Professional Staff: Please use this form to communicate any concerns you have regarding the client and place in the client's file. Please be as detailed as possible and specify the full nature of the concern.

Narrative: _____

_____

_____

_____

_____

Behaviors and Affect of Client: _____

_____

_____

_____

_____

Additional Information of Note: _____

_____

_____

_____

_____

©2018, *Dialectical Behavior Therapy With Adolescents*, K. Michelle Hunnicutt Hollenbaugh and Michael S. Lewis, Routledge

Handout 4.1

My Target Behaviors

In the below spaces list the target behaviors you and your counselor have agreed to work on, and skills you can use that will help you reach your goals.

Target Behavior: Stop Stealing
    Skill: Weigh Pros and Cons
    Skill: Alternate Rebellion

Target Behavior: _____
    Skill: _____
    Skill: _____

Target Behavior: _____
    Skill: _____
    Skill: _____

Target Behavior: _____
    Skill: _____
    Skill: _____

Target Behavior: _____
    Skill: _____
    Skill: _____

Target Behavior: _____
    Skill: _____
    Skill: _____

©2018, *Dialectical Behavior Therapy With Adolescents*, K. Michelle Hunnicutt Hollenbaugh and Michael S. Lewis, Routledge

Handout 4.2

Mindfulness Exercises

Try some of these mindfulness activities to improve your skill level

Mindful Breathing: Close your eyes or focus on one spot in the room. Take a nice long deep breath in through your nose and then release slowly through the mouth. Be aware of how the air feels entering your body and leaving it. Imagine that all your thoughts are written on a piece of paper and fold that paper mentally until it's small enough to put in your pocket. Simply focus on the sensation of your breathing. If stray thoughts come, simply brush them away and refocus on the sensation of your breathing. Feel the rhythm of your breaths as you breathe in to the beat of 4 (1…2…3…4) and then do the same as you exhale. Do this for five minutes noticing how your body feels and changes.

Take It All In: Stop what you're doing and simply observe your surroundings. Take in everything using your senses. What do you see — notice the colors, shadows, light, dark, and shapes that you can see. What are the aromas you can smell, sounds you can hear? How does your body feel? Touch the environment to take in their textures or imagine what it would be like to touch things you can't reach. Do this for five minutes.

Be Intentional: Take an activity you do everyday, often mindlessly, like shower, eat, or wash the dishes. Be intentional and allow the fullness of the activity to consume you. Connect with the gestures you use, the physicality of the task, and take your time completing it.

Name It: Take time throughout your day to find things you are thankful for. Use your first name as a guide — for each letter, find something that begins with that letter. Often these are small things that we take for granted, like the knowledge of how to complete a task, the connections we make with other people, or even simply a light breeze.

Source: Adapted with permission from Rathus, J. H. & Miller, A. L. (2015). *DBT® skills manual for adolescents*. New York, NY: Guilford Press.

©2018, *Dialectical Behavior Therapy With Adolescents*, K. Michelle Hunnicutt Hollenbaugh and Michael S. Lewis, Routledge

Handout 4.3

Interpersonal Effectiveness Myths

Challenge these common myths we tell use when worried about interacting with others

Myth: People are thinking the worst about me
Challenge: _____

Myth: I can't take it if others disagree with me
Challenge: _____

Myth: If I ask for something, I'll look weak
Challenge: _____

Myth: People only look out for themselves, so I should too
Challenge: _____

Myth: Saying no to someone is selfish and greedy
Challenge: _____

Myth: It doesn't make a difference what I say or do, so I just won't care
Challenge: _____

Myth: If someone is kind to me it's because they want something
Challenge: _____

Myth: I don't deserve compliments or other's attention
Challenge: _____

Myth: This is the worst possible thing that could have happened
Challenge: _____

Myth: Come up with your own example: _____
Challenge: _____

Source: Adapted with permission from Linehan, M. M. (2015). *DBT® skills training manual* (2nd ed.). New York, NY: Guilford Press.

©2018, *Dialectical Behavior Therapy With Adolescents*, K. Michelle Hunnicutt Hollenbaugh and Michael S. Lewis, Routledge

Handout 4.4

DEAR MAN

Use the below acronym to think through a given situation and choose how best to respond in a healthy and helpful way.

Describe the situation to help you and others understand fully what's happening

Express your feelings and thoughts calmly and openly

Assert what you want clearly

Reinforce how others react

Mindful of the situation and don't get distracted

Appear confident with your body language and tone of voice

Negotiate — be willing to give in order to get

GET WHAT YOU WANT!

Think of a recent situation where DEAR MAN would have helped _____
_____
_____
_____

How would these skills have changed the situation? _____
_____
_____
_____

Source: Adapted with permission from Linehan, M. M. (2015). *DBT® skills training manual* (2nd ed.). New York, NY: Guilford Press.

©2018, *Dialectical Behavior Therapy With Adolescents*, K. Michelle Hunnicutt Hollenbaugh and Michael S. Lewis, Routledge

Handout 4.5

Understanding My Emotions

Emotions impact all areas of the mind and body. To best understand your emotions take a moment to evaluate what happens when you feel particular emotions.

o When I feel _____, my body reacts by _____. I think about _____, and I want to _____.

Anger

Body	Thoughts	Behaviors

Happiness

Body	Thoughts	Behaviors

Sadness

Body	Thoughts	Behaviors

Fear

Body	Thoughts	Behaviors

Source: Adapted with permission from Linehan, M.M. (2015) *DBT® Skills Handouts and Worksheets*. New York: Guilford Press.

©2018, *Dialectical Behavior Therapy With Adolescents*, K. Michelle Hunnicutt Hollenbaugh and Michael S. Lewis, Routledge

Handout 4.6

Emotional Myths

Mark as many below that you believe to be true for you:

— There is a right way and wrong way to feel for every situation

— Crying is not okay for men

— My emotions happen for no reason

— Some emotions should just be ignored

— I often feel stupid for the way I feel

— Emotions like stress and anger are damaging and to be avoided

— Other people are better at knowing how I feel

— Talking about my emotions is a sign of weakness

— Being emotional means I'm out of control

— Bad emotions are a result of a bad attitude

— Other people will judge me based on how I feel

— I simply need to "get it together" when I feel bad

What are some other "myths" you can think of?

_____
_____
_____
_____
_____

Source: Adapted with permission from Linehan, M. M. (2015). *DBT® skills training manual* (2nd ed.). New York, NY: Guilford Press.

©2018, *Dialectical Behavior Therapy With Adolescents*, K. Michelle Hunnicutt Hollenbaugh and Michael S. Lewis, Routledge

Handout 4.7

EMOTIONAL THESAURUS

There are essentially four core emotions: happy, sad, anger, and fear. All other emotions come from of these emotions. Under each of these emotions list as many emotions as you can think of—then rank them from 1 (not very intense) to 10 (extremely intense). For example, happy is a 5, content is a 1, and overjoyed could be a 10.

HAPPY	SAD	ANGER	FEAR

Source: Adapted with permission from Linehan, M. M. (2015). *DBT® skills training manual* (2nd ed.). New York, NY: Guilford Press.

©2018, *Dialectical Behavior Therapy With Adolescents*, K. Michelle Hunnicutt Hollenbaugh and Michael S. Lewis, Routledge

Handout 4.8

Acting the Opposite

You've heard of "fake it 'til you make it"—sometimes that's how our emotions work too. If we act the opposite to how we feel, often our emotional state will change for real. Our brain works in funny ways, and the more we believe something to be true the more it will be true.

What does the current emotion (anger, hurt, apathy, etc.) feel like to you? _____
_____
_____
_____

What would the opposite look like? _____
_____
_____

How do you see this working? _____
_____
_____

After trying it, how did it work? _____
_____
_____

Source: Adapted with permission from Linehan, M. M. (2015). *DBT® skills training manual* (2nd ed.). New York, NY: Guilford Press.

©2018, *Dialectical Behavior Therapy With Adolescents*, K. Michelle Hunnicutt Hollenbaugh and Michael S. Lewis, Routledge

Handout 4.9

Cope Ahead

Instead of waiting for a situation to come up and figure out what to do, think ahead and figure out how you might best handle it.

Think of a upcoming situation you think you might have difficulty handling or will prompt strong emotions. Be specific. _____
_____
_____
_____

What skills would help out in this particular situation and why? _____
_____
_____
_____

Imagine yourself in the situation NOT using the skill. How does it go? _____
_____
_____
_____

Imagine yourself in the situation using the skill. How does it go? _____
_____
_____
_____

Now practice mindfully through the situation until you feel prepared!

Source: Adapted with permission from Linehan, M. M. (2015). *DBT® skills training manual* (2nd ed.). New York, NY: Guilford Press.

©2018, *Dialectical Behavior Therapy With Adolescents*, K. Michelle Hunnicutt Hollenbaugh and Michael S. Lewis, Routledge

Handout 4.10

Radical Acceptance

Radical acceptance means fully taking in the reality of the situation. That the facts are the facts even if you don't care for them. What is the reality of the current situation? _____
_____
_____
_____

Acceptance doesn't mean approval—you don't have to like it, or think it is fair. Acceptance is a way of understanding the current situation.

What are the emotions you feel?_____
_____
_____
_____

Changing the future requires accepting the present.

What are the changes you can foresee yourself making and what are the current hurdles you must accept to make this change?_____
_____
_____
_____

Source: Adapted with permission from Linehan, M. M. (2015). *DBT® skills training manual* (2nd ed.). New York, NY: Guilford Press.

©2018, *Dialectical Behavior Therapy With Adolescents*, K. Michelle Hunnicutt Hollenbaugh and Michael S. Lewis, Routledge

Handout 4.11

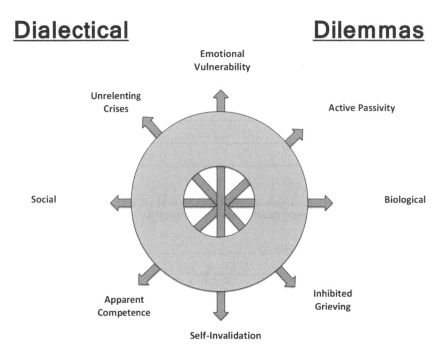

Source: Adapted with permission from Linehan, M. M. (2015). *DBT® skills training manual* (2nd ed.). New York, NY: Guilford Press.

©2018, *Dialectical Behavior Therapy With Adolescents*, K. Michelle Hunnicutt Hollenbaugh and Michael S. Lewis, Routledge

Handout 4.12

Walking the Middle Path

Move yourself beyond thinking in extremes—instead view yourself as walking steadily between two seemingly opposite ideas. Below are some examples as well as an opportunity to think of some of your own. Move from either/or to both/and

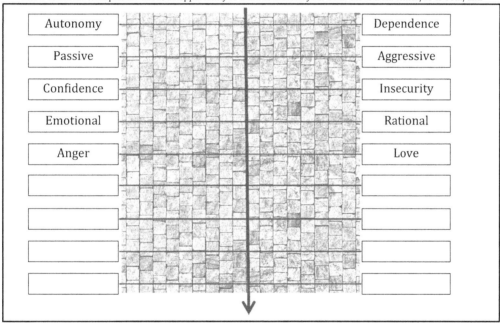

Image © Shutterstock

Source: Adapted with permission from Rathus, J. H. & Miller, A. L. (2015). *DBT® skills manual for adolescents*. New York, NY: Guilford Press.

©2018, *Dialectical Behavior Therapy With Adolescents*, K. Michelle Hunnicutt Hollenbaugh and Michael S. Lewis, Routledge

Handout 4.13

Validation

Validation of Others: Acknowledge and let the other person know that you recognize his or her thoughts and feelings and they are clear to you. Validation does not mean agreement; rather instead it lets a person know that you've heard them and their thoughts and feelings are important to you. You can do this through eye contact, nodding your head, not being critical, and in general showing them respect.

Self-Validation: Acknowledge your own thoughts and feelings as real, accurate, and clear. You can do this by being mindful of your thoughts and emotions in a situation and naming them to yourself and others. Don't judge them or assign them as "stupid" but simply notice them and let them be.

What did you do to **Validate Others** today? _____

_____

_____

_____

What did you do to **Validate Yourself** today? _____

_____

_____

_____

How would you grade yourself on validation today? (1—needs a lot of work—10—did great): _____

How can you improve tomorrow? _____

_____

_____

_____

Source: Adapted with permission from Rathus, J. H. & Miller, A. L. (2015). *DBT® skills manual for adolescents*. New York, NY: Guilford Press.

©2018, *Dialectical Behavior Therapy With Adolescents*, K. Michelle Hunnicutt Hollenbaugh and Michael S. Lewis, Routledge

Handout 4.14

Changing Behavior

There are four primary ways to modify behavior: Reinforcement, Punishment, Extinction, and Shaping.

- Reinforcement: using consequences (positive or negative) to increase a desired behavior. Positive reinforcement uses a reward such as praise or a treat while negative reinforcement removes an unwanted experience such as stopping an annoying noise.

- Punishment: an action that attempts to decrease an unwanted behavior. Examples of punishment could include being grounded for misbehaving or getting a poor grade on a test after not studying.

- Extinction: a decrease of a behavior because reinforcement is no longer provided. For example, you clean your room because you get $5 for doing so. When you stop getting paid, you stop cleaning the room.

- Shaping: reinforcing small behaviors that are leading to the desired behavior. We use shaping to teach our pets how to do tricks by giving them a treat when they get close to the desired behavior and increase it as they get it more and more correct.

Which of these do you think is most effective and why? _____

_____

_____

Think of an example when one of these was used effectively for you. _____

_____

_____

_____

Think of a behavior you want to increase or decrease—how can you use one of these methods to accomplish it?

_____

Source: Adapted with permission from Rathus, J. H. & Miller, A. L. (2015). *DBT® skills manual for adolescents*. New York, NY: Guilford Press.

©2018, *Dialectical Behavior Therapy With Adolescents*, K. Michelle Hunnicutt Hollenbaugh and Michael S. Lewis, Routledge

Group Orientation

Working with others in a group setting provides you with feedback, support, and a connection with others dealing with similar concerns as yours. It is normal to feel apprehensive or uneasy, have concerns and questions about how this will work, or worry if it will even work at all. Rest assured this is completely expected. In fact, since most others are feeling the same way it can be helpful to address these concerns in group.

Groups come in different sizes, for different purposes, and have different topics but what remains consistent is than the more you put into the group process the more you'll get out of it. Some days will be more difficult than others but if you keep coming and allow yourself to be honest, you'll get out of it what you need.

> To help you get the most of the experience we recommend the following guidelines

Be Patient: The group process can take time and there will be sessions that are frustrating. Commit to attending five group sessions before passing judgment on how useful this is for you

Be Honest: Be open with others and allow yourself to be vulnerable at times.

Be Present: Both physically (as in on time for group) and psychologically (as in aware and attentive) during group time.

Offer Support: Give feedback and encouragement to other group members when you see opportunities. Giving support is not the same as advice—instead of making suggestions, allow members to decide what's best for them while you cheerlead.

Test With New Behaviors: Group is a great place to try new techniques ina safe environment.
Be open to trying and getting feedback from others on how it went. It'll make it easier to try it later.

Confidentiality: What is said in group stays in group. We need to be able to trust one another with our information. Don't share anything with anyone else outside of group and only talk about group topics during group time.

Respect: Be sensitive to others. No name calling, poking fun, or in general picking on other group members.

Focus on the Topic: Therapy works best when we can stay on topic and explore what that entire topic has to offer. It can be easy to get diverted or think of another topic. Hold those comments for later or ask a group facilitator when it would be appropriate to bring it up.

Be Yourself: Relax and have fun with the process. Let us get to know the real you and we'll do the same.

©2018, *Dialectical Behavior Therapy With Adolescents*, K. Michelle Hunnicutt Hollenbaugh and Michael S. Lewis, Routledge

Handout 4.16

Group Rules

In order for the group to work well together and get the most out of this experience, we ask that you follow the following rules and guidelines. Please hold yourself and others accountable to these rules.

Confidentiality: Information and stories shared here are not to be discussed outside of group. If it's said here, leave it here.

Punctuality: Be mindful of the work members are doing in group and how coming late can disrupt that process. If you are late alert a team member and we can insert you when it is appropriate to do so.

Participation: All members help others and your feedback can be invaluable to the others. Showing care and support is the reason group therapy works.

Respect: Be kind to other members' thoughts, ideas, and feelings. Group is a place of vulnerability and we want to provide a safe space for all members to share without fear of being put down. This also includes members who are not present.

Complete Assignments: Homework will be discussed in group and it is disruptive to have to work around a member who hasn't done the work.

Socializing Outside of Group: Your first duty is to the group and becoming friends outside of the group confuses the boundaries of group relationships and can be disruptive to the group process.

Sobriety: Coming to group intoxicated moves the focus unfairly to you and takes away from the progression of the group as a whole.

"I" Statements: Speak from your own point of view and own your thoughts, feelings, and behaviors.

©2018, *Dialectical Behavior Therapy With Adolescents*, K. Michelle Hunnicutt Hollenbaugh and Michael S. Lewis, Routledge

Handout 5.1

Family Genogram

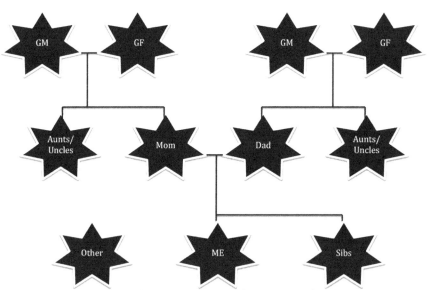

To better understand how family history impacts the present, work with your parent(s) to examine problem behaviors or invalidating patterns that may have existed among or between family members.

©2018, *Dialectical Behavior Therapy With Adolescents*, K. Michelle Hunnicutt Hollenbaugh and Michael S. Lewis, Routledge

Handout 5.2

Relational Mindfulness

Being mindful of your own thoughts, feelings, and behaviors is only half the battle. We are also called to connect with others. Take time to be aware of their thoughts, feelings and behaviors as well. Below are some of the important skills that improve interpersonal skills. Can you be mindful to improve these skills? What are some others you can think of?

Source: Adapted with permission from Linehan, M. M. (2015). *DBT® skills handouts and worksheets*. New York, NY: Guilford Press.

©2018, *Dialectical Behavior Therapy With Adolescents*, K. Michelle Hunnicutt Hollenbaugh and Michael S. Lewis, Routledge

Handout 5.3

Family Chain Analysis

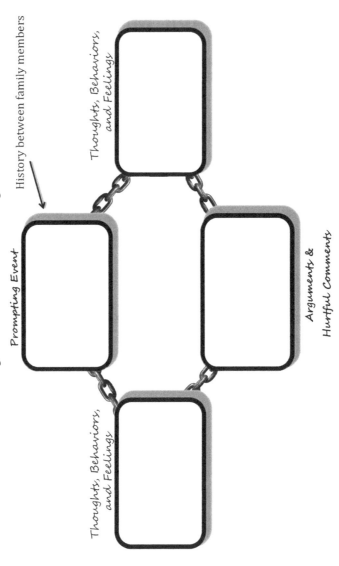

Source: Adapted with permission from Fruzzetti, A. E., Santisteban, D. A., & Hoffman, P. D. (2007). Dialectical behavior therapy with families. In L. A. Dimeff, K. Koerner (Eds.), *Dialectical behavior therapy in clinical practice: Applications across disorders and settings* (pp. 222–244). New York, NY: Guilford Press.

©2018, *Dialectical Behavior Therapy With Adolescents*, K. Michelle Hunnicutt Hollenbaugh and Michael S. Lewis, Routledge

Handout 6.1

Partial Hospital Teen Daily Goal Sheet

Name: _____ Day: _____ Date: ____/____/____

PROGRAM TARGET GOAL: _____

PLAN TO REACH GOAL: _____

PATIENT'S SUMMARY OF DAY:

1	2	3	4	5
* Commitment absent or weak * Willful in response to coaching and skill use * Little participation * Therapy-destroying and/or persistent therapy-interfering behavior	* Some willfulness in response to coaching and skill use * Little or inconsistent participation * Some therapy-interfering behavior * Some commitment present	* Both willfulness and willingness present * Tries some skills and makes some effort to participate * Few or no therapy-interfering behavior * Adequate commitment	* Generally willing and responsive to coaching/skill use and solution analysis * Good participation * Sometimes asks for help * Committed to goals	* Willing, asks for help * Very effective participation * Makes effort to apply skills to problems * Follows up on solutions * Strong commitment to reaching goals

PROGRAM POINTS:

1	2	3	4	5
(0-14 Points Earned)	(15-18 Points Earned)	(19-22 Points Earned)	(23-26 Points Earned)	(27-28 Points Earned)

STAFF COMMENTS (Behavior, Assignments, Information Attached, etc.)   TIBS: _____

_____

_____

MEDICATION TAKEN AT DAYBREAK: _____ STAFF SIGNATURE: _____

HOME TARGET GOAL: _____

PLAN TO REACH GOAL: _____

Patient Summary: I am up to date on Diary Card: ____ YES ____ NO
                   Completed my DBT Homework: ____ YES ____ NO

USED SKILLS:

1	2	3	4	5	6
Didn't think about them	Crossed my mind but didn't use them	Tried to use them but didn't help	Tried to use them and they helped some	Tried to use them and they helped	Used automatically and they helped

PATIENT'S SUMMARY OF AFTERNOON AND NIGHT:

1	2	3	4	5
*Unpleasant *Poorly self motivated *Disrespectful *Did not follow adult instruction	*Unpleasant at times *Difficult to motivate *Willful *Minimal compliance with adult instruction	*Some self-motivation *Responded to adult instruction *Moderate self control *Improving attitude	* Fairly self motivated *Fairly engaged	*Demonstrated initiative *Excellent attitude *Used/taught skills

MEDICATION TAKEN AT HOME   **WAS MEDICATION TAKEN AS DIRECTED?**

Name of Med.(s) / Time Given / Dosage (mg's)

1. _____/_____/_____   Yes No (Why)_____
2. _____/_____/_____   Yes No (Why)_____
3. _____/_____/_____   Yes No (Why)_____

Parent Comment: remember to practice validation and a non-judgmental attitude with suggestions for problem-solving

_____

Signed:_____

©2018, *Dialectical Behavior Therapy With Adolescents*, K. Michelle Hunnicutt Hollenbaugh and Michael S. Lewis, Routledge

Handout 6.2

Missing Links Analysis

Name: _____ Date: _____ Missing Behavior: _____

To understand missing effective behaviors, do a missing link analysis
Use this sheet to first figure out what got in the way of doing things you needed or hoped to do or things you agreed to that others expected you to do.
Then use that information to problem solve so that you will be more likely to do what is needed, hoped, or expected next time

1: Did I know what effective behavior was needed or expected? YES ____ NO ____
If NO to question #1, DESCRIBE what got in the way of knowing:
_____
_____
_____

DESCRIBE problem-solving: _____
_____
_____ STOP

2: If YES to question #1, was I willing to do what was needed? YES ____ NO ____
If NO to question #2, DESCRIBE what got in the way of wanting to do what was needed
_____
_____
_____

DESCRIBE problem-solving: _____
_____
_____ STOP

3: If YES to question #2, did thoughts of doing what was needed or expected ever enter my mind? YES ____ NO ____
If NO to question #3, DESCRIBE problem solving:
_____
_____
_____ STOP

4. If YES to question #3, Describe what got in the way of doing what was needed or expected right away:
_____
_____
_____

DESCRIBE problem solving: _____
_____
_____ STOP

Source: Used with permission from Linehan, M. M. (2015). *DBT® skills handouts and worksheets*. New York, NY: Guilford Press.

©2018, *Dialectical Behavior Therapy With Adolescents*, K. Michelle Hunnicutt Hollenbaugh and Michael S. Lewis, Routledge

Handout 6.3

Lunch Time Tasks

Name: _____ Date: _____ Missing Behavior _____

Everyone is responsible for various tasks each day. You will be assigned various tasks throughout the week. Initial to the right when they've been completed

Task: Monday   Tuesday   Wednesday   Thursday   Friday   _____

Task: Monday   Tuesday   Wednesday   Thursday   Friday   _____

Task: Monday   Tuesday   Wednesday   Thursday   Friday   _____

Task: Monday   Tuesday   Wednesday   Thursday   Friday   _____

Task: Monday   Tuesday   Wednesday   Thursday   Friday   _____

Task: Monday   Tuesday   Wednesday   Thursday   Friday   _____

Task: Monday   Tuesday   Wednesday   Thursday   Friday   _____

Task: Monday   Tuesday   Wednesday   Thursday   Friday   _____

Task: Monday   Tuesday   Wednesday   Thursday   Friday   _____

Task: Monday   Tuesday   Wednesday   Thursday   Friday   _____

Task: Monday   Tuesday   Wednesday   Thursday   Friday   _____

Task: Monday   Tuesday   Wednesday   Thursday   Friday   _____

Task: Monday   Tuesday   Wednesday   Thursday   Friday   _____

Task: Monday   Tuesday   Wednesday   Thursday   Friday   _____

Tasks may include cleaning tables, sweeping the floor, cleaning the microwave, emptying the trash, etc. at the discretion of the staff

©2018, *Dialectical Behavior Therapy With Adolescents*, K. Michelle Hunnicutt Hollenbaugh and Michael S. Lewis, Routledge

Handout 6.4

DBT HOMEWORK:
Teach Your Parent(s) a Skill

Today we learned the: _____

Skill of: _____

TEACH YOUR PARENTS THE SKILL YOU LEARNED TODAY AND HAVE THEM SIGN THIS FORM.

COMMENTS:

Parental/Guardian Signature that you learned and understand the skill: _____

©2018, *Dialectical Behavior Therapy With Adolescents*, K. Michelle Hunnicutt Hollenbaugh and Michael S. Lewis, Routledge

Handout 6.5

Top 10 Thinking Errors

All-or-Nothing Thinking: Thinking of things in absolute terms (always, every, never). If something isn't 100% then it is a total failure. **To Defeat:** Understand the only absolute is that there are no absolutes. Ask yourself disputing questions such as "Can I think of a time when it was NOT that way?" or find exceptions to the thinking. Investigate best and worst case scenarios to test the validity of thinking.

Overgeneralization: Taking isolated situations and using them to make wide-sweeping generalizations. **To Defeat:** Understand that the past does not predict the future—that one event happened does not necessarily mean it will always happen. Keep things in perspective of their own unique situations.

Mental Filter: Focusing exclusively on certain, usually negative, aspects of something while ignoring the rest (usually positive). This often includes generalizing the negative ("I'm stupid") and discounting the positive. **To Defeat:** Train yourself to look for the positive in most any situation. Counter negative comments or thoughts with positive ones to help maintain balance.

Disqualifying the Positive: Continually "shooting down" positive experiences for arbitrary reasons. This way you maintain a negative belief that is contradicted by your everyday experiences. Basically, the good stuff doesn't count because everything else is so miserable. **To Defeat:** Make a list of your personal strengths and accomplishments and remind yourself of them often. Accept compliments from others with a simple "thank you."

Jumping to Conclusions: Assuming something negative when there is no actual evidence to support it. Assuming the intentions of others (mind reading), you conclude that someone is reacting negatively to you without bothering to check it out. In another instance you anticipate things will turn out poorly (fortune telling) and assume this is a foregone conclusion before the event. **To Defeat:** Ask yourself what evidence you have to support your conclusions and if they are grounded in truth. Are there other possible explanations that you haven't considered? Ask for clarification before assuming someone else's intentions, thoughts, or feelings. If all else fails, simply let go of the thought and conclude you don't have enough evidence to hold on to it.

Magnification and Minimization: Exaggerating negative and understating positives. Often positive characteristics of other people are exaggerated and negatives understated. Focusing on the worst possible outcome (catastrophizing), however unlikely, prohibits you from considering other outcomes and that you're simply "doomed." **To Defeat:** Ask yourself how/why this is so bad/good/much/little/etc. and compared to what exactly. Attempt to scale your thoughts and match your response to given situation.

Emotional Reasoning: Making decisions and arguments based on how you feel rather than objective reality. Becoming blinded by feelings and reacting to it as facts. **To Defeat:** Ask yourself what is it about the present situation that produces the feelings and what thoughts are behind them. What is the nature of these thoughts—do they perhaps fall into one of these other thinking error categories?

Shoulding: Focusing on what you believe you, others, and the world ought to do/not do. Applying expectations that go against the objective reality of the situation. Replacing goals and objectives with expectations, which lead to guilt and shame when they aren't met. **To Defeat:** Remove the word should/ought/must from your vocabulary and replace them with goal-oriented language that better represents the rational reality.

Labeling and Mislabeling: Explaining by naming rather than describing a specific behavior. Assigning a label to someone or yourself that puts them/you in an absolute, unalterable negative light. This is a logic-level error by which we make a leap from a behavior/action to an identity (he was rude to me . . . therefore he's a jerk). **To Defeat:** Specify thoughts and comments to specific situations and avoid broad, wide sweeping statements or names. Remember we are not defined by our behaviors and can change.

Personalization and Blame: Occurring when you hold yourself personally accountable for an event that isn't entirely in your control. **To Defeat:** Ask yourself how specifically you are to blame and what portion of fault can you own. Is this a situation you can resolve and/or change in the future?

Source: Adapted with permission from Rathus, J. H. & Miller, A. L. (2015). *DBT® skills manual for adolescents*. New York, NY: Guilford Press; Linehan, M. M. (2015). *DBT® skills handouts and worksheets*. New York, NY: Guilford Press.

©2018, *Dialectical Behavior Therapy With Adolescents*, K. Michelle Hunnicutt Hollenbaugh and Michael S. Lewis, Routledge

Handout 6.6

B.E.A.T.

Learning to solve problems effectively involves implementing new skills. Using the B.E.A.T. skill is an easy way to assess, break down, and defeat any problem.

B—Behavioral: Identify problem behaviors to decrease and skillful behaviors to increase
- Decrease avoidance behaviors
- Eliminate substance use
- Eliminate emotional and vocational outbursts
- Decrease family power struggles and conflict
- Eliminate self-injury

E—Educational: Learn a proven set of problem solving skills and acceptance strategies
- Mindfulness skills—increase awareness of emotions and tolerate destructive urges
- Distress tolerance skills—increase skills to get through difficult situations without making them worse
- Emotional regulations skills—increase skills to identify and change emotions
- Interpersonal effectiveness skills—increase skills to effectively ask for what you want, keep relationships positive, and accept "no" when needed
- Middle path skills—increase skills to solve family problems

A—Action Oriented: Learning skills involves practice
- Rehearse skills in new situations
- Seek guidance when stuck
- Allow yourself to try and fail
- Acknowledge your successes

T—Teamwork: Partner with your therapist and treatment team to identify problems that you want to solve and goals you want to reach
- Commit to your treatment
- Ask for help
- Review options with therapist

©2018, *Dialectical Behavior Therapy With Adolescents*, K. Michelle Hunnicutt Hollenbaugh and Michael S. Lewis, Routledge

Handout 6.7

Understanding Goals and Problems

What is a goal? Anything you want to achieve or accomplish. It can be about school, work, family, or friends; it can be about activities, skills you want to acquire, or places you'd like to visit. In other words, the sky is the limit. Write down as many goals as you have or that come into your mind _____

_____
_____
_____
_____
_____
_____

What is a problem? Usually a problem is something that will get in the way of reaching your goals. A problem can be a *feeling* (anger, sadness, fear, etc.), a *behavior* (avoiding, arguing, hiding, attaching, etc.), a *thought* (self-doubt, worthlessness, wondering what friends think, family concerns, etc.), a *bodily sensation* (tight muscles, stomach pains, rapid heart rate, etc.), or a *situation* (family changes, conflicts with family or friends).

What are the problems that are challenging you right now? _____

_____
_____
_____

Which of these problems feels the most important for you to solve and why? _____

_____
_____
_____

Which of these problems feels the easiest for you to solve and why? _____

_____
_____
_____

Which of these problems feels the most difficult for you to solve and why? _____

_____
_____
_____

©2018, *Dialectical Behavior Therapy With Adolescents*, K. Michelle Hunnicutt Hollenbaugh and Michael S. Lewis, Routledge

Handout 6.8

Phases of Treatment

Entering: Begins with admission and identifying your goals and behaviors targets with your therapist
- Complete the DBT Treatment Contract
- Begin self-monitoring with your Diary Card

Working: Involves skills building and self-monitoring
- Monitoring your targets progress with your therapist
- Learning new skills to reach your goals in DBT Skills Group
- Applying skills in Problem Solving Process Group
- Staying on track in individual therapy
- Learning to ask for help from family and staff and by using phone coaching

Exiting: Learn to extend treatment outside of the treatment environment and maintenance of skills
- Create a continued care plan
- Place focus on maintaining gains in targets to avoid readmission
- Identify crisis plans and social support systems

©2018, *Dialectical Behavior Therapy With Adolescents*, K. Michelle Hunnicutt Hollenbaugh and Michael S. Lewis, Routledge

Handout 6.9

Partial Hospital Behavioral Expectations and Rules of Conduct

Therapy Enhancing:
1. Report any thoughts to self-harm, harm others, or run away to staff or parent.
2. Attend program every day and arrive on time.
3. Ask for help when you need it.
4. Be willing to try out behavioral suggestions.
5. Accept no for an answer without argument or complaint, verbal or nonverbal.
6. Follow the rules and guidelines for the program the first time instruction is given.
7. Practice mindfulness every day.
8. Complete Diary Card every day.

Therapy Destroying:
1. Possessing dangerous contraband.
2. Leaving the building without staff permission.
3. Refusal to accept consequences.
4. Physical aggression.
5. Verbally abusive, hostile, or threatening behavior towards others or yourself.

Therapy Interfering:
1. Not following adult instructions the first time.
2. SUBGROUPING: Contact between patients after program hours. This also includes exchanging notes, phone numbers, e-mails, addresses, screen names, social media handles, etc.
3. Being late. If you are late, you need a dated signed note from your parent stating why you are late.
4. Not bringing a completed signed goal sheet and/or educational folder from home. It is expected that both are brought in complete and signed every day.
5. Not keeping your hands to yourself.
6. Not treating peers, staff, and yourself with respect. (No put downs, disrespectful behavior, critical comments, etc.)
7. Whispering, giving the appearance of whispering, or nonverbal communication.
8. Communication with students in TIBS or on protocol.
9. Talking about movies, TV, music, violence, weapons, illegal substances, or any other topic that is overtly and predominantly dark, aggressive, or antisocial.
10. Going to any other area of the program without staff approval.
11. Not bringing your lunch every day. If you do not bring a lunch you must sit in silent lunch.
12. Having any personal electronic device during program hours. Any personal electronic devices must be given to staff every morning before or during AM group.

Ten General Guidelines and Rules:
1. Bring all materials and supplies to class and have them labeled with your full name.
2. In the classroom and specified groups, raise your hand for staff permission before speaking.
3. Do not write in or on any program property.
4. Put your name and date on your lunch every day.
5. Do not share your lunch without staff approval.
6. To purchase a soda or snack, you must bring a nutritional lunch approved by staff.
7. You may not borrow or exchange money from peers or staff.
8. Backpacks and purses are not allowed in the program.
9. Students driving to the program must give keys to staff upon arrival.
10. Sign in and out of the bathroom with your name and the time you are signing in.

I understand the above rules and agree to follow them. I also understand that if the rules are not followed, consequences will occur.

_____   _____

©2018, *Dialectical Behavior Therapy With Adolescents*, K. Michelle Hunnicutt Hollenbaugh and Michael S. Lewis, Routledge

Handout 7.1

Willingness vs. Willfulness

Here's an interesting dialectic. Willingness means that you know what is needed in a situation and mindfully set to complete the task. Willfulness indicates that you know what is required but refuse to do it. Interestingly, we can be willing when we want to feel willful and vice versa. Can you think of examples when you've been willing and willful? What were the positive or negative outcomes?

Willing	Outcome	Outcome	Willful

Source: Adapted with permission from Linehan, M. M. (2015). *DBT® skills handouts and worksheets*. New York, NY: Guilford Press.

©2018, *Dialectical Behavior Therapy With Adolescents*, K. Michelle Hunnicutt Hollenbaugh and Michael S. Lewis, Routledge

Handout 7.2

My Daily Goals

Name: _____ Date: _____

Today's Goals:

1: _____
_____

2: _____
_____

3: _____
_____

Describe How You Are Going to Accomplish These Goals Today:
_____
_____

Rate Your Success Today (1 = Not at All; 10 = Total Success)   How Can You Improve Tomorrow?

1   2   3   4   5   6   7   8   9   10   _____
                                                _____

©2018, *Dialectical Behavior Therapy With Adolescents*, K. Michelle Hunnicutt Hollenbaugh and Michael S. Lewis, Routledge

Handout 9.1

Dialectical Abstinence

On the below spectrum, where am I relative to never engaging in binging and purging behaviors again?

Regularly Engaging |——————|——————|——————| Never Engaging

I, _____, am committing to abstaining from binging and purging behaviors. Instead I will use the following skills to keep the course of a healthy and mindful life:

-
-
-
-

Signature: _____

Source: Adapted with permission from Wisniewski, L., Safer, D., & Chen, E. (2007). Dialectical behavior therapy and eating disorders. In L. A. Dimeff, K. Koerner (Eds.), *Dialectical behavior therapy in clinical practice: Applications across disorders and settings* (pp. 174–221). New York, NY: Guilford Press.

©2018, *Dialectical Behavior Therapy With Adolescents*, K. Michelle Hunnicutt Hollenbaugh and Michael S. Lewis, Routledge

Handout 9.2

Burning Bridges

Burning bridges means eliminating the pathway between you and your past harmful behaviors. What are the some roadblocks you can put in the way of moving from the impulse and the behavior? Identify the components below.

Impulse ~ *Harmful Behaviors*

Harmful Behavior: _____

Burning Bridge Method #1: _____

Burning Bridge Method #2: _____

Burning Bridge Method #3: _____

Burning Bridge Method #4: _____

Burning Bridge Method #5: _____

Burning Bridge Method #6: _____

Source: Adapted with permission from Wisniewski, L., Safer, D., & Chen, E. (2007). Dialectical behavior therapy and eating disorders. In L. A. Dimeff, K. Koerner (Eds.), *Dialectical behavior therapy in clinical practice: Applications across disorders and settings* (pp. 174–221). New York, NY: Guilford Press.

©2018, *Dialectical Behavior Therapy With Adolescents*, K. Michelle Hunnicutt Hollenbaugh and Michael S. Lewis, Routledge

Handout 9.3

Urge Surfing

Sometimes it's impossible to ignore something — just trying not to think about it causes you to think about. Quick — don't think of a red T-Rex! Impossible! You have to think of them in order to then NOT think of it. The same is true for negative behaviors and wanting to do them. The more you try to ignore it the stronger it seems to get. Even if you are successful in ignoring them, the energy needed is huge.

So let's do the opposite! Instead of fighting against the urge, roll with it. Have you ever tried to swim into a wave? The wave always wins, but if we learn to go with the wave we can ride through it all the way until it dies. That's what we're doing here too. When an urge hits, ride through it, be mindful of how it feels as it gets worse and then slowly starts to get better. This will pass if you give it time. A general rule of thumb is that urges rarely last longer than seven minutes. You can ride the wave for seven minutes! Next time you feel the urge try to ride it!

When faced with an urge, how did this technique work? _____
_____
_____
_____

Source: Adapted with permission from McMain, S., Sayrs, J. R., Dimeff, L. A., & Linehan, M. M. (2007). Dialectical behavior therapy for individuals with borderline personality disorder and substance dependence. In L. A. Dimeff & K. Koerner (Eds.), *Dialectical behavior therapy in clinical practice: Applications across disorders and settings* (pp. 145–173). New York, NY: Guilford Press.

©2018, *Dialectical Behavior Therapy With Adolescents*, K. Michelle Hunnicutt Hollenbaugh and Michael S. Lewis, Routledge

Handout 9.4

Mindful Eating

Approach eating in a new way

Use all Your Senses: Take in the aroma of the food, take time to smell it and try to identify the different scents. Look at it fully—the colors and layout on your plate. When you place it in your mouth, allow it to sit on your tongue. Take in the textures of the food. Explore the various flavors you taste.

Take it Slow: Take inventory of how you feel before you eat both emotionally and physically. As you eat, take time between each bite to reassess how you're feeling. Take time to enjoy the quality of each bite fully. Set your utensil down between bites to force yourself to take your time. Eat until you're satiated and stop.

Remove Distractions: Allow eating to be its own activity. Turn off the TV and music. Turn off the phone. Just be present with your eating experience.

Use the space below to journal your experience

Source: Adapted with permission from Wisniewski, L., Safer, D., & Chen, E. (2007). Dialectical behavior therapy and eating disorders. In L. A. Dimeff, K. Koerner (Eds.), *Dialectical behavior therapy in clinical practice: Applications across disorders and settings* (pp. 174–221). New York, NY: Guilford Press.

©2018, *Dialectical Behavior Therapy With Adolescents*, K. Michelle Hunnicutt Hollenbaugh and Michael S. Lewis, Routledge

Handout 9.5

Alternate Rebellion

Choosing new, healthier behaviors isn't always easy. The urge to do something impulsive is still going to come. However, there might be ways to choose behaviors that aren't destructive. You can still break the rules but stay on the road to recovery. Below are some ideas—and some spaces for you to brainstorm your own.

Write a nasty letter to someone . . . but don't send　_____

Wear eccentric or mismatched clothes　_____

Shave your head or dye your hair　_____

Do something kind of random　_____

Have a heated debate with a friend　_____

Read a book instead of being bored at church　_____

Eat some exotic food　_____

Go exploring outside your normal boundaries　_____

Express an honest opinion instead of being polite　_____

Stretch your normal roles—surprise people　_____

Leave your room unorganized

Turn the music up loud

Source: Adapted with permission from Linehan, M. M. (2015). *DBT® skills handouts and worksheets*. New York, NY: Guilford Press.

©2018, *Dialectical Behavior Therapy With Adolescents*, K. Michelle Hunnicutt Hollenbaugh and Michael S. Lewis, Routledge

Handout 9.6

Food Log

Date:	Meal	Contents	Emotions	Notes
	Breakfast			
	Lunch			
	Dinner			
	Drinks			
	Other			
	Meal	Contents	Emotions	Notes
	Breakfast			
	Lunch			
	Dinner			
	Drinks			
	Other			
	Meal	Contents	Emotions	Notes
	Breakfast			
	Lunch			
	Dinner			
	Drinks			
	Other			
	Meal	Contents	Emotions	Notes
	Breakfast			
	Lunch			
	Dinner			
	Drinks			
	Other			
	Meal	Contents	Emotions	Notes
	Breakfast			
	Lunch			
	Dinner			
	Drinks			
	Other			
	Meal	Contents	Emotions	Notes
	Breakfast			
	Lunch			
	Dinner			
	Drinks			
	Other			

©2018, *Dialectical Behavior Therapy With Adolescents*, K. Michelle Hunnicutt Hollenbaugh and Michael S. Lewis, Routledge

Handout 10.1

Do What Works

It can be easy to get caught up in the details of a situation and lose sight of the bigger picture. It's often not a matter of what is "right" or "wrong" or "fair" versus "unfair" but rather: does what I'm doing get me to my ultimate goal? Use the questions below to outline how this process works.

Describe a recent situation in which you felt you had to stand up for what was "right." _____
_____
_____

What was the outcome of the situation? _____
_____
_____

What did you gain? Lose? _____
_____
_____

Did it work towards your ultimate goal? Why or why not? _____
_____
_____

How could you have handled it differently? _____
_____
_____

©2018, *Dialectical Behavior Therapy With Adolescents*, K. Michelle Hunnicutt Hollenbaugh and Michael S. Lewis, Routledge

Handout 10.2

Acts of Kindness

Taking care of others is just as important as taking care of you. It's easy to get lost in our own problems, situations and life. Let's be mindful and focus on being good to our friends, family, neighbors, and even strangers. There are even real benefits to being kind—we tend to feel better about the world, feel healthier, experience reduced anxiety and depression, and in general see life a little more brightly. Below are some ideas on ways to be kind . . . what can you add?

- Volunteer at a food bank
- Open a door for someone
- Buy a stranger a cup of coffee
- Email a friend just to say hi
- Listen intently
- Cook a meal
- Give your leftovers to the homeless
- Write your grandparents or family members a physical letter and mail it
- Bring snacks to school for your class
- Give a hug to your parents
- Donate old clothes and eyeglasses

Write something nice on someone's Facebook page
_____
_____
_____
_____
_____

- Write a positive message on a sticky note and leave it somewhere fun
- Include everyone in a conversation
- Smile at your teacher
- Pick up litter
- Hold the elevator for someone
- Say thank you to the janitor
- Text someone good morning
- Rake a neighbor's leaves
- Give up your seat to someone else
- Offer those around you a piece of gum

Source: Adapted with permission from McCann, R. A., Ball, E. M., & Ivanoff, A. (2000). DBT with an inpatient forensic population: The CMHIP forensic model. *Cognitive and Behavioral Practice*, 7(4), 447–456. doi:10.1016/S1077-7229(00)80056-5

©2018, *Dialectical Behavior Therapy With Adolescents*, K. Michelle Hunnicutt Hollenbaugh and Michael S. Lewis, Routledge

Handout 11.1

Clear Mind

Addict Mind: Singularly focused on using. Thoughts and behaviors are all geared towards using or preparing to use. Impulsive.

Clean Mind: Not using but not well. Naïve to potential dangerous situations, prone to high risks, and open to falling back into using behaviors. Believes self to be safe and invincible to future problems.

Clear Mind: Both clean and aware of the potential for relapse. Safeguards the self from potential people, places, and things that might trigger old behaviors. Sets up a support system to help with cravings.

Source: Adapted with permission from McMain, S., Sayrs, J. R., Dimeff, L. A., & Linehan, M. M. (2007). Dialectical behavior therapy for individuals with borderline personality disorder and substance dependence. In L. A. Dimeff, K. Koerner, L. A. Dimeff, K. Koerner (Eds.), *Dialectical behavior therapy in clinical practice: Applications across disorders and settings* (pp. 145–173). New York, NY, US: Guilford Press.

©2018, *Dialectical Behavior Therapy With Adolescents*, K. Michelle Hunnicutt Hollenbaugh and Michael S. Lewis, Routledge

Handout 11.2

Apparently Irrelevant Behaviors

It can be quite easy to overlook the thoughts, feelings, and behaviors that lead to negative and harmful consequences such as eating disorders, crime, and substance abuse. Just like we can't go from A to Z without going through LMNO. Identify below the people, places, and things that while they don't seem problematic at the time can lead to the behaviors you're trying to avoid.

A. _____
B. _____
C. _____
D. _____
E. _____
F. _____
G. _____
H. _____
I. _____
J. _____
K. _____
L. _____
M. _____

N. _____
O. _____
P. _____
Q. _____
R. _____
S. _____
T. _____
U. _____
V. _____
W. _____
X. _____
Y. _____
Z. Problem Behavior

©2018, *Dialectical Behavior Therapy With Adolescents*, K. Michelle Hunnicutt Hollenbaugh and Michael S. Lewis, Routledge

Handout 11.3

Building Bridges

Building bridges means creating pathways between our goals to not use drugs and alcohol and to combat cravings. These can be new triggers for sobriety, urge surfing, mental activities, and using our senses. What are the some things you can put in your way to build a successful bridge? Identify the components below.

Goal: _____

Building Bridge Method #1: _____

Building Bridge Method #2: _____

Building Bridge Method #3: _____

Building Bridge Method #4: _____

Building Bridge Method #5: _____

Building Bridge Method #6: _____

Source: Adapted with permission from Linehan, M. M. (2015). *DBT® skills handouts and worksheets*. New York, NY: Guilford Press.

©2018, *Dialectical Behavior Therapy With Adolescents*, K. Michelle Hunnicutt Hollenbaugh and Michael S. Lewis, Routledge

Handout 11.4

Adaptive Denial

Cravings to use will hit . . . it's a fact of addiction. As an alternate to trying to logically think through it, give yourself a break. No arguing with yourself, simply deny that it's a problem in the first place!

— "I don't have a problem, in the first place; I'm safe and sound"

— "I never wanted to use in the first place"

— "What I really want is something else anyway"

— "Even if I could use right now, I wouldn't so who cares"

— "My body feels great and I have no discomfort at all"

Write your active denial script here:

When you've finished reciting your script, find a non-using related behavior for seven–ten minutes. If the craving hasn't subsided start over and recite your script again and find another alternative behavior. Repeat until the cravings are gone.

Source: Adapted with permission from McMain, S., Sayrs, J. R., Dimeff, L. A., & Linehan, M. M. (2007). Dialectical behavior therapy for individuals with borderline personality disorder and substance dependence. In L. A. Dimeff & K. Koerner (Eds.), *Dialectical behavior therapy in clinical practice: Applications across disorders and settings* (pp. 145–173). New York, NY: Guilford Press.

©2018, *Dialectical Behavior Therapy With Adolescents*, K. Michelle Hunnicutt Hollenbaugh and Michael S. Lewis, Routledge

Index

Page numbers in italics indicate figures and in bold indicate tables on the corresponding pages.

12-step support groups 141
24-hour skills coaching 8

absence of alternatives 23–24
abstinence, dialectical 115, 138–139, 222
acting the opposite skill 44, 151, 154, 199
active passivity *vs.* apparent competence 17
acts of kindness 130, 229
adaptive denial 140–141, 233
addict mind 138
administrators in partial hospital program settings 78
admissions director in partial hospital program settings 79–80
Adolescent Family Life Satisfaction index 61
Alcoholics Anonymous 141
Allen, J. P. 68
alternate rebellion 116, 140, 226
American Association for Ambulatory Behavioral Healthcare (AAABH) 63
ancillary modes 9
ancillary team members 33; therapy-interfering behaviors by 35
Andolfi, M. 72
Angelo, C. 72
anger management 130–131
Antonishak, J. 68
anxiety 149–151
apparent compliance *vs.* active defiance 114
apparently irrelevant behaviors 139–140, 231
assessment: of comorbid diagnoses 166; initial diagnostic 24; overall program evaluation 25; of treatment outcomes 24–25
attrition 49–50

Ball, E. M. 130
B.E.A.T. 216
Beck Anxiety Inventory (BAI) 157

Beck Depression Inventory (BDI) 157
Beck Scale of Suicide Ideation 162
behavioral contingencies and expectations in partial hospital program settings 77–78
behavioral skills, increasing of 16; with comorbid diagnoses 168
Behavioral Tech 20, 50, 174
behavior chain analysis 182; for life-threatening behaviors 163–164
Behavior Chain Analysis (BCA) 11
behaviorism 46
Ben-Porath, D. D. 112–113
billing 50–51
binge eating disorder 109; *see also* eating disorders
biosocial theory 3–4, 177; conduct disorder and criminal behaviors and 125, *126*; eating disorders and 111–112
bipolar disorder 154–156
borderline personality disorder (BPD) 1
Brief Symptom Inventory (BSI) 167
building bridges 140, 232
bulimia 109; *see also* eating disorders
burning bridges 115, 140, 223
burnout, clinician 16

care, continuity of 33–34
case management strategies 12
case managers 32; in partial hospital program settings 80
changing behavior 205
cheerleading 24
Child Behavior Checklist 134
clean mind 138
clear mind 138, 230
client report 191
clinical directors in partial hospital program settings 78–79
clinician interfering behaviors 16

INDEX

clinicians: burnout 16; inpatient 88; major points for 171–173; outpatient 87–88; primary 31; *see also* treatment team
coding scale, validating and invalidating behaviors 60–61
Cognitive Behavioral Therapy (CBT) 1, 152
Cognitive-Behavioral Treatment of Borderline Personality Disorder 10
commitment strategies 22–24, 184
commitment to treatment 172; in conduct disorder, probation, and juvenile detention settings 134–135
communication problems 35–36
community mental health (CMH) settings 39–40
comorbid diagnoses 166–168
conduct disorder, probation, and juvenile detention settings 123–124; adaptations to DBT for 128–131; additional treatment team members and roles 128; biosocial model of 125, *126*; challenges and solutions 134–135; considerations before implementing DBT for 124–125; group session format 131–133; treatment targets in 126–128
confidentiality 34–35, 188
connecting of present commitments to prior commitments 23
consultation group 9, 74; in school sites 101
contingency management 90
continuity of care 33–34
cope ahead skill 44, 92, 130–131, 150–151, 200
criminal justice system *see* conduct disorder, probation, and juvenile detention settings
Crisis Stabilization Scale (CriSS) 93–94

daily goals 221
Daily Progress Report (DPR) 105
Daybreak Treatment Center 68–69, 68–73
DBT *see* Dialectical Behavior Therapy (DBT)
DBT-Linehan Board of Certification 78, 174–175
DEAR MAN 43, 195
denial, adaptive 140–141, 233
depressed mind 155
depression 152–154
devil's advocate, playing 22–23

dialectical abstinence 115, 138–139, 222
Dialectical Behavior Therapy (DBT): ancillary modes 9; for anxiety 149–151; assessment in 24–25; for bipolar disorder 154–156; commitment strategies 22–24, 184; for comorbid diagnoses 166–168; for conduct disorder (*see* conduct disorder, probation, and juvenile detention settings); consultation group 9; current and future directions in 173; for depression 152–154; dialectics and 4–5; difference of 1–2; for eating disorders (*see* eating disorders); in family counseling (*see* family counseling); homework 214; implementation (*see* implementation); individual sessions 8–9; information sheet 189; in inpatient settings (*see* inpatient settings); intersession skills coaching 8; for life-threatening behaviors 14, 126, 161–166; major points for clinicians 171–173; multicultural considerations in 25–26; other resources on 173–175; in outpatient settings (*see* outpatient settings); in partial hospital programs (*see* partial hospital program (PHP) settings); for post-traumatic stress disorder (PTSD) 152; in school sites (*see* school sites); for substance use disorders (*see* substance use disorders); team (*see* treatment team); terminology 2, **3**; as third wave CBT 1; *see also* treatment
dialectical dilemmas 16–17, 45–46, 202; multicultural considerations 25
dialectical milieu 64–66
dialectical strategies 10
dialectics 4–5, 45–46
diary cards 41–42, 48–49, 178, 179, 180, 181; conduct disorder, probation, and juvenile detention settings 133–134; family 58, 60; inpatient 93; life-threatening behaviors and 162; skills 183; substance use disorders and 145
different populations, implementation with 21–22
Difficulties in Emotional Regulation Scale (DERS) 49
Dimeff, L. A. 61, 81, 143

directors of education in partial hospital program settings 80–81
distress tolerance 7, 44–45, 57, 131
dodge 68
doing what works 228
do what works skill 129

eating, mindful 225
eating disorders: adaptations to treatment targets for 112–114; additional treatment team members 112; biosocial model and emotion dysregulation in 111–112; challenges and solutions in treating 120; considerations before implementing DBT for 109–111; group session format 117, **117–119**; specific skills and adaptations related to 115–117
educational therapy and academic preparation 70, 80–81
emotion, mindfulness of 156
emotional myths 197
emotional thesaurus 198
emotional vulnerability vs. self-invalidation 17
emotion dysregulation, biosocial theory of 3–4; conduct disorder and 125, *126*; eating disorders and 111–112
emotion regulation 7, 43–44; in conduct disorder, probation, and juvenile detention settings 129–130; in relationships 58
emotions, understanding 196
excessive leniency vs. authoritarian control 17

Family Adaptability and Cohesion Evaluation Scale (FACES) IV 61
family-based treatment for eating disorders 110
family chain analysis 210
family counseling: adaptation to treatment targets in 54; challenges and solutions with 60; considerations for implementing DBT in 53–54; family skills group format in 59; outcome evaluation 60–61; in partial hospital program settings 80; skills adaptations in 54–59
family genograms 56, 208
family therapy-interfering behaviors 15–16
food log 227

foot in the door/door in the face 22
forcing autonomy vs. fostering dependence 17
freedom to choose 23–24
Frieburg Mindfulness Inventory (FMI) 82
Fruzzetti, A. E. 53–55, 57–58, 60
funding of inpatient care 94

genograms, family 56, 208
goals and problems, understanding 217
Goldstein, T. R. 154
Grizenko, N. 64
group orientation 206
group rules 207
groups: consultation 9, 74; problem-solving, in partial hospital program settings 71; skills 5–6
group session formats 46–47, **47–48**; conduct disorder, probation, and juvenile detention settings 131–133; eating disorders treatment 117, **117–119**; family 59; inpatient 92–93; substance use disorders 143; Teen Talk 102, **103–104**
Gunderson, J. G. 64, 65

Harvey, P. 138, 143
health insurance issues 50–51
Health Insurance Portability and Accountability Act (HIPAA) 34
Hoffman, P. D. 53, 55
homework, DBT 72, 214

implementation: for conduct disorder, probation, and juvenile detention settings 124–125; with different populations 21–22; in different settings 21; for eating disorders 109–111; in family counseling 53–54; in inpatient settings 85–87; in outpatient settings 39–42; in partial hospital program (PHP) settings 64–68; in school sites 97–99; standard DBT vs. DBT informed 19–20; structural/financial considerations in 21; for substance use disorders 137; training in 20; *see also* treatment
individual sessions 8–9; in partial hospital program settings 80
information sheet, DBT 189

informed treatment, DBT 19–20
initial diagnostic assessment 24
inpatient settings 85; adaptations to treatment targets in 88, **89**; additional treatment team members in 87–88; challenges and solutions 94–95; considerations before implementing DBT in 85–87; group session format in 92–93; outcome evaluation 93–94; specific skills and adaptations for 89–92
interpersonal effectiveness 6–7, 43, 151; myths 194
Interpersonal Sensitivity (INT) 81
intersession skills coaching 8, 116–117; conduct disorder, probation, and juvenile detention settings 131
Ivanoff, A. 130

juvenile detention *see* conduct disorder, probation, and juvenile detention settings

Kelly, E. 111
Kiddie-Sads-Present and Lifetime Version 167
kindness: acts of 130, 229; loving 153

Latino clients 25–26
leaders, team 31
life-threatening behaviors 14, 126, 161–166; with comorbid diagnoses 167
Linehan, Marsha 1–2, 10, 11, 56, 65–66, 71, 151, 172; on co-leading treatment 21; DEAR MAN acronym 43; on dialectical dilemmas 16–17; on loving kindness 153; on mindfulness activities 42; on nurturance *vs.* benevolent demandingness 66; on phone coaching for life-threatening behaviors 165; on skills trainers 31; on stages of treatment 13; on unwavering centeredness *vs.* compassionate flexibility 67; on willingness *vs.* willfulness 91–92
log, food 227
loving kindness 153
lunch time tasks 213

making repairs 58
managers, case 32

manic mind 155
Matzner, F. J. 68
McCann, R. A. 125, 130
McMain, S. 139
Medicaid 39
Medicare 39
Menghi, P. 72
Miller, A. L. 1, 10, 11, 17, 71, 172; on co-leading treatment 21; on do what works skill 129; on family crisis plans 57; on genograms 56; on mindfulness activities 42; on phone coaching for life-threatening behaviors 165; on treatment targets in family counseling 54; Walking the Middle Path skills module 45
mind, clear 230
mindfulness 6; conduct disorder, probation, and juvenile detention settings and 129; of current thoughts, in inpatient settings 90–91; in eating 116, 225; of emotion and bipolar disorder 156; exercises in 42, 193; of others for interpersonal effectiveness 151; in partial hospital program settings 70; relational 56–57, 129; relationship 209; states of mind and bipolar disorder 155; of worry thoughts 150
miscommunication 35–36
missing links analysis 212
Monroe-DeVita, M. 61, 81, 143
multicultural considerations 25–26

Narcotics Anonymous 141
Native American clients 26
Nicholò-Corigliano, A. 72
no activity *vs.* over-activity 114
nonjudgmental stance 125
normalizing pathological behaviors *vs.* pathologizing normative behaviors 17
nurses 88
nurturance *vs.* benevolent demandingness 66–67
nutritionists 112

old school *vs.* new school 25
orientation and commitment strategies 10
outcome evaluation 172–173; for additional diagnoses 156–157; conduct disorder,

probation, and juvenile detention settings 133–134; eating disorders treatment 119–120; in family counseling 60–61; in inpatient settings 93–94; in outpatient settings 48–49; in partial hospital program settings 81–82; in school sites 102–105; substance use disorders treatment 143–146
outcomes assessment 24–25
outpatient settings: challenges and solutions in 49–51; considerations before implementing DBT in 39–42; diary cards in 41–42; group session formats 46–47, **47–48**; outcome evaluation in 48–49; standard skills modules for adolescents in 42–46; traditional treatment targets in 40–41
outpatient therapists 87–88
over-protection *vs.* under-protection 25

panic attacks 150–151
Papineau, D. 64
parental involvement and commitment to treatment for conduct disorder, probation, and juvenile detention settings 124
parenting skills 58–59, 73, 141
partial hospital program (PHP) settings 63–64; adaptations to DBT for 68–73, **73–74**; behavioral expectations and rules of conduct in 219; considerations before implementing DBT in 64–68; outcome evaluation in 81–82; teen daily goal sheet 211; treatment adherence in 74–78; treatment team roles in 78–81
phases of treatment 218; in partial hospital program settings 75–77
phone coaching: for life-threatening behaviors 164–166; rules for 116–117
physicians 32, 112
post-traumatic stress disorder (PTSD) 152
pretreatment stage 12–13
primary clinicians 31; in partial hospital program settings 80
private practice 39
probation *see* conduct disorder, probation, and juvenile detention settings
probation officers 128

problem-solving strategies 11; in family counseling 57; in partial hospital program settings 71
program coordinators in partial hospital program settings 81
pros and cons 23, 91
provider communication form 190
psychiatrists 33, 80, 88
psychoeducation 56
psychoeducational skills 5–6

quality-of-life interfering behaviors 16, 126; with comorbid diagnoses 168

radical acceptance skill 44–45, 156, 201; in family counseling 57–58
Rathbone, B. H. 138, 143
Rathus, J. H. 1, 10, 11, 17, 71, 172; on co-leading treatment 21; on do what works skill 129; on mindfulness activities 42; on phone coaching for life-threatening behaviors 165
rational *vs.* dynamic milieu models 68
rebellion, alternate 116, 140, 226
relational mindfulness 56–57, 129
relationship mindfulness 209
residential staff and conduct disorder, probation, and juvenile detention settings 128
Ricard, R. J. 104
Rizvi, S. L. 61, 81, 143

school counselors 128
school sites 97; adaptations to DBT for 99–100, **101**; challenges and solutions in 105–106; considerations before implementing DBT in 97–99; consultation team members and roles in 101; group session format in 102; program evaluation in 102–105; treatment targets in 101, **102**
secondary treatment targets, stage one 16–17; eating disorders and 112–113
self, validation of 151
self-injury 63, 161–166
self soothing 91
Shaller, Esme 76
Silva, R. R. 68

INDEX

Silvan, M. 68
skills adaptations: for anxiety 149–151; in conduct disorder, probation, and juvenile detention settings 128–131; for depression 152, **153**; in eating disorders treatment 112–117; in family counseling 54–59; in inpatient settings 90; major points 171; in partial hospital program (PHP) settings 68–73, **73**–**74**; for post-traumatic stress disorder (PTSD) 152; in school sites 99–100, **101**; in substance use disorders 137–141
skills diary card 183
skills groups 5–6
skills modules in outpatient settings 42–46
skills trainers 31; in partial hospital program settings 78
Skills Training for Emotional Problem-Solving for Adolescents (DBT STEPS-A) 99–100
smart phone applications 175
Social Interaction Questionnaire (SIQ) 104
staff turnover 50
stage four 14
stage one 13; secondary treatment targets 16–17; treatment targets 14–16
stages, treatment 12–14; in partial hospital program settings 75–77
stage three 13–14; eating disorders and 110–111
stage two 13
standard DBT 19–20; adaptation for substance use disorders 137–141
standard skills modules in outpatient settings 42–46
State-Trait Anger Expression Inventory-2 (STAXI-2) 134
STOP skill 45, 131
strategies, treatment 10–12
structural/financial considerations with implementation 21
structured eating plans *vs.* no eating plan at all 114
stylistic strategies 11–12
Substance Abuse Subtle Screening Inventory-Adolescent 145–146
substance use disorders 137; adaptations from standard DBT for 137–141; additional treatment modes 141–142, **142–143**; additional treatment team members and roles 141; challenges and solutions 146; clear mind, clean mind, and addict mind in 138; considerations before implementing DBT for 137; group session format 143; key points to consider 146; outcome evaluation 143–146
suicide 63, 161–162
Suicide Attempt Self-Injury Interview (SASII) 162
super groups 68
Swenson, C. R. 53, 55, 90

target behaviors 192; stage one 14–16; traditional 40–41
team *see* treatment team
Teen Talk 100, **101**; group session format 102, **103–104**
terminology, DBT 2, **3**
therapy-interfering behaviors 15–16; by ancillary team members 35; with comorbid diagnoses 168; in inpatient settings 94–95; in partial hospital program settings 78
thinking errors 215
training 36, 172; implementation 20; in school sites 99
treatment: adherence in partial hospital program settings 74–78; ancillary modes 9; commitment 172; commitment to, in conduct disorder, probation, and juvenile detention settings 134–135; with comorbid diagnoses 167–168; consultation groups and 9; context in partial hospital program settings 68–69; fidelity to 50; individual sessions 8–9; intersession skills coaching 8; life-threatening behaviors and 163; modes of 5–7; stages of 12–14; strategies 10–12; 24-hour skills coaching 8; *see also* implementation
treatment targets: conduct disorder, probation, and juvenile detention settings 126–128; in eating disorders treatment 112–114; in family counseling 54; in inpatient settings 88, **89**; in outpatient settings 40–41; in school sites 101,

240

102; stage one 14–16; in substance use disorders 142, **142–143**
treatment team 21, 185; additional members in inpatient settings 87–88; challenges and solutions 34–36; conduct disorder, probation, and juvenile detention settings 128; contacts 186; continuity of care and 33–34; for eating disorders 112; members and roles 29–33; role in school sites 101; roles in partial hospital program settings 78–81; for substance use disorders 141; turnover 50

unrelenting crises *vs.* inhibited experiencing 17
unwavering centeredness *vs.* compassionate flexibility 67–68
urge surfing 116, 139, 224
urine screens 143

validation 46, 204; in conduct disorder, probation, and juvenile detention settings 125; in family counseling 57, 60–61; in partial hospital program settings 78; of self 151
validation strategies 11

Walking the Middle Path skills module 7, 45, 151, 203
Ways of Coping Checklist (WCCL) 49
websites for DBT 174–175
weekly medication management 187
willingness *vs.* willfulness 91–92, 220
Wisnewski, L. 111–113, 115
worry thoughts 150

Youth Outcome Questionnaire (Y-OQ) 105, 156–157

Zeldow, P. B. 65